Advances in Computer Security Management

VOLUME 1

HEYDEN ADVANCES LIBRARY IN EDP MANAGEMENT

Edited by Thomas A. Rullo

Other Advances Series in the Library

ADVANCES IN DATA PROCESSING MANAGEMENT Volume 1
ADVANCES IN DATA BASE MANAGEMENT Volume 1
ADVANCES IN COMPUTER PROGRAMMING MANAGEMENT Volume 1
ADVANCES IN DISTRIBUTED PROCESSING MANAGEMENT Volume 1
ADVANCES IN DATA COMMUNICATIONS MANAGEMENT Volume 1

Advances in Computer Security Management

VOLUME 1

Edited by
THOMAS A. RULLO

Philadelphia • London • Rheine

Heyden & Son Inc., 247 South 41st Street, Philadelphia, PA 19104, USA
Heyden & Son Ltd., Spectrum House, Hillview Gardens, London NW4 2JQ, UK
Heyden & Son GmbH, Münsterstrasse 22, 4440 Rheine, Germany

ISSN 0197 1514
ISBN 0 85501 606 X

PRINTED IN THE UNITED STATES OF AMERICA

CONTENTS

CHAPTER 7: A Survey of Computer-Based Password
Techniques—
Helen M. Wood

CHAPTER 8: Application of Cryptography—
Rein Turn

CHAPTER 9: Department of Defense Network Security
              Considerations—
              **James D. Scharf, Virgil Wallentine, and
              Paul S. Fisher**

CHAPTER 10: The Federal Aviation Administration Computer
               Security Program—
               Lynn McNulty

LIST OF CONTRIBUTORS

FRANCIS Y. CHIN, Professor, Department of EE and CS, University of California—San Diego, La Jolla, California 92093, U.S.A. (p. 57).

STEVEN CUSHING, Ph.D., Higher Order Software, Inc., 806 Massachusetts Avenue, Cambridge, Massachusetts 02139, U.S.A. (p. 79).

PAUL S. FISHER, Professor, Department of Computer Science, Kansas State University, Fairchild Hall, Manhattan, Kansas 66506, U.S.A. (p. 122). (p. 202).

I. A. GILHOOLEY, Inspection Department, Bank of Nova Scotia, 181 University Avenue, Toronto, Ontario, Canada (p. 33).

RICHARD M. McCONNELL, Diagnostics Inc., P.O. Box 10171, Oakland, California 94610, U.S.A. (p. 106).

LYNN McNULTY, Security Division, Federal Aviation Administration, 800 Independence Avenue, S.W., Washington, DC 20591, U.S.A. (p. 231).

GÜLTEKIN ÖZSOYOĞLU, Department of Computer & Information Science, Cleveland State University, Cleveland, Ohio 44115, U.S.A. (p. 57).

JOSEPH J. RODRIGUEZ, Department of Computer Science, Kansas State University, Fairchild Hall, Manhattan, Kansas 66506, U.S.A. (p. 122).

JAMES D. SCHARF, Defense Communications Agency, Command & Control Technical Center, Washington, D.C. 20310, U.S.A. (p. 202).

JAMES E. SMITH, Insurance Corporation of America, 2205 Montrose Blvd., Houston, Texas 77006, U.S.A. (p. 1).

REIN TURN, Professor, Computer Science Department, California State University, 18111 Nordhoff Street, Northridge, California 91330, U.S.A. (p. 168).

VIRGIL WALLENTINE, Department of Computer Science, Kansas State University, Fairchild Hall, Manhattan, Kansas 66506, U.S.A. (p. 202).

HELEN M. WOOD, Computer Science Analyst, Institute for Computer Science and Technology, National Bureau of Standards, Washington, DC 20234, U.S.A. (p. 140).

PREFACE TO THE HEYDEN ADVANCES LIBRARY IN EDP MANAGEMENT

During the past few years the rapid advances in EDP technology have been more than matched by a flood of published materials. It would be impossible to absorb all this new material and still be able to function in a working environment. Because of the information manager's plight, the HEYDEN ADVANCES LIBRARY IN EDP MANAGEMENT has been developed to provide a more useable information system.

A unique concept in the EDP information management field, the Library consists of six individual series, each dealing with a different area of information processing.

ADVANCES IN DATA PROCESSING MANAGEMENT
ADVANCES IN DATA BASE MANAGEMENT
ADVANCES IN COMPUTER PROGRAMMING MANAGEMENT
ADVANCES IN DISTRIBUTED PROCESSING MANAGEMENT
ADVANCES IN DATA COMMUNICATIONS MANAGEMENT
ADVANCES IN COMPUTER SECURITY MANAGEMENT

These series focus on the most current topics of interest across a broad spectrum. They are not, however, merely collections of papers or readings. Rather, each series presents chapters which have been selected with a specific information need in mind and developed by authors chosen for their expert knowledge and experience. This combination of breadth of material and depth of author knowledge results in a unique and concentrated information management program.

We intend to review the EDP information management field regularly and add to each series so that managers can gain insights into the latest developments. We will also be researching new areas of potential impact. The HEYDEN ADVANCES LIBRARY IN EDP MANAGEMENT is a continuing and expanding effort, and we would welcome any suggestions or guidance from our readers.

THOMAS A. RULLO
Editor

PREFACE

Several factors have combined to raise the problem of computer security to its current level of concern. First, the positive contributions of computer systems to modern organizations have caused them to become integral parts of a company's operations. Sensitive data are not only stored and processed within the computer but, in many cases, exist only through the processing power of the system. Further, as the integration of EDP systems into an organization becomes more pervasive, they become essential to accomplish the mission of the organization.

These two factors—the storage and processing of sensitive information, and the integration of computers into operations—provide incentives for different types of security breaches. On the one hand is the opportunity to access and either acquire or modify vital information for either personal gain or malice. On the other hand, the disruption of a computer systems operation can cause severe harm to an organization.

Technological factors compound the problem since the advancing sophistication of systems has brought the problem of preventing security breaches to a new level. In simpler times, unauthorized access to the information being processed and to the system itself was prevented by locking the data center door and monitoring the staff that were admitted. With the prevalence of communications capabilities on sophisticated systems, this checking becomes more difficult. When the central processor is in Chicago and several hundred terminals across the Midwest have access to the system, that is a lot of doors to lock.

In this book, we deal with a full spectrum of computer security issues. Some of the more advanced approaches are discussed, and practical methodologies are presented as both tutorials and case studies. The authors selected to unravel this material have developed their expertise through working experience.

In "Risk Management for Small Computer Installations," Jim Smith presents a practical, easy to use, risk management plan. After discussing basic risk management concepts and the way they relate to corporate goals, he shows how to implement a security plan. He deals specifically with the problem of assessing security risks through a Probability/Severity Matrix, which is provided as an appendix. Detailed management and user risk analysis forms are also included as separate appendices.

I. A. Gilhooley deals with the protection of business and system data against unauthorized disclosure, modification, or destruction in "Data Security." The chapter deals with physical security, employee education and logical security, and discusses four kinds of controls: deterrent, preventive, detective, and corrective. He concludes with a discussion of the role of the auditor in assessing the adequacy, effectiveness, and efficiency of the system of internal control.

In "Security of Statistical Data Bases," Francis Chin and Gültekin Özsoyoğlu discuss the specific security problems associated with statistical data bases. The primary security problem for a statistical data base is to limit its use so that only statistical information is available and no sequence of queries is sufficient to deduce protected information about any individual. This chapter first examines several proposed protection policies and then argues that the security problem should be elevated to the conceptual data model level. Proposed is the design of a statistical data base which utilizes a statistical security management facility to enforce several security constraints on the conceptual model level.

The Higher Order Software (HOS) system specification technique, which was developed to help guarantee system reliability, is discussed by Steven Cushing in "Software Security and How to Handle It." Since its purpose is to eliminate timing and data conflicts in the specification of large programming systems, it thus contributes as well to the requirements of system security. Besides discussing protection models, security models, and hierarchical security modelling, he describes the theory behind Higher Order Software and specifies a security model for HOS.

In "Designing for Privacy: The Data Vault," Richard McConnell defines the role of members of our industry as "data keepers" rather than as data processors. To fulfill the conflicting demands placed upon our systems for both freedom of information and rights to privacy, he proposes that we reevaluate our basic assumptions. In particular, he views systems designed around the concept of a Central Storage Unit (CSU) rather than a Central Processing Unit (CPU) as providing a fresh approach to the problem. He concludes that if program logic is a reflection of work procedures, and file structure is a reflection of our basic mental categories, a shift from central processing to central storage orientation may finally lead us to data management. The Data Vault System that he describes is predicated upon the Central Storage Unit approach.

A survey of both potential security problems and system security techniques is presented by Paul Fisher and Joseph Rodriguez in "Security Problems in a Data Base Environment." Here the authors deal with managers' concerns about system penetration. Next, they propose a planning methodology to minimize this risk. The compromising of data base security through inference techniques is discussed and controls are suggested. Finally, surveillance techniques and a set of security policies and goals are provided.

In "A Survey of Computer-Based Password Techniques," Helen Wood reviews passwords and their effective application to the problem of controlling access to computer resources. In addition to describing the need for and uses of passwords, she categorizes password schemes according to selection technique, lifetime, physical characteristics, and information content. Password protection, in both storage and transmission, is dealt with. Current implementations and cost considerations are addressed. While the author notes that rapid advances are being made in other personal authentication methodologies, until they become more cost-effective, the password will most likely remain the most widely used means of controlling access to remote computing systems and services.

In "Application of Cryptography," Rein Turn examines the use of cryptographic techniques to provide data security in distributed data processing systems, computer networks, and record-keeping systems. He also reviews the use of these techniques in terms of digital signatures for providing data and message authentication and integrity. Basic terminology, concepts, and design principles are presented, and the governmental-approved Data Encryption Standard (DES) is described. The public-key cryptosystems are examined, and the generation of digital signatures is discussed. The approach to the topic is from the point of view of managers responsible for implementing data security, data integrity, and private protection requirements.

Secure Department of Defense networks currently in use and some for which research is now being done are discussed by James Scharf, Virgil Wallentine, and Paul Fisher in "Department of Defense Network Security Considerations." This chapter focuses specifically on DOD networks since they are where the majority of research in network and computer security originated and is still heavily supported. In addition to describing both the developmental efforts and technical characteristics of these systems, the authors provide substantial background information on the DOD system security philosophy and implementation strategies.

In "The Federal Aviation Administration Computer Security Program," Lynn McNulty takes us down the rocky road that agency had to follow to implement an effective program. The existence within the FAA of two distinctly different data processing communities that serve operational and administrative needs compounds their security problems. The route taken to solve this problem should prove of interest to others attempting to implement a security program on a large scale.

THOMAS A. RULLO

Chapter 1

RISK MANAGEMENT
FOR SMALL COMPUTER INSTALLATIONS

James E. Smith

Insurance Corp. of America, Houston, Texas

The issue of security and privacy is an old one—as old as record keeping, which is almost as old as man. Record keeping dates back to the cave dwellers. The need for identity was probably the causal force that urged the cave dweller to draw crude symbols on the cave walls where he lived. An interpretation of the symbols will reveal such facts as family membership, diet, attire, battles, births, and deaths.

Record keeping progressed to clay tablets and papyrus scrolls about 4,000 years ago. With the Industrial Age came machines which could print many copies of the same material making the dissemination of information easier and faster.

The most dramatic change in record keeping was to come after the invention of the computer, ENIAC, in 1946. As early as the 1950 census, the Bureau of the Census used a computer to aid in the capture and interpretation of census data. From this meager start were born the disciplines of records management and electronic data processing.

Why, then, the concern about record keeping? The answer is deeply rooted in the complex nature of our industrial society. Man's knowledge has proliferated as the result of science and technology. He knows more about his world, his institutions, and himself.

Figure 1-1 illustrates the dramatic increase in knowledge as a function of time.

Consider something as fundamental as medical care. The proper treatment of patients today calls for collecting large amounts of data, which physicians study and file for future reference. Few records are more sensitive than those that reveal a patient's physical condition. The existence of the record represents a major risk. It could be stolen, misused, or inaccurate. But its existence might also save the patient's life someday.

Individuals now expect services that were far beyond the reach of their forbears. Higher education, instant credit, and insurance coverage of all kinds are daily needs today. No organization could administer these services on a large scale without the aid of a computer. A process to collect, update, and verify the information would soon overwhelm the staff.

Business organizations must cope with ever-increasing volumes of information.

1

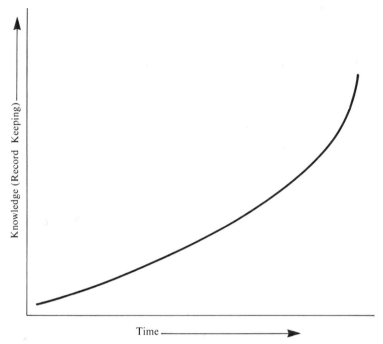

Fig. 1-1.   Knowledge as a function of time.

Management must have *timely and accurate information* about its operation to make sound business decisions.   Many business firms have implemented management information systems to consolidate large volumes of information into common data bases that can provide access to current data.   The centralized files represent a risk.   These business records could be inadvertently destroyed or fall into the wrong hands.   Most people would agree that the risk is more than offset by the gain.   The organization can now improve its efficiency, upgrade its services, and compete effectively in the market.

Record-keeping problems predate the computer.   But the computer—with its capacity to store, process, and retrieve large volumes of data at great speeds—has magnified both the potential risks and benefits.   The objective is to minimize the risks and maximize the benefits.

Today, data security presents special considerations.   The capability of computers to share resources, run many jobs concurrently, and communicate with remote terminals introduces many unknown variables into the data security picture for which physical and procedural controls are inadequate.   Excluding such inadequacies,[3] even conventional methods of protection are not being practiced.   While the percentage may be open to challenge, the fact remains that information security has not been given enough priority in either the public or private sector.

PRIVACY VERSUS DATA SECURITY

Privacy and data security are not interchangeable terms. They are related but wholly different issues. Privacy is an end that society would like to achieve. It pertains to the kinds of information about individuals that should be allowed to flow into, and through, record-keeping systems of all kinds. Privacy is primarily concerned with:

- How and what information will be collected.
- How, and by whom it will be used.
- How it can be reviewed, modified, and corrected.

A more comprehensive definition follows:

Information privacy includes the right of the individuals to know that recorded personal information about them is accurate, pertinent, complete, up-to-date, and reasonably secure from unauthorized access—either accidental or intentional . . . The concept of information privacy includes the right of the individual to influence the kind, quantity, and quality of information contained in your system which is readily identifiable to him or her. Regardless of whether this information is open to the view of the general public or specifically required to be confidential by Law, these privacy guidelines should be observed by all operators and users of information systems. This control extends from the time the information is collected, through processing and use, to the information's final disposition.[2]

Data security is neither a social nor a legal issue. Rather, it is a procedural matter, which involves the way organizations protect their information from unauthorized or accidental modification, destruction, and disclosure.

Historically, the protection of critical business records has been the prime incentive for data security. Recently, however, the rise of the privacy issue has also helped organizations to recognize the importance of protecting personal records.

An organization that has data must accept responsibility for protecting such data. It must decide what information it needs, who has access to it, how the data will be used. It must also make sure the data are accurate and determine how they will be protected. In short, the organization must select the combination of operating procedures and physical security measures, as well as hardware devices and programming tools, it needs to safeguard both business and personal records.

Security and integrity considerations, while not synonymous, cannot be separated. While security is primarily concerned with the protection of privacy, integrity is concerned with fraud and error problems. Good integrity means that the computer hardware and operating system are performing to design objectives; that data files contain accurate and complete information; that personnel are honest and obey security procedures; and that computer programs perform legitimately and without error.

There is no such thing as perfect security. Most organizations can achieve a level of protection appropriate to their needs. The objective of a data security program is to cut the risk and probability of loss to the lowest affordable level and also to be capable of implementing a full recovery program if a loss occurs.

EFFECT OF COMPUTERS ON SECURITY

With the number of computers now in the hundreds of thousands and their monetary value in the billions, executive management has demonstrated a knowledge of the benefits of data storage and manipulation.

Before the computer was considered a management tool for decision-making, it was a technological novelty. Glass walls were built around the computer to aid executives in "showing off" the computer facilities to visitors and employees. A false sense of need for bigger and faster computers greatly aided poor systems design, the collection of more than the minimal data required, and easy access through remote terminals. Although the political unrest of the 1960s quickly put the computer behind concrete and steel walls, the use of remote terminals continued at a rapid pace.

Simple economics has removed computers from the arena of novelty only to place them in the hands of management as a tool for making decisions. The ease and speed with which information can now be manipulated has caused management to discount the data being manipulated and the manipulator (computer) and add emphasis to the end result. While it is important to use all available resources when trying to arrive at decisions affecting company goals, it is equally important that management recognize the value of the commodity called information.

Personal identifiable information about a subject is a valuable commodity which is "owned" by that subject. Your right to maintain that information within your system is predicated on the principle of "informed consent." Whenever your system accepts information from an individual, your acceptance generates a sort of "silent agreement" between the subject and you.

The subject is saying in effect, "You have a service in which I wish to participate. I understand that in order to participate, you must have certain personal information about me. Otherwise, your system cannot operate. I accept that fact, and I therefore give you the information you desire in order that I may avail myself of your services."

When you accept the information, you are agreeing to take the information into your system, guarantee its accuracy each time its physical format is changed, protect the information from others with whom the subject has not made an agreement, and to not use the information for any purpose other than that to which the subject agreed.[2]

The threat of computer-related crimes is real. Unlike an armed robber who often steals only small sums of money, the computer criminal may steal millions of dollars. The electronic speed with which the fraudulent transactions are carried out help ensure that the dollar amount will be large. The head teller of Union Dime Bank in New York embezzled more than $1,500,000 by manipulating amounts via his terminal. Mark Rifkin illegally transferred $10,200,000 from Security Pacific National Bank in Los Angeles to his own account in New York using a computer security code without authorization. Perhaps the most dramatic case involved the Equity Funding Corporation. Over $2,000,000,000 of dummy life policies were generated on nonexistent people without detection by the auditors.

THE EFFECTIVE SECURITY PROGRAM

The first step in providing an effective security program is that all levels of management must become aware of the importance of information management and its consequences. H. R. J. Grosch says it well:

Technology is neutral. It can invade privacy or protect it, penetrate security or enhance it, conceal embezzlements or facilitate audits. And computer technology is not only neutral but exceedingly flexible; unlike the site of a nuclear reactor or a pipeline, computer hardware and especially software systems can be remodelled quickly and extensively.

The cost of "bad" systems and "good" systems are both within reach. If executives responsible for data management face up to their only recently recognized opportunities, if they calculate the cost—including the social, the humanitarian cost—of building and operating systems balanced between economy and efficiency on the one hand, and security and accuracy and personal rights on the other, they will find support from the professional community, and an increasingly alert society.[2]

Understanding the terminology of risk management is essential to introducing an effective program into any organization. The following paragraphs analyze the objectives of risk management, outline the steps in the risk management process, describe where and how the risk management process is performed, and evaluate the contributions of effective risk management to a company.

Exposures to loss involve the chance that a company will suffer an economic loss. Some losses do occur. These losses have three elements: (1) the item subject to loss, (2) the force(s) that may cause the loss, and (3) the potential economic impact of the loss. Perhaps the last element is more applicable to business than games.

Loss implies the existence of an item of value. Valuable items such as data files, libraries, and hardware immediately come to mind whenever a data processor thinks of loss. Regardless of the type of loss—fire damage, theft, operator error, whatever—the result is that the entity bearing the loss has a reduced value. For example, the salvage value of a computer destroyed by fire is less than its cash value prior to being destroyed.

Causal forces are another element of loss exposure. Knowing what is subject to loss is not enough.   One must be aware of the cause to apply risk management skills intelligently in a particular situation.

Perils, as causal forces may be referred to, can be grouped according to origin as: (1) natural, (2) human, or (3) economic.   Natural perils include fire, flood, hurricane, war, and other disasters.   Examples of human perils include dishonesty, vandalism, theft, negligence, and incompetency.   Finally, economic perils, such as recession, inflation, and lagging sales, can present a strong blow to any company.

The last category is really a logical sequence to the first two.   Financial impact is essentially a relative, as opposed to a fixed, term.   For example, poor customer relations may cause a company to lose $1 million in annual sales revenue.   If the annual sales volume is $100 million, impact is minor; however, if the annual sales revenue is $5 million, the company will suffer a severe economic impact.

Loss exposures come in two types: (1) pure and (2) speculative.   A pure loss exposure is characterized by two outcomes—loss or no loss.   Stated differently, things get worse or remain the same.

Computer operating systems are not provably secure.   Thus, the user can only assume that the operating system is performing error-free.   Should the operating system fail, then the user is assured that the operating system is not secure.

The costs of pure losses are predictable.   Assets such as computer hardware have known financial value.   Destruction of the asset assures the user of a predictable financial loss.

Speculative losses have the additional outcome of potential gain.   An illustration would be the investment in a new product that a company wants to market. Anything could happen, from the company going bankrupt to rapid growth and record sales.

Sometimes, the possibility of loss becomes a reality.   The financial impact may range from a minor inconvenience to a setback large enough to force a company out of business.   The domino principle is very much in evidence here.   When a company's survival is severely threatened, creditors may refuse to lend money and employees are then forced out of work.   There are other, direct losses to the community, such as lost services and goods as well as a reduced tax base.

Few businesses suffer severe losses.   However, all fear that they will be among the unfortunate few that do.   This uncertainty generates fear and worry directly related to the degree of uncertainty, the magnitude of potential loss, the ability to bear the loss, and the personalities of the individuals facing the potential loss.

Less than optimum use of resources is a real cost of uncertainty.   It costs money to retain information no longer needed.   Unnecessary backup costs money in time and storage.   With an uncertain future, chances are that management will use short-range planning methods as opposed to long-range plans.   For example, it may be decided to lease rather than purchase assets such as computer hardware.

Some businesses hedge against uncertain loss by hoarding resources.   Instead of investing in modern machinery, expanding sales territories, and implementing training programs, all of which might produce a greater rate of return, the company may decide to invest in lower yielding bank accounts in order to have money available to meet losses that may occur.

RISK MANAGEMENT

Risk management involves the application of general management concepts to a specialized area. Henri Fayol defines management as follows:

> To manage is to forecast and plan, to organize, to command, to coordinate, and to control. To foresee and provide means of examining the future and drawing up the plan of action. To organize means building up the dual structure, material and human of the undertaking. To command means maintaining activity among the personnel. To coordinate means binding together, unifying, and harmonizing all activity and effort. To control means seeing that everything occurs in conformity with established rule and expressed command.[1]

Risk management also requires planning future action, organizing material and individuals for the undertaking, maintaining activity among personnel for the objectives involved, binding together and unifying all the activities and efforts, and finally, controlling this activity and seeing that everything occurs in conformity with established rules and objectives.

Of these four tasks, risk management is more interested in the planning task. Planning involves decision-making, and the four stages of decision-making are: (1) identifying and analyzing the loss exposures, (2) determining what to do about these exposures, (3) implementing the decisions made, and (4) monitoring the decisions made and, when necessary, modifying them.

Objectives

Using physical and human resources, risk management can accomplish certain post-loss and pre-loss objectives. Survival is the most important and basic objective to be met. No matter how severe a loss a company sustains, it should be able to resume operation, albeit on a much smaller scale.

A more ambitious objective is continuity of operations. In some cases, such as a utility company, contractual obligations require continuous service. In most cases, after a period of interruption, resumption of partial operations and service to selected clients is adequate. Otherwise, clients may turn to other companies to fulfill their needs.

The third objective is earnings stability. It is important to provide replacement funds for earnings lost during an interruption of operations. The objective is to minimize the impact of the loss on the financial statement.

Continuing growth is an important objective for a company on the rebound from a loss. Proper planning means that resources will be available to continue new product and services development.

Finally, social responsibility or good citizenship is an objective to be considered. Seldom does a severe loss affect only the officers or owners of a business. Employees, customers, vendors, employees' families, and the general public may all be affected. In addition, public relations must be considered. A good image is helpful when applying for a bank loan to finance a new inventory, trying to close a big contract, or just trying to start over.

With respect to losses that may occur, a company must address certain pre-loss objectives: (1) economy, (2) reduction of anxiety, (3) meeting of externally imposed responsibilities, and (4) social responsibility. Preparing for what may happen in the most economical way is the economy goal. These costs may include insurance programs, safety programs, and time spent analyzing potential losses and preparing to handle them.

Reduction of anxiety is one important goal. Fear and worry are strong motivators. When all responsible parties can "sleep comfortably," then this goal may have been reached. Risk management must satisfy some externally imposed regulations, as do other management functions. For instance, a secured creditor may require additional property insurance. Government regulations may require capital improvements to meet minimum safety standards. Finally, social responsibilities surface again. The employees and customers must feel secure in their relationships to the company.

Conflicts do exist between post-loss and pre-loss objectives. To achieve post-loss objectives costs money. Off-site backup is not cheap. Time, materials, labor, and storage cost money. A security system may require additional people, software, and hardware. It is obvious that trade-offs are a difficult, but necessary task.

A problem identified is half-solved. Identifying and analyzing loss exposures is the beginning step of risk management. It consists of identifying what is exposed to loss and what can cause loss, obtaining information on how likely it is that such a loss may occur, and, if it does occur, how severe it will be. This determination must be done on a periodic basis, as exposures are constantly changing. A missed exposure could present you with catastrophic results if peril strikes.

Corporate Goals and Risk Management

Three corporate goals govern all policies established by the executive management:

1. Continued growth
2. Earnings stability
3. Survival

There is no doubt about the importance of continued growth and earnings stability to an organization. Ambitious marketing strategy and sound investment programs are reflected in the annual statement. However, survival is perhaps the most important goal of the three. If an organization suffers a severe loss and survives, then the incentive is there to strive again for the first two goals.

The existence of potential data security problems is fact, not fiction. The cases of criminal incursion cited previously undergird that fact. When corporate management accepts the reality of security problems, a call for commitment to a policy of risk management will surely gain unified support.

Management support should come in the form of establishing a security administration organization to study, implement, and monitor the security program. According to company size, the organization could be one person or a whole department. For example, a small company could retain the services of a security consultant to ensure impartial review and recommendation.

However, security is not the responsibility of a small functional group. It is the responsibility of all employees. To ensure the involvement of employees, the security group should educate them in security procedures and problems. The remaining responsibilities of the security organization include:

- Establishing a policy
- Developing a plan
- Performing cost/risk analysis
- Determining measures needed
- Implementing security measures
- Monitoring and, where necessary, modifying security procedures

Development of a plan is of prime importance—first, because it is necessary for budgeting and organizational support, and second, because it gives management an awareness of data security and its value to the organization.

IMPLEMENTATION OF A SECURITY PLAN

Prior to implementing a security plan, each person in the organization must be convinced (1) that there is a problem, (2) that he can do something about it, (3) that it is advantageous for him to do so.

The following quotation from a paper presented at the IBM Data Security Forum of September, 1974, serves as an excellent guide for creating a security policy manual.

INFORMATION SECURITY POLICY CONSIDERATIONS

DEFINING PURPOSE AND POLICY

Purpose

The objective is to ensure that official information of the Company is protected, but only to the extent and for such period as necessary to minimize volumes of data, and preclude needless safeguarding. This policy establishes the bases for identification of information to be protected; prescribes a system for classification, downgrading and declassification; prescribes safeguarding policies and procedures to be followed; and establishes a monitoring system to ensure the effectiveness of the Information Security Program.

Policy Statement

Within the Company, there is some official information and material which, because it bears directly on the effectiveness of the operation and conduct of our business, must be subject to some constraints and whose disclosure could result in harm to the Company. To protect against such disclosure by either overt or covert means, it is essential that such official information and material be given limited dissemination.

SETTING CLASSIFICATION PRINCIPLES AND CRITERIA

This action is probably one of the most important in establishing the Information Security Policy. The criteria established herein determine what should be classified. Without this step, disclosure of information is almost certain to occur. The government has three classification levels. It is important that levels be kept to a minimum so that clear distinctions can be made to avoid confusion and prevent over-classification and, hence, possible over-protection.

UPGRADING, DOWNGRADING, AND DECLASSIFYING

This section gives the Company's rules and procedures for changing the classification level of its information. It should be noted that some information may change its classification automatically over time.

MARKING

This section covers the marking of information and material in accordance with the procedures established under classification. As a consequence of this marking, the information or materials may be easily protected to the level required. Markings also facilitate downgrading and declassification action.

SAFEKEEPING AND STORAGE

Sensitive information or material must be secured in storage at the level appropriate to its asset value and its security classification.

EVALUATING HARM FROM INFORMATION COMPROMISE

If absolute security could be assured, which it cannot, then compromise would not be a consideration. In this section it is necessary to establish the seriousness of the compromise and take measures to negate or minimize the adverse effect, as well as regain custody of the information or material. Additionally, it will be necessary to identify and correct the cause of the compromise.

RESTRICTING ACCESS AND DISSEMINATION: REQUIRING ACCOUNTABILITY

Access and dissemination of sensitive information should be limited to those who have a need for such data in order to perform their required function. Prior to granting access, it is necessary to have background checks which are periodically updated to determine their reliability. Accountability permits the assessment of who had access to what information when.

TRANSMITTING DATA

This section of the Policy should describe the permissible methods and procedures by which sensitive information may be transmitted or transported to prevent its disclosure.

DISPOSING OF AND DESTROYING DATA

These subjects are often overlooked. As a result, classified waste may permit a competitor to obtain sensitive information.

PROVIDING SECURITY EDUCATION

Security education permits all persons handling sensitive information to become aware of their responsibilities, as well as the handling procedures.

Security education occurs through indoctrination briefings and refresher briefings.

The security policy should be documented in a manual, and any questions regarding its interpretation should be referred to the security administrator.[4]

For a policy to be effective, there must be:

1. A firm commitment by management.
2. Complete support by every employee.
3. Understanding by trained and competent personnel.
4. Constant monitoring to ensure adherence to the policy.

The size of an organization may have great impact on long-range planning and motivation to spend money for non-revenue generating goals such as data security. Government bodies, as well as most large corporations, are open to public scrutiny. Policing can be accomplished in the voting booth in the case of governing organizations. Publicly held corporations (mostly large ones) are scrutinized by customers, stock analysts, trade unions, and governmental watchdogs such as the Occupational Safety and Health Administration (OSHA) and the Environmental Protection Agency (EPA).

Customers may examine an organization to determine whether it can supply the required material (e.g., machine, parts and paper) for a specified period of time. If any doubt arises, a different supplier can usually be located.

Stock analysts often examine the long-range goals of companies when making investment decisions. Where the concern is to locate a growth stock to invest in, analysts look for plans to diversify through acquisition and/or market expansion and protection of current assets among other things. As data security becomes an even more vital issue, company policy in this matter will also come under closer examination. A breach of privacy, if it were to precipitate a class action suit, could prove devastating.

Trade unions are concerned that organizations have prudent plans and goals. This will ensure job stability as well as additional jobs. Matters in question are often resolved at the bargaining table and are subsequently included in legal, contractual agreements.

Governmental agencies have various methods of control, all of which can be upheld in a court of law. The IRS, OSHA, and EPA are among these institutions. While both large and small companies can be prosecuted, it is usually the large company that comes under attack because it has political appeal. Prosecution of a large company can solve a problem and launch a political career at the same time.

Management training and promotion programs have only recently begun to include DP personnel. Often the DP personnel have been considered technical staff and not professional management staff. As legal and ethical matters concerning data security are being raised, the need for management personnel knowledgeable about information management and mismanagement becomes paramount. The executive staff has almost exclusively drawn from the financial and marketing departments in the past when filling senior management positions.

SECURITY IN SMALL ORGANIZATIONS

Small organizations (most are privately held) may elect not to spend money for non-revenue generating goals and, because of size and stock status, may avoid severe public scrutiny. They are usually established to meet the needs of a handful of clients, maybe as few as one client. The limited production of specialized widgets or government-funded research could not be profitably accomplished by large organizations. Therefore, the number of management personnel could be as few as one. Most financial arrangements will also be made with small financial institutions. With such a small circle of people to "answer" to, decisions have less review.

The DP center is often designated as an extension of the accounting department. Not only are proper audit rules broken, but the chance of including a DP-educated person on the executive staff is greatly reduced.

Long-range planning would require a small company to plan growth from manual to automated record keeping, which is not often the case. Usually, automating the record keeping occurs after a crisis of poor customer or employee service. The project is undertaken with a sense of urgency and is almost always underfinanced. A small insurance company ($5 million in premium) in Texas will illustrate the problem.

The company was experiencing rapid growth and decided that (1) new and larger offices were needed and that (2) in-house computing services would soon be necessary in lieu of service bureau processing which was not providing adequate and secure services. The first step was to move to new facilities. Then a consultant was employed to assist in developing the information system. Recommendations for site development, hardware selection, software design, and employee training were presented by the consultant. After the necessary contracts were signed and work had begun, the president and sole owner had a change of mind after a poor financial decision (the consultant was unaware of it) and feared that certain data had been accessed without authorization at the service bureau. Contracts were broken, the consultant was fired, and another consultant who promised quicker results at a lower price got the job. Within three months the original consultant was called in to straighten out an expensive mess that could have been avoided. The actual money and time needed to complete the project exceeded the original estimates.

Data Center Security

Establishing a secure data center requires planning and financial commitment, often the two things lacking in the small organization. The following is a list of those mistakes most often made by small organizations:

1. The need for a computer arises out of crisis, not planning.
2. The data center is wherever the machine can fit, often a small office. Physical security measures, if any, consist of a new key lock on the door.
3. Financial constraints make it necessary to purchase the cheapest machine available.
4. Time constraints make it necessary to purchase the machine that can be installed the quickest.
5. Software is rushed through development, and testing usually occurs on live data.
6. DP personnel selection, either staff or consulting, occurs *after* hardware selection.
7. DP functions and personnel come under direct control of one of the departments it services.
8. Management believes that the computer will solve all of its problems.
9. Management will not admit to a lack of knowledge about computers.

Some of the problems described in the following paragraphs may not apply in some circumstances, while other issues may be underemphasized. Nevertheless, each vulnerable area must be investigated in detail to determine all potential risks. Only after identification can risks be quantified and controlled.

A computer center can become the target of adverse criticism and even criminal action not because of misconduct, but because of affiliation with an organization whose objectives may not commend public approval. The public may have reservations based on at least one of the following:

- Pollution of the environment, by noise, smell or contamination, or by biological or chemical warfare work, for example, nuclear energy.
- Company incompetence, such as incorrect billings or out-of-date credit files.
- Personal injustice due to computing errors.
- Misconceptions of the computer controlling private lives.

Radical pressure groups may be prepared to resort to violence and criminal acts to achieve their objectives. Knowing that the computer center is the nucleus of business activity, it is a prime target. Such action will also ensure publicity for the cause.

Difficulties can arise from a difficult economic situation. Data security depends on the orderly operation of the data center. Interruptions due to cash flow problems could certainly stop or at least slow down the operation. The first cutbacks to occur may well be in the area of security since security does not contribute directly to the "bottom line." As money loses value, replacement costs of hardware, software, property, and other assets will increase. Inflation has a direct effect on premiums. There is always the danger that supply organizations will run into financial difficulties or be unable to obtain raw materials to supply the finished products.

While it is rare for a large computer manufacturer to cease operations, peripherals manufacturers and mini/micro-computer manufacturers come and go. Acquisition of a small company by a large company may change company objectives and product line so as to be incompatible with previously manufactured equipment. Ideally, this matter should be considered during the original evaluation of system proposals, as follows:

1. Could the application software be converted to run on a different computer?
2. What would be the penalties in terms of performance, cost of conversion, and replacement of hardware?
3. Will the change be too disruptive to the operations staff?

Inflation affects DP personnel in two ways. First, as company profit margins take a dip, management will be reluctant to grant pay increases to offset increases in the cost-of-living. Second, as budgets shrink, companies trim the work force. Trade unionism becomes more dominant and the picture is set for confrontation in the form of a walk-out and total stoppage of company production. Militant employees could threaten sabotage.

Physical Security

Fires, floods, windstorms, and earthquakes are classified as natural disasters. These disasters threaten DP operations by destroying the equipment or disrupting operations.

Of all the problems which threaten the computer operations, those affecting the physical environment are the easiest to comprehend and to safeguard.

1. Boundary protection is necessary to prevent unauthorized access to the computer center.
2. Fires may be started from several sources:

   - a chemical manufacturing plant in the vicinity.
   - sharing premises with production and warehousing.
   - poorly constructed and maintained buildings in the immediate vicinity.

3. Water, or any other liquid for that matter, can be a real threat to a computer center. Water damage can be caused by:

   - flooding from heavy rainfall.
   - bursting water pipes in or outside the building.
   - fire fighting.

4. Other mishaps can occur. (The following list is by no means comprehensive, but it may provide some guidance.)

   - If the building is in close proximity to an airport, there is the risk of crashing aircraft. The constant noise may also cause poor employee performance.

- Closeness to main roads may increase the risk of a vehicle crashing into the building.
- The computer center is situated near a target building for extremists such as a foreign embassy.
- Vandalism is much more likely in a high crime area.
- Pollution may cause machine malfunctions and/or employee sickness.

MONITORING SECURITY

Management's needs and data processing capabilities have become more complex and have also merged. As more business functions have become computerized, management has become dependent upon data processing and internal controls that ensure accuracy and completeness. Traditional control and audit methods, tools, and techniques have become outmoded as computer applications change in form and structure. With a greater reliance on computers comes a greater potential for loss.

Traditional methods for auditing manual records as a whole do not apply to auditing automated records. Manual methods have always allowed for exception handling and do provide excellent audit trails. Before the use of terminals and data base concepts, simple batch processing afforded some degree of control and auditability. However, database concepts and terminals drastically altered the picture. With the new methods up and operating, transactions automatically "flowed" through the system. Thus, a single transaction error could be greatly magnified and have significant impact on the total system rather than just one group of files.

Data processing applications using real-time and database techniques are heavily dependent upon application controls to identify errors and omissions and report them for subsequent manual resolution. Auditors are now developing test procedures to verify application program controls. These procedures will be used to test computational routines, programs, or whole applications in order to evaluate controls or verify processing accuracy and continued compliance with specified processing procedures.

The *Test Data Method* executes computer application programs or systems using test data and verifies processing accuracy by comparing processing results with predetermined test results. This type of testing is easy to use and may be as simple or complex as desired.

Parallel Operation is a procedure to verify the accuracy of new or revised application system programs by processing production data using both the existing and newly developed procedures and comparing results to identify unexpected results.

The *Integrated Test Facility* procedure is a method of processing test data concurrent with production processing and comparing test results with predetermined test results. Care must be taken not to impact production files.

Parallel Simulation is an involved process. Although similar to the method of parallel operation, the variable becomes the application program instead of the data. Such a method requires the auditor to be knowledgeable in computer programming. Some generalized audit software is now being developed to relieve the programming burden.

Application system development is an excellent time for audit assessment. Standards of control for both the automated procedures and the supporting manual procedures can be established. To retro-fit such controls is not only more costly, but may force major design changes in the application programs.

The DP center needs to be audited by reviewing job accounting history and forcing execution of the disaster recovery plan.

Job Accounting Data Analysis is a procedure for monitoring the persons submitting jobs for processing and, where terminals are involved, for checking the source of the request. This is an excellent method, albeit after the fact, to identify unauthorized system use.

Disaster Testing is a little used, but very important audit method. Forcing execution of backup/restore procedures will ensure an orderly recovery from disaster, if and when it strikes. As management is becoming more dependent upon the flow of information, disaster testing is becoming more important.

THE ROLE OF THE EDP AUDITOR

It is commonly accepted that the function of auditing and controlling data processing systems in many organizations is lagging behind data processing capabilities. Expanding the use of the computer seems to have taken precedent over the implementation of controls in the applications.

The large company has several advantages over the small company with respect to systems auditing. First, most large companies have internal auditing staffs and may even employ risk managers. Systems auditing would most definitely be a part of the job descriptions, thus ensuring involvement. Second, the small number of computer mainframe models in use today makes it much less costly for auditing firms to develop and use generalized audit software.

Management awareness in the small company for systems auditing may be low, or even nonexistent. As a novice user, management may just simply be unaware of the need for such services. Not requesting the counsel of a consultant or the auditing firm could also leave management in the dark. It is not uncommon for a small company to install computer hardware and software using the "crisis" method. This approach focuses on getting the system up and running in the least amount of time, for the fewest dollars, while using live data for testing. Working under crisis precludes devoting time to adequate application control features.

The auditing firm may provide peer advice when there is no resident EDP auditor on the staff. However, this group can and may give insufficient or erroneous advice, particularly if the auditing firm is small. Consultants may be hired for technical expertise only. If so, they may have no knowledge of systems audit procedures to inject into the project, or management may simply not want their advice.

The large number of computer models in use today presents a special challenge with respect to EDP auditing. It is almost impossible to develop generalized audit software that can be used on multiple CPU models from different vendors. In many cases, the language in which the software is written may not be compatible across vendor lines. Lack of familiarity with the computer system and auditing software may cause the auditor to take only a casual glance at the application controls while paying great attention to areas with which he is more familiar.

HARDWARE/SOFTWARE CONSIDERATIONS

While the number of vendors of large mainframe computers has increased slightly, the vendors of small computers have greatly increased in number. The challenge facing the small computer user is obvious. Making the right selection of hardware has gone from hard to complex. Although the risks facing the buyer are much the same as they were years ago, the order of severity has changed. Cost, reliability, service, and the financial stability of the manufacturer must be considered in the final decision of which computer best meets the needs of an organization.

The cost of data processing is always of prime importance to an organization, especially a small one. Most organizations are small when the need for a computer arises, so withstanding the heavy costs of starting up and budgeting a DP center is a difficult task at best.

Hardware cost, despite inflation, has continued to drop. In addition, technological advances have brought about a machine that is significantly faster, smaller, and more reliable; using even less electricity than previous computers. The low cost and high performance have tempted many small businessmen to buy a computer, and thus a large market for business software has sprung up among the micro computer users.

Reliability has become an accepted feature of today's computers. With few exceptions, most computers are rarely inoperative. Most micro computers are sold with 30- to 90-day warranties and no service contracts are available. At least one micro computer manufacturer is offering a "throw-away" computer since estimated repair costs exceed the cost of replacing defective parts. The user simply returns the defective board and receives a replacement board for a small fee. Although the larger manufacturers are still offering maintenance service, regularly scheduled preventive maintenance procedures have been discontinued on most recent models.

Service has been the primary criterion when choosing a computer. However, it is not the factor it once was because of the increased reliability of the hardware. Preventive maintenance is not even performed on more recent models. In its place, some manufacturers offer a "dial-in" service. The "sick" computer is connected by a communication line to a computer at the service center, which then performs diagnostics. A service technician soon appears on site to replace the defective parts.

Vendor software has made a quantum leap in reliability in the last 10 years. Operating systems can be upgraded and changed with a minimum of disruption and operating failures. However, operating system software for small computers has been reduced to a more primitive state for marketing purposes. Initial lower cost plus the shorter development time required are the primary reasons for the step backward.

The simpler operating systems are a disservice to the user. The lack of job accounting and control, library and file security, and terminal control open many doors for invading the private information in the computer. Software developments lag significantly behind hardware advances, and this factor contributes to the primitiveness of the operating system software that is currently available.

If software developments lag behind hardware developments, then security developments must be further behind. With the primary issue being to get the system operable, security measures often become an afterthought. To illustrate the lagging efforts toward safety and security, the automobile has been a valuable commodity since the 1920s. No apparent concern for occupant safety began until the 1960s. Yet, the advancements made in both crash and health (exhaust emission controls) protection have not been significant in 20 years of research, testing, and use. The same holds true in data processing. The outmoded systems security practices of yesterday are still in use today. This unfortunate state of affairs stems primarily from the following notions:

- Security protection is primarily aimed at keeping outsiders away from organizational data.
- Primitive password protection, unsupported by proper supervision, audit, and controls, is sufficient to prevent unauthorized access.
- All programmers should have access to all systems facilities.
- Programming is a private function so programs are not subject to review.

The "add-on" approach to security is one in which the law of diminishing returns holds true. Even when all security risks have supposedly been considered, the emergence of one missed risk is a potential threat to the whole system. Unfortunately, no method is available to prove the completeness (security) of the operating system and application programs. Some of the most successful application software is predicated upon the ability to steal control away from the operating system. Job scheduling and print spooling programs are the classic examples. Security functions, if added on instead of designed into the operating system, would likely be very vulnerable.

Mini and micro computers face security threats by virtue of their design. Security functions may be left out of the operating system because of the significant increase in memory required for implementation. Without sufficient user memory available, the machine would be worthless. CPU speed may also be a constraint. Most small computers are relatively slow in comparison to their big brothers. The additional overhead of security software may degrade performance so as to make it unacceptable.

The rapid growth of the computer industry has also fostered the birth of many new companies. As a new computer chip is announced, another company appears on the scene ready to package and market the new chip. The financial community has much faith in the future of computers to keep investing in new companies and participating in acquisitions. Because of the newness of many companies, their product lines may not be fully developed. When company growth is a factor, purchasing one of the many new models may have such serious drawbacks as (1) hardware/software growth and compatibility and (2) the lack of hardware/software support should the vendor become insolvent or be acquired by another company.

THE PEOPLE SIDE OF SECURITY

Identifying current company risks requires that management review the past. Each manager brings to his job prior experiences. From these experiences comes valuable information. Having once suffered from flooding, it is likely that a manager would insist on keeping the DP center on a floor other than the basement or ground level. Theft often ensures the tightening of physical security measures. Figure 1-2 illustrates what is likely to happen in any risk management program.

Risk identification needs to be a task in the user departments as well as the DP center. This function will serve as a good cross-check and may point out possibilities that have been discounted or overlooked by people in charge of the risk analysis study. The user usually takes a more zealous approach to identifying risks that may impair his work productivity. For this reason, a user survey will place more emphasis on procedural matters than financial ones. Because of the large investment in equipment and personnel, the EDP survey will emphasize cost in dollars rather than procedural mistakes. See Appendix A for the user survey and Appendix B for the EDP survey.

People are undoubtedly the most important function of the DP department. No facility can function without a trained staff dedicated to performing its job. Personnel controls should reflect the need for carefully selecting mature, trustworthy employees as well as protecting these employees from unnecessary temptation.

One of the most important objectives in hiring employees should be to hire individuals who are competent for the tasks to be performed. This may result in the lowest cost over time by reducing errors and training cost. It will also help avoid employee frustration that arises from inability to perform assigned tasks.

Hiring procedures should provide as much information on qualifications as is

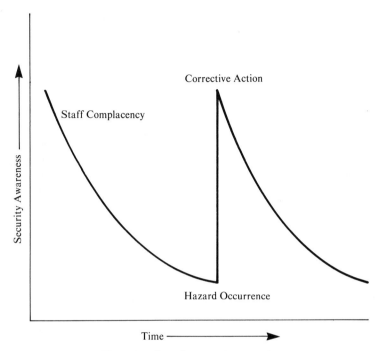

Fig. 1-2.   Security awareness cycle.

necessary to make a judgment on competency.   Data should include past employment verification, character reference checks, educational accomplishments, and criminal history, if any.

A surprising number of problems and security breaches result from improper training.   Training is essential to the circumvention of procedural errors.   Employees trained in proper security methods probably will not circumvent them.

The small company may lack any formal training program simply due to size; the DP department may be as small as one or two people.   In such situations, training is often given on-the-job with little or no formal program.   When the responsibilities of the whole department are placed on a small group of individuals, little time and expense can be devoted to training programs because the need for productivity is so great.   The use of consulting services does not necessarily ensure better training.   Chances are the consultant also lacks the resources for training. users and may even use the lack of such resources as a way to bid jobs at a lower price.

It is imperative that management review the productivity and work habits of the DP personnel.   Staff compliance with security procedures is a "must" if security measures are to be effective.   Competency can be determined only by review.   Job review acts as a deterrent to computer crime just as a policeman walking a beat deters robberies on that beat.   Structured programming serves as an excellent control because it forces involvement of several people reviewing each program. Such review may well thwart crime as it is less likely for a collusion to subvert system controls than it is for one individual to do so.

Personnel should be restricted in access, not only to the physical location of the computer but also to its capabilities. The most obvious breach of security comes in this area. The small company, having a limited staff, may require that each employee be cross-trained to perform all DP functions. This situation is especially likely where the department is staffed with only one or two people. Where possible, at least the users should be restricted from the computer center. Programmers should not have access to the production library and files, or the operating system. Unrestricted access to these areas involves too great a threat of a security breach.

A policy of vacation and job rotation is essential for boosting morale and reducing the perpetration of fraud. The probability of discovery of fraud increases greatly when the perpetrator's job is taken over by someone else. This practice has been the most effective tool of fraud discovery, although credit is usually given to "accident."

An essential element of personnel security is the termination of employees when the evidence justifies this action. Also, the prosecution of an employee for criminal acts may discourage other employees from contemplating such a crime. Collecting identification materials, revoking all powers of attorney, and auditing areas in which the employee had control will reduce the likelihood of future criminal acts by the employee and absolve the successor from responsibility for prior acts.

ASSESSING THE SECURITY PROBLEM

Once management has made a commitment to security procedures, a plan must be developed and put into action. To assist the designated risk manager in assessing the probability and severity of perils affecting the company, a matrix of probability/severity has been developed and is included as Appendix C. Use Appendices A and B as well as the previous paragraphs to aid in identifying all the risks. The following terminology definition will aid in the understanding of the matrix:

Probability Rating:

Improbable—extremely unlikely to happen, for example, significant damage due to a hurricane in Utah.
Remote—the chance of occurrence is remote, such as an aircraft crashing into the building.
Possible—a reasonable chance of occurrence, i.e., fire or storm.
Probable—very likely to happen, i.e., operator or programming error.

Severity Rating:

Low—small monetary loss with little impact on the organization, small delays, general inconvenience.

Medium—the loss causes small cash flow problems.

High—the loss is significant enough to impact the annual statement.

Catastrophic—the loss causes permanent damage, such as insolvency.

Loss in Dollars:

The actual cash value of the loss if incurred.

Loss in Time:

Number of productive hours lost if the loss is incurred.

After the questionnaires have been filled out and reviewed, the manager must list each peril and check the appropriate columns and fill in the dollar and time figures. A few simple computer programs can then be written to sequence and list the perils in many different orders. Grouping perils by probability/severity categories helps in determining the priority and cost of implementing the control techniques.

Once all the perils have been categorized and prioritized, control methods need to be identified and put into action. A brief description of the categories follows:

Method to be Used:

Avoidance—not exposing the organization to a risk. For example, locating the data center on a high floor in a building when the area is flood prone avoids risk due to flood damage to equipment.

Reduction—minimize the possibility of a risk occurring; i.e., jobstream procedures will reduce operator error.

Retention—the organization accepts full responsibility for the loss incurred.

Transfer—the risk is assigned to another party; insurance is a form of transfer.

Control Method in Action:

Briefly explain how the risk is to be controlled or avoided.

CONCLUSION

There are as many risk management plans as there are risk managers. No doubt, many of these plans are very good. However, the plan outlined in this chapter has been presented because of its ease of use, flexibility, ease of maintenance, and visual impact. Once the first study has been completed and the plan is put in use, it will be much easier to maintain. Using a computer file to store the matrix will allow the manager easy flexibility in generating graphs or reports that have strong visual impact.

If a security plan is to be effective at all, it must be well institutionalized and justified by the organization it is to serve. This justification must include a business look at the economics involved, an examination of the effect on personnel, and an honest, objective assessment as to its need. The principal concern is not the "fixes available," but a program that brings together, early in the process, the appropriate decision-makers and the community that will be impacted by a security program.

Security, the protection of assets, is sometimes perceived as costly, difficult to assess, sinister, contrary to maximizing productivity, and contrary to good employee relations. It is imperative, then, that the expenditures for a security program be based on economics and not emotion.

There is sufficient evidence to justify the need for controls that can prevent improprieties in DP. The staggering losses from computer-related crimes imply that a program of reaction may be one that is too little, too late. The organization that survives will be one that plans ahead.

APPENDIX A

RISK ANALYSIS

FOR _____SYSTEM

LOCATED AT _____

PERFORMED ON _____

BY _____

_____

_____

_____

Note: Circle value definition utilized.

A. HARDWARE

What would it cost to replace:

1. Your principal computer system? . . . .$_____
2. Other computers? . . . .$_____
3. On-site terminals? . . . .$_____
4. Peripheral stand-alone equipment? . . . .$_____
5. Card processing equipment (keypunch, tab, etc.)? . . . .$_____
6. Decollating and bursting equipment? . . . .$_____
7. Diskette? . . . .$_____
8. Other support equipment? . . . .$_____
9. $_____
10. $_____

                                    SUBTOTAL $_____

B. FACILITIES

What would it cost to replace your physical computer facility? Consider such elements as:

1. Site preparation . . . .$_____
2. Construction . . . .$_____
3. Heating and plumbing . . . .$_____
4. Electric including UPS . . . .$_____
5. Air conditioning and humidity control . . . .$_____
6. Fire prevention and protection . . . .$_____
7. $_____
8. $_____

                                    SUBTOTAL $_____

C. SPECIAL ITEMS

What would it cost to replace:

1. Your magnetic tape inventory? . . . .$_____
2. Your disk packs? . . . .$_____
3. Other storage media? . . . .$_____
4. Operating supplies (forms, cards, etc.)? . . . .$_____
5. Special maintenance equipment (tape cleaner, etc.)? . . . . . .$_____
6. $_____

7. $_____

                                              SUBTOTAL $_____

D. FURNISHINGS

What would it cost to replace:

1. Office furnishings (e.g., desks, chairs)? ....$_____
2. Specialized storage units (e.g., tapes, disk packs)? ....$_____
3. Custom furnishings (e.g., work stations)? ....$_____
4. $_____
5. $_____

                                              SUBTOTAL $_____

E. COST TO RE-CREATE

In your present environment, what would it cost to re-create your principal tape/disk data and production program files? Consider the following elements:

1. Source document and data preparation   HOURS   DOLLARS
   (keypunch and related clerical support)
   a. Regular labor ...._____ $_____
   b. Overtime labor ...._____ $_____
   c. Purchase services ...._____ $_____
   d. Travel and accommodations requirements ....$_____
   e. Transportation of computer jobs and related items .....$_____
   f. Material ....$_____
   g. Extra manpower ....$_____
   h. $_____
   i. $_____

                                              SUBTOTAL $_____

2. Restoration from backup files
   a. Computer rental ....$_____
   b. Regular labor ....$_____
   c. Overtime labor ....$_____

    d. Travel and accommodations ....$_____

    e. Transportation and computer jobs and related items ....$_____

    f. Extra manpower ....$_____

    g. Materials ....$_____

    h. $_____

    i. $_____

                            SUBTOTAL $_____

3. Documentation Reproduction

    a. Reproduction equipment rental or purchase ....$_____

    b. Extra labor ....$_____

    c. Overtime labor ....$_____

    d. Travel and accommodations ....$_____

    e. Transportation of material ....$_____

    f. Materials ....$_____

    g. $_____

    h. $_____

                            SUBTOTAL $_____

4. Consider the impact if you were unable to re-create some or all of your data and program files.

    If your company could still function, estimate the cost to continue operation. Consider the following:

    a. Utilize software program packages and consultant
       EDP services ....$_____

    b. Modify your EDP procedures to accommodate such
       packages ....$_____

    c. Initiate re-analysis and re-programming effort.
       Estimate the labor costs to return your operation
       to its former level ....$_____

F. **WEEKLY COST TO CONTINUE OPERATION AT BACKUP SITE**

    1. Purchased computer time (mainframe) ....$_____

    2. Input/output charges (if separately billed) ....$_____

    3. Media space rental (tape/disk if applicable) ....$_____

    4. Extra labor costs ....$_____

    5. Extra overtime costs ....$_____

    6. Travel and accommodations ....$_____

    7. Transportation of material ....$_____

    8. Materials ....$_____

    9. Special security precautions ....$_____

   10. $_____

   11. $_____

                WEEKLY CONTINUITY SUBTOTAL $_____

G. BUSINESS INTERRUPTION

Estimate the potential loss of revenues due to your inability

to function ....$_____

APPENDIX B

USER RISK ANALYSIS

for the _____Application

Completed By

_____

_____

_____

_____

_____

    On _____

                      (date)

I. Uses of the Application Output (List)

    A. _____

    B. _____

    C. _____

    D. _____

II. Dependencies

    Are there other uses of the application output outside your specific area _or_ uses dependent on your manual analysis of the application output (e.g., reports) utilized outside your area?

    Please List:

Use	_User_
_____	_____
_____	_____
_____	_____
_____	_____
_____	_____
_____	_____

III. Critical Dates or Time Periods

    List any Critical Dates or Time Periods (e.g., January 31 for W-2 forms)

Date	Reason	Brief Description of Criticality

IV. Dollar Risk vs EDP Application Outage Duration

V. Critical Files

    A. List Critical Files

        _____

        _____

        _____

        _____

        _____

    B. File Backup Requirements
        1. Are the files backed up by the EDP resource?   _____
        2. If so, how often?   _____
        3. How are the files backed up?

       a. Magnetic tape in vault   _____

       b. Microfilm   _____

       c. If microfilm, where stored   _____

       d. Estimate time to recover if
          microfilm or listing is only
          backup remaining   _____

       e. If backup is by microfilm,
          how often is it updated?   _____

VI. Revenue Estimate

   A. Revenue earned by Company associated with this application
is _____per _____.

   B. Cost or loss by Company associated with this application
is _____per _____.

VII. Fallback Modes

   A. Is a manual fallback system feasible?

      1. If so, how long to put in place? _____

      2. Cost to put in place? _____

      3. Estimated running cost of manual system is
         _____ per _____.

   B. Time frame when manual fallback system ceases to be
feasible? _____.

VIII. Estimated Business Loss as Result of Interruption

IX. Remote Access System Data

Is the application run remote from the computer center?

_____

If yes:

A. What type of terminal is used? _____

B. Is your terminal connected to the computer via:

      1. Leased lines _____

      2. Dial-up plus acoustic coupler _____

      3. Other (state) _____

C. Is your terminal in the same building as the computer? _____

D. Would you consider the information transmitted/received over the terminal?
   1. Private _____
   2. Customer private or sensitive _____
   3. Information whose dissemination should be controlled_____
   4. Information or data that is used in auditing proofs, etc. _____
   5. Information that may be disseminated to anyone within/without the Corporation without control
   _____
   6. Used in making management decisions _____

E. Do you use a password to sign on to the system? _____

   If so:

   1. Who determines the password? _____
   2. How? _____
   3. How often is it changed? _____
   4. Do you change the password when an employee that knows the password terminates employment?
   _____
   5. How many people know the password? _____

F. Do you feel that the security measures in the system are adequate for your needs? _____Explain:
   _____
   _____
   _____

G. Do you employ any cryptographic methods to protect vital data? __

   If so:

   1. Are software or programmatic techniques used? _____
   2. Are hardware devices used? _____
      If so, name the manufacturer and model number.

H. What programming languages can you utilize from your terminal? Please list:
   _____
   _____
   _____
   _____
   _____

X. What have we missed?

APPENDIX C
PROBABILITY/SEVERITY MATRIX

Hazards / Perils	Probability Rating				Severity Rating				Loss in Dollars	Loss in Time	Control Method Used				Control Method in Action
	Improbable	Remote	Possible	Probable	Low	Medium	High	Catastrophic			Avoidance	Reduction	Retention	Transfer	

REFERENCES

1. Fayol, H.: General and Industrial Management. Pitman Publishing Corporation, 1942.
2. IBM: *Data Security and Data Processing,* Vol. 3, Part 1, June, 1974.
3. Leavitt, D.: 90% of sites lack orderly security plan. Computer World Volume VIII, No. 19, May 8, 1974.
4. Short, G. E.: Establishing a Company Security Program. IBM Data Security Forum, September, 1974.

Chapter 2

DATA SECURITY

I. A. Gilhooley

Inspection Supervisor, Bank of Nova Scotia

Data security can be defined as the standards and procedures that protect data against unauthorized disclosure, modification or destruction, whether accidental or intentional.

Within a computer environment, it is convenient to categorize data into two types:

1. *Business Data,* comprising all the computer-held information maintained by the various application programs in support of the business requirements of the company.
2. *System Data,* comprising the vendor-supplied operating system, utility programs (e.g., sorts, merges, copies), compilers, and the application programs developed or purchased to meet the business requirements of the company. The controls pertinent to the introduction of new or amended versions of the operating system, utility programs, or compilers will not be addressed specifically in this chapter although many of the concepts which will be introduced are relevant (e.g., segregation of duties).

This chapter will outline events which can lead to the unauthorized modification, disclosure, or destruction of data and the measures which can deter, prevent, detect, or correct the occurrence of these events.

TRENDS IN DATA PROCESSING

Data security is essential to the success of any company regardless of the degree of computerization. Whether data are maintained in filing cabinets within each department or in an integrated data base covering all aspects of the company's operation, it is desirable to protect such data against unauthorized disclosure, modification, or destruction.

Computerization has centralized the maintenance of data previously distributed throughout the many departments of the company and allowed extremely fast and efficient access to these data. The exposures relating to computer-held data are the same as those relating to manually or electromechanically maintained data, but the magnitude of the exposure has increased greatly. This aspect is particularly relevant in the light of the current trend toward the data base environment and the resultant significant increase in opportunities for the unauthorized modification, disclosure, or destruction of sensitive data.

Another significant trend at the present time is toward the use of minicomputers both as stand-alone systems and as components in a distributed processing network. The proliferation in the use of stand-alone minicomputers is attributable to the significant reduction in price due to recent technological advances which have brought minicomputers within the reach of smaller businesses and the continuing awareness by businessmen of the advantages of computerization. The problem with this advancement in the use of minicomputers is that the management of these smaller installations probably has little experience or knowledge of the need for data security in a computerized environment.

CAUSES OF EXPOSURE AND RESULTANT EXPOSURE

Causes of exposure are the situations and events that could lead to a financial loss to the company. An exposure can be defined as the effect (expressed in financial terms) of the occurrence of an identified cause of exposure multiplied by the probability of it happening within a given timeframe. It is apparent that the evaluation of exposures is a subjective matter based on estimates of the probability of the occurrence of a cause of exposure and the resultant financial loss. The method of calculation illustrated has been taken from an IBM publication on data security.

1. Assign a weighting factor (c) based on the cost to the company should the event occur. This cost may be based upon the cost of recreating data that has been altered or destroyed or may be the cost of the competitive disadvantage incurred by the disclosure of sensitive information to a competitor.
2. Assign a weighting factor (p) based on the probability that the event will occur within particular timeframes.
3. Calculate the exposure (e) in terms of $ per annum using the following formula:

$$e = \frac{10^{(p+c-3)}}{3}$$

Suggested weighting tables in keeping with this exponential form of equation are:

Probability	p	Value	c
Never	0	$0	0
Every 300 years	1	$10	1
Every 30 years	2	$100	2

Every 3 years	3	$1K	3
Every 100 days	4	$10K	4
Every 10 days	5	$100K	5
Once per day	6	$1M	6
10 times per day	7	$10M	7

If an installation is not to misapply its budget for security, some evaluation of potential exposures must be conducted. The security budget can then provide controls designed to have an effect on the greatest exposures.

TYPES OF SECURITY

A data security program covers many aspects of security. To be effective, the program must be well balanced among these various aspects. Too often, management has concentrated its efforts in one area leaving gaping holes elsewhere. This happens for a variety of reasons:

1. Management has not adequately assessed what it is trying to protect against and operates in react mode, instituting controls after "something has happened."
2. Management reacts according to the latest publicized computer frauds, instituting controls based on how the fraud occurred without assessing how these controls fit in the overall system of control.
3. Management opts for the more visible, prestigious controls, perhaps to show senior management or the board of directors that something is being done about data security.

This chapter has categorized security as follows:

1. *Physical Security.* Physical security is concerned with safeguarding the hardware used during the processing of data and the media on which the data reside. Physical security includes protection against fire, flood, explosion, malicious destruction, and the provision of contigency planning arrangements to take effect in the event of a catastrophic occurrence at the main computer facility, resulting in a prolonged downtime of hardware, software, or telecommunications.
2. *Employee Education.* An aware employee educated to the needs of system security and privacy safeguards is perhaps the strongest control against many of the causes of exposure relating to data security. The employee must also be made aware of the disciplinary action which will be taken against anyone who violates company guidelines in this area.
3. *Logical Security.* Logical security refers to the software or hardware-wired controls built into the system to prevent or detect unauthorized entry into the system or unauthorized access to system or business data.
   Logical controls include the use of passwords to gain entry into the system

and cryptography techniques which ensure that sensitive data are only available in clear text mode to authorized programs which process those data.

CONTROLS

Within each of the categories of security described in the preceding section, there are several categories of controls which can be implemented to act upon a particular cause of exposure. Again, it is imperative to take a balanced approach toward the introduction of controls. It would be courting disaster, not to mention the height of arrogance, to rely solely on preventive controls without providing adequate detective and/or corrective controls.

The various categories of controls are as follows:

1. *Deterrent*
   - These controls are designed to deter people (primarily employees) from trying to penetrate the security system. An example of this type of control is a management policy statement clearly defining what will happen to anyone caught violating security measures.
2. *Preventive*
   - These controls prevent the cause of exposure from occurring at all or at least minimize the possibility; for example, password control at the terminal level in an on-line system will prevent unauthorized access to the system.
3. *Detective*
   - Where an exposure has occurred, detective controls will report its existence in an effort to minimize the extent of the damage. Certain fire precautions (e.g., heat detectors) fall into this category.
4. *Corrective*
   - These controls are necessary to recover from a loss situation. Without corrective controls a company may go out of business because of inability to recover essential data after a catastrophe.

PHYSICAL SECURITY

Physical security refers to the controls within the data center, designed to safeguard the hardware used during the processing of the data and the media on which the data reside. Physical security also involves the administrative controls that ensure a smooth and secure interface between people and the computer.

Threat Analysis

The budget to make provisions for security will undoubtedly be limited so it must be used effectively. The installation of closed-circuit TV and complex man-traps will be meaningless if proper control is not maintained over the creation of back-up files or if the administrative procedures for the handling and distribution of sensitive reports are inadequate.

Physical security measures are the most visible, and there may be a tendency to concentrate on the more glamorous (and expensive) of these measures (such as closed-circuit TV and man-traps) to the exclusion of less ostentatious but equally effective ones.

A balanced approach to the introduction of physical security measures will ensure that the budget is applied for maximum coverage. To this end it is necessary for the company to address the following specific tasks:

1. Evaluate the physical threats to the data center (e.g., fire, flood, and power failure) and determine the probability of occurrence for each threat (i.e., cause of exposure).
2. Estimate the potential losses to which the data center is exposed in the event of an occurrence of one of the causes of exposure previously identified. The objective of calculating the potential loss estimate is to identify critical aspects of the data center operation.
3. Determine the annual loss expectancy by combining the estimates of the value of potential loss and probability of loss. A possible formula is presented on page 34.
4. When the estimate of annual loss has been completed, management will have a clear picture of the significant threats and will be able to assess the relevancy of various security measures in relation to their cost and their effect on the significant threats.

Segregation of Duties

Prior to the introduction of computers, segregation of duties was effectively implemented by placing specific responsibilities in distinct departments within the company. It was not possible, therefore, for one person to control all aspects of any portion of the business. Accountants and auditors have built up a great deal of experience and expertise in the area of segregation of duties within manual systems. However, segregation of duties is often overlooked when a computer system is introduced. Fundamentally, segregation of duties ensures that one person cannot initiate, authorize, and process a transaction and have sole possession of the output (e.g., cash or goods) from that transaction.

Within a computerized environment the functions which were previously split between several departments may now be centralized within the data center. Although the responsibility for the initiation and authorization of transactions should remain within the originating department, the recording of these transactions onto computer-readable media will be the responsibility of the data center. In some instances the computer programs designed to process these transactions will au-

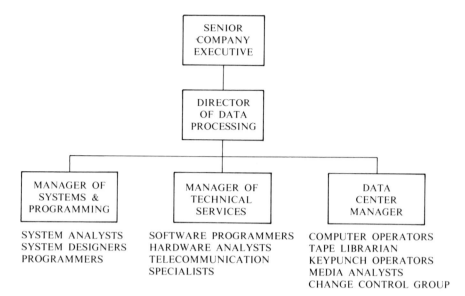

Fig. 2-1.   Organization chart for a medium-sized data processing department.

thorize them based on certain predetermined conditions; for example, if a check drawn on an account will overdraw the account, the system may authorize payment based on an overdraft limit maintained for that account.

It is obvious that adequate segregation of duties must exist within the data processing department (of which the data center forms a part) and that this segregation must include the interface between the data processing department and the user groups.   Figure 2-1 gives a suggested organization chart for a medium-sized installation to provide adequate segregation of duties.

The data center has custodial responsibility for all data (i.e., business and system data) held on computer-readable media (e.g., on tapes and disk packs).   The physical security measures are, therefore, the responsibility of the data center. Responsibility for the integrity of the data maintained on computer media, however, remains with the appropriate user or technical department.

Although the controls to protect the integrity of this data may be designed and implemented by the system designers and programmers responsible for the system, ultimately the user department is still responsible for the integrity of its business data.

Changes to production libraries should be physically effected by one of the groups within the data center.   The initiation, authorization, and actual change will be the responsibility of an applications group with the approval of the appropriate user department.

Figure 2-2 gives an example of the segregation of duties desirable to control the integrity of business and system data.

	BUSINESS DATA	SYSTEM DATA (Application Programs)
Initiation of change	User officer	Computer user group
Authorization	User supervisor	User management
Change vehicle	Application update program	Programmer update
Custody of media	Data center	Data center
Change effected in production environment by	Data center running the Application Program	Data center copying program into production environment

Fig. 2-2. Segregation of duties to ensure data integrity.

Controlled Access

The provision of elaborate security measures is meaningless unless they are specific in their application. Before deciding on controlled access devices (e.g., armed guards, identification badges), the data center management must assess exactly what they are trying to protect. Keeping non-personnel out of the building is fine, as far as it goes, but if personnel have the run of the building once inside the main door, then the overall security of the data center is minimal (e.g., where programmers and user department personnel are allowed access to the computer room, tape library, or printer area).

Once the data center management has assessed which areas should be considered as sensitive, only those employees whose work routine requires access on a daily basis should be allowed unrestrained access. An important part of any controlled access system concerns the administrative procedures which give direction on allowing access, on a controlled basis, to anyone who has a legitimate cause to be in a restricted area (e.g., service engineers).

Environmental Safeguards

Fire Precautions

Fire precautions can be considered in the categories of those that *prevent* the fire from occurring, those that *detect* the fire's occurrence or the imminence of a fire, and those that endeavor to *correct* the situation with the minimum of damage. Within each of these categories the controls (i.e., precautions) can be further broken down into those that are people dependent and those that are mechanical.

1. *Preventive Controls*
   - The materials used in the construction of the data center should have an adequate fire rating.
   - The design of the building should minimize the possibility of fire spreading from one area to another.
   - Administrative procedures should be designed and implemented to avoid the risk of fire (e.g., the storage and disposal of combustible materials).
2. *Detective Controls*
   - Detective controls should be designed to detect the early signs of a fire (e.g., excessive heat, smoke), activate the corrective device, and provide an audible warning to employees of the danger.
   - Heat detectors, smoke detectors, and manually activated fire alarms should be placed in strategic areas within the data center.
   - Administrative procedures should describe the people-dependent functions to be activated in the event of fire.
3. *Corrective Controls*
   a. *Mechanical*
      - Water is still widely used as an extinguishing agent for fire and can be applied at the scene of the fire by means of a sprinkler system activated by the detection controls mentioned previously. The advantage of using water in fire fighting is its low cost relative to other means.
      - Halon and carbon dioxide are gases used in fire fighting especially where electrical equipment may be involved. The use of carbon dioxide must be carefully controlled and the area evacuated before its use because of its harmful effects on people. Halon, when used in small quantities, does not have this harmful effect on people but is very expensive to use.
   b. *People Dependent*
      - Personnel should be trained in what they are to do in the event of fire.
      - Fire marshals should be appointed for each department or functional area with specific responsibilities for their area.
      - Emergency exits and all fire fighting equipment should be clearly sign-posted.
      - The fire department should be invited to review the fire precautions within the data center. Since the fire department may be called in to fight a fire, it would be advantageous if they were aware of the layout of the data center and what fire fighting facilities were readily available and their location.
      - After the fire has been brought under control and extinguished, there should be clearly defined procedures for getting the data center back into production status.

In addition to the controls for the prevention, detection, and correction of fire, there must also be ancillary controls to recover from the smoke and water damage which accompanies fire damage.

Power Supply

Computer hardware is built to withstand variances in the power supply, but only within certain tolerances depending on the particular piece of hardware.

An uninterruptable power supply can be effected by using a bank of batteries designed to smooth out variances in the power supply. Where the power supply is completely shut down, this power from the batteries will cut in, enabling an orderly shutdown of computer operations. The amount of time these batteries can operate in a stand-alone manner depends on the number of batteries in the bank and the amount of equipment which has to be serviced, but typical times range from a few minutes to 15 minutes.

Other less expensive methods for dealing with a sudden surge in current include voltage regulators. Again, data center management must take into account what it is trying to protect and evaluate the exposures before deciding what specific protection is required.

Good Housekeeping

The reasons for following good housekeeping habits are innumerable:

- Large amounts of paper stored in the computer room can create a fire hazard; allowing operators to smoke while working is another potential source of fire.
- Food and drink should not be allowed into the computer room. A drink spilled down the back of the CPU is virtually guaranteed to cause a system failure.
- Inadequate filing of tapes and disks can cause operational problems and a security exposure. If files are continually misplaced, it may take a long time to realize that a file has been stolen.
- Management tolerance of poor housekeeping habits is not conducive to establishing the level of awareness about security desirable among employees in a computer environment.

Insurance

Insurance should be considered as a component of an integrated system of security and not as a substitute. Even the best thought-out plans for security cannot possibly cover every eventuality. Insurance should be taken out as a conscious effort to cover exposures which cannot be totally eliminated by other means and whose cost of occurrence would be too high to absorb.

Many types of insurance policies are available, each with its own limitations and endorsements. Generally speaking, the wider the coverage, the greater the cost. Listed below are high-level descriptions of the types of policies available. Again, it should be stressed that insurance is only a part of the security program. The premiums payable or indeed the availability of insurance will depend on the other components of the program.

- Policies to cover physical damage or destruction (through fire, flood, or storm) of the hardware and media (e.g., tapes and disks).
- Policies to cover the cost of recreating data (as opposed to simply replacing the media on which the data were held) are available at additional cost. Adequate back-up procedures, including the use of off-site storage, can reduce the need for a policy of this type.
- Policies to cover the loss of business due to an insured peril. A company may suffer from severe competitive disadvantage if its data center is put out of action for an extended period of time owing to a fire. Contingency planning can effectively counter this eventuality and may either nullify the need for such a policy or substantially reduce the premiums payable.

Contingency Planning

Contingency planning concerns establishing procedures and facilities to counteract a prolonged (i.e., in excess of 24 hours) failure or unavailability of hardware, software, or telecommunications. The increased use of computers has resulted, in many cases, in a reliance to the point where the company would cease to function if the computer facilities were unavailable for any length of time. Considering this fact, the number of computer users who do not give serious thought to contingency planning or who go no farther than the thinking stages is astonishing.

Effective contingency plans can range from establishing a second site with comparable facilities to the main processing center, to establishing procedures for returning to the manual system that was in place before the introduction of the computer system. The extent of the alternate arrangements depends upon the degree to which the company relies upon the computer and the size, complexity, and criticality of the applications run on the computer.

Contingency planning requires a commitment on the part of senior company management and not just data processing management. The following points are suggested as a possible approach to contingency planning:

- Establish a task force with specific responsibilities for contingency planning.
- Define objectives and scope as they relate to contingency planning.
- Establish specific tasks, timetable, and checkpoints.
- Define the review process and levels of responsibilities.

Specific tasks which should be addressed include:

- *Threat Analysis.* Evaluate the threats to the data center (e.g., fire, flood, and power failure) and determine the probability of occurrence for each threat and the estimated time to recover from such an occurrence.
- *Loss Potential Analysis.* Estimate the potential losses to which the data center is exposed. The objective is to identify critical aspects of the data center operation and to place a dollar value on the loss estimate.
- *Annual Loss Expectancy.* Combine the estimates of the value of potential

loss and probability of loss to develop an estimate of annual loss expectancy. The purpose of this exercise is to pinpoint the significant threats as a guide to the selection of contingency arrangements. The cost of contingency arrangements should relate to the loss(es) against which they provide protection.

- *Remedial Measures.* When the estimate of annual loss has been completed, management will have a clear picture of the significant threats and critical applications. It will then be necessary to evaluate the recovery plans already in place to counter short-term failures and determine what additional measures, if any, are required to provide a cost-effective, secure environment which can handle both short-, and long-term failure or unavailability of hardware, software, or telecommunications.

EMPLOYEE EDUCATION

Systems analysts, programmers, computer operators, and employees of the various user departments serviced by the computer are among the employees who must be made aware of what security means to the company, and that people are perhaps the most important component of any security system.

- Many cases of unauthorized disclosure of information have been caused by the careless actions of authorized recipients of this information.
- The most elaborate entry systems are meaningless where employees exercise "common courtesy" and hold the door open for the person following to enter into secure areas.
- Password systems are meaningless unless the employees are made aware of the reasons for maintaining the confidentiality of their password.

One of the expected results of any security education program is to familiarize personnel with existing security safeguards, including why safeguards are employed, what safeguards are designed to protect against, how these safeguards work, and what is the result of utilizing each safeguard. Further, this education program should bring about a general attitude of "security awareness" on the part of all personnel:

1. Awareness of what security problems exist and what opportunities for improvement are available.
2. Awareness of the employee's own security responsibilities as well as those of his co-workers.
3. Awareness of what to do when security violations are detected.

Management must educate employees in the requirements of a security system, and must also clearly define the disciplinary action against anyone who violates company guidelines in this area.

The security requirements of the company should be clearly stated in writing and readily available to all employees. New employees should be made aware of the company requirements and requested to read the appropriate documentation. Existing employees should be given refresher courses and also kept up-to-date with any enhancements or changes in the security program. A possible method of ensuring that employees are periodically reminded of the security requirements is to ask them to complete a staff declaration to the effect that they are aware of the security requirements and have no knowledge of any breach in them. The staff declarations could be completed on an annual basis (e.g., on the individual's anniversary of starting work with the company) or at whatever frequency is deemed necessary.

LOGICAL SECURITY

Logical security refers to the software or hardware-wired controls built into the system to prevent or detect unauthorized entry into the system or unauthorized access to system or business data.

Vendor Controls

Vendor controls are primarily to ensure that data are not lost or amended during transmission from the media into main storage.

1. *Parity-Bit Checking*
   Parity-bit checking entails adding one bit (i.e., the parity bit) to each character processed. Computers are built to accept either even or odd parity. The parity bit is added to ensure that the count of "on" bits is odd or even depending on the type of computer. When the computer accepts odd parity, the count of all "on" bits within a character (including the parity bit) must be an odd number. Even parity would indicate an error in this case.
2. *File Labels*
   Vendor-supplied software will generally attach header and trailer labels to data files created.
   The header labels can be used to determine that the correct file is being used and can also protect the file from being overwritten before a specified date. Trailer labels can contain the number of blocks written into the file. This block count can then be checked after the file has been read to ensure that all the blocks have been read and that additional data have not been inserted. There may, however, be an option to bypass this label processing. Although this option may be a necessary feature in some installations, it should be the subject of stringent administrative and detective controls.

Cryptography

The growing trend toward the data base environment has caused a significant increase in opportunities for the unauthorized access to or disclosure of sensitive information. Additionally, more and more applications are being designed as real-time, on-line systems, with the result that an increasing amount of confidential or sensitive data is being transmitted over telecommunication lines.

Encryption techniques are designed to scramble the data into a form which is unintelligible to the unauthorized observer. Decryption techniques are then used to translate this scrambled text back into its original form.

The advantages of encryption are that the encrypted data are secure from unauthorized disclosure or amendment, including the addition of any information. The introduction of the computer has enabled the creation of extremely complex algorithms for encryption, which are almost impossible to decrypt without detailed knowledge of the algorithm or, in some cases, without the actual key used in the encryption.

1. *On-Line Communications*

   Cryptography has been used almost since the introduction of the telegraph and is widely used to scramble telephone communications as a protection against wiretapping.

   Devices now available can be attached between the modem and the computer or terminal. Used in pairs, the sending encryption device translates the text into its encrypted form. The receiving device then translates the encrypted text back into its original form.

2. *Data Files*

   A great deal has been written about cryptography as it relates to on-line communications. However, the majority of a company's data resides on data files stored on tapes and disks resident either in the data center or at an off-site storage location. There is no reason why sensitive data held on external media should not also be protected by data encryption.

The objective of the following is to present a viable approach which will (1) ensure that sensitive data are made available only in clear text to authorized programs, (2) centralize the responsibility for data privacy and security, (3) be transparent to individual programs which access the data, and (4) keep the additional processing overhead to a minimum.

Data held on external media are most often held in clear text forms; i.e., assuming that individuals have access to the file, the data are readily accessible and in a readable form.

Obviously, not all data maintained would be considered sensitive. It would be the responsibility of individual companies to determine which information, if disclosed, could cause competitive disadvantage, breach of good faith, or other problems.

The organizational structure of the data processing department would have to be expanded to include a data administrator responsible for maintaining an administration data set describing which files within the installation are considered to contain sensitive data. The administration data set would contain an entry for each production file deemed to contain sensitive data.

Each entry would contain the following information:

- Position and length of the fields to be encrypted/decrypted.
- The key to be used for encrypting the data. Each application would have the facility of specifying a unique key.
- The job names and passwords which are to be considered as authorized; i.e., only certain job names supported by the correct password will be allowed access to the data in clear text format. All other jobs may gain access to the file but would obtain sensitive data only in an encrypted form.

As each file is opened, the administration data set would be accessed using the file name as a key. If an entry is found, the job name corresponds to an authorized job name and the correct password is specified; then an indicator within the data control block (DCB) will be set on to indicate that encryption/decryption is required for this file. The remaining pertinent information from the administration data set entry will be stored in core and an address pointer to this information will be stored in the DCB. (If the file to be accessed does not have an entry in the administration data set or the job being run is not authorized to read clear text data, then the data are made available to the program as it appears on the external device, i.e., in its encrypted form.)

After each record has been read from the file into core storage, the associated DCB will be interrogated to determine whether any data must be decrypted. (The decryption module will use the field positions and key extracted from the administration data set when the file was opened. On return from this module, the previously encoded data will be in clear text form.)

When a record is to be written to an output file, the associated DCB will be interrogated to determine whether any data must be encrypted before being physically written to the output device. (The encryption module will use the field positions and key extracted from the administration data set when the file was opened.)

The basis of this proposed system lies within the administration data set. Security over the information held within this data set is imperative if the proposed system is to attain the desired level of data security. The data administrator also has a key role in ensuring the completeness, accuracy, and authenticity of the entries within the administration data set.

The advantages of this approach to data security are as follows:

1. Actual possession or availability of a production file does not represent an exposure since sensitive information cannot be interpreted.
2. Sensitive data are made available only in clear text to authorized programs.
3. By amending the open, read, and write procedures for all files, the security routines are transparent to individual programs. All programs must go through these routines whenever data are to be accessed or created.
4. The creation of a data administration function with responsibilities as pre-

viously described centralizes the responsibility for data privacy and security.

5. The processing overhead will be minimized by determining at open time which files are to be subject to encryption/decryption and by storing all other pertinent information in high-speed core storage.

6. The data processing department will derive benefit from the standardization of data protection practices. Test files could be created directly from production files as any sensitive data would be encrypted and therefore not readily available to other than authorized production programs.

Identification/Authentication of On-Line Users

In a batch environment, control over access to the computer and therefore the data held by the computer is relatively easy to maintain.

Typical examples of these access controls are:

- The remote job entry (RJE) station or card reader is maintained in a restricted access area within the data center with an operator present whose responsibility is to take the jobs and input them into the system.
- Physical recognition of any person submitting a job is possible owing to the fact that jobs have to be handed in at a central location.
- Each job has to have a job submission card which possibly even requires an authorization signature or initial. This card will state the name of the person submitting the job, the purpose of the run, the computer resources required (including the names of any files to be used), and the expected output.

However, an on-line system operated with terminals does not offer the same possibilities for the centralized control over access to the system. An on-line system must devise alternative methods to identify the person operating the terminal. Once an individual has been accurately identified, it is then possible to restrict that person's access to certain transactions or data files. Identification is usually made by the operator providing some kind of password to the system. The passwords can either be keyed into the system by the operator or can be contained on a badge or card which is inserted into a reader attached to the system.

Ideally, access to an on-line system would consist of two stages. First is the identification stage, where the operator identifies himself to the system. The operator identification can be considered as non-secure information. It may be the surname of the individual, employee account number, or some other type of ID. The second stage concerns the authentication that the operator is who he says he is. This authentication password should be unique to each operator and should be kept confidential. It is the authentication of identification which has the direct bearing on the security of the system. Some computer packages can generate passwords randomly. User-selected passwords have been found to be the most easily discovered.

The following points should be considered when designing controls to protect against unlimited access to an on-line system.

- Maintain a password data set identifying authorized personnel who may access the system.
- Establish and document the administrative functions responsible for maintenance of this password data set.
- Clearly define who has access to this data set and ensure that it is protected from unauthorized disclosure or modification.
- Generate passwords (i.e., the authentication password) randomly by the computer and change as frequently as practicable.
- Suppress the display or printing of any passwords. In this way it is not possible for anyone to gain knowledge of a password by looking over the shoulder of an operator or by reviewing printed output.
- Educate the user to the importance of non-disclosure of passwords and clearly state management policy in the event of unauthorized disclosure.

Various means are being developed for identifying terminal operators by some physical personal characteristic (e.g., finger prints or voice prints). Although these methods have the greatest potential for unerring identification, they are not yet commercially available.

Data File Protection

Passwords

It is possible for the "owner" of a data file to assign a password to the data file at the time of its creation. Access to this file is only available when the password is correctly presented to the system. The advantage of the password system for data file security is that it provides a reasonable level of protection at low cost.

The disadvantages are:

- In a batch environment, the password must be supplied by the computer operator. This may appreciably slow down job throughput depending on the number of files which require a password and also presents a security exposure in that the password must be shared with someone who is not the owner of the data. In an on-line environment, the terminal operator will be requested to supply the password for any protected files that he tries to access. This, therefore, obviates having the "owner" of the data share the password with anyone else.
- All the data on the file are protected from anyone who does not have knowledge of the password. There may, however, be a legitimate case for allowing someone access to certain portions of the data. If that person is given the password, he has access to all the data but if he is not given the password, he cannot access the portion to which he is entitled.
- The password may not be unique to any individual. Where multiple users

have access to a protected data file, additional measures are necessary to identify precisely who has accessed that file.

Date Protection

Data files normally have labels at the beginning and at the end (i.e., header and trailer labels). Part of the information held in the header labels is the date of expiration for the particular file. If an attempt is made to write onto that file prior to the expiration date, a message will appear on the console log. The operator has the option of cancelling the job or of continuing by overriding the date protection.

Where date protection is used as a measure for data security, appropriate administrative controls must be introduced to ensure that only authorized overrides are submitted by the console operator. Reliance on the date protection facility is not a strong control, but it can be strengthened by writing a report to management detailing each system request for date protection override.

- Overriding date protection should be the exception not the rule.
- The report must be reviewed and acted upon.
- There should be a clearly stated management policy regarding any instances of unauthorized override.

Access Control Software

The growing awareness of the need for comprehensive treatment of data security has led to the introduction of several access control software packages designed to protect data from unauthorized disclosure, modification, or destruction, and to permit access to each user on a strict need-to-know basis. Each package has its own features, strengths, and weaknesses. They are all, however, attempting to provide a level of security based on the following criteria:

- Access authorization is user based.
- Access by the user is limited to information he needs to know to perform his function within the company.
- All attempts at unauthorized access are detected, rejected, and reported.

Before access control software can be introduced, the installation must complete a great deal of preplanning, including setting up the organizational and administrative function necessary to support the software, classifying users according to what they require access to and classifying data according to its relative need for security.

Testing

Before new or amended programs are placed into the production environment, they must be tested using data specially suited to the particular needs of the test. Testing can be carried out by the programming team responsible for creating or amending the programs, the user department that will ultimately use the output from the programs, or the data center in the form of an acceptance test designed to ensure that the programs will run successfully in the production environment.

Using "Live" Data

The transaction data for the test may be relatively simple to create. In fact, there may not be suitable data on any live transaction files. It may, however, be considered necessary and/or expedient to use a live master file for the test.

The advantages of using a live master file are:

- the majority of possible conditions will already exist on the master file.
- the master file will be up-to-date. The problem with maintaining a test master file is that it is often not kept current.

The disadvantages of using "live" files are obvious. The increase in the potential for unauthorized modification, disclosure, or destruction of these files is tremendous. Where it is considered necessary to use live files in the test environment, consideration should be given to the following points:

- Encrypt all production data and allow the data to be decrypted only by authorized programs running in the *production* environment (see p. 45).
- Do not allow access to the actual live file. Insist that a copy of the file is taken and that the copy be used in testing. This procedure will eliminate the risk of modification or destruction of a live file during testing although the risk of disclosure remains.
- Establish and document procedures and standards for copying production files into the test environment. The copying should be under control of the data center as they should have custodial responsibility for all production data.
- Establish procedures for controlling the output (printed and otherwise) from test runs which use live production files.
- Ensure that *all* copies of production files are scratched after use in the test environment.
- Make use of system reporting facilities to detect unauthorized accesses to production files and clearly state management policy in the event of such an occurrence.

Testing Alternatives

The preceding discussion assumed the necessity of using production files in the test environment. Careful planning at the design and development stages of a system can, however, remedy this necessity to a large degree.

Regression Testing Facility

A regression testing facility requires setting up a master file and transaction file containing all known conditions. Each record is documented, stating the content of the record and its purpose during the running of a test. The documentation for the transaction file should also contain a section on the expected results after application of the transaction. Tests of the system are run using these files. Whenever the system is changed, the tests can be rerun and the two sets of output compared (i.e., the output before and after the change was made). Any unexpected discrepancies must be followed up by the person conducting the test. Output results can be compared either visually, which can be a long, tedious, error-prone task, or by the use of an automated file-compare facility. A regression testing facility requires a high degree of documentation and a commitment to keep both the documentation and the files in line with the current production environment; as an example, when a new condition is encountered in the production environment, the testing files and documentation should be updated to incorporate this new condition.

Integrated Test Facility (*ITF*)

An integrated test facility entails the incorporation of certain records into the live master file for use as a testing vehicle. Tests are conducted using these records, and they can be created and amended according to the needs of the test. The main advantages of an integrated test facility are in problem determination, auditability, and training.

- Where an error condition is suspected, the condition can be recreated in a live situation without affecting the "authentic" records on the file.
- The auditors have the opportunity of submitting transactions for processing by the production sytem in its production environment without disrupting the run.
- Employees training on the system can use these "dummy" records until they have sufficient knowledge to work on the authentic records.

Care must be taken, however, to ensure that the ITF records are not confused with live data and are not used in reporting actual company results. An ITF combined with a regression testing facility can provide a powerful tool in ensuring that systems are properly tested prior to their introduction into the production environment.

Library Management System

A Library Management System (LMS) consists of the standards and procedures to ensure the security of an installation's program libraries and the integrity of the members that reside on these libraries.

Earlier sections discussed some of the available techniques to protect the business data of the company from unauthorized disclosure, modification, or destruction. Now the security of the programs developed to process these data will be considered. It is essential that the application programs executed in the production environment be authorized, meet the criteria for which they were designed, and not perform any additional, unauthorized functions.

An effective LMS, therefore, consists of the administrative and logical (i.e., software) controls to ensure that new or amended library members to be migrated into the production environment are authorized, properly documented (i.e., audi-

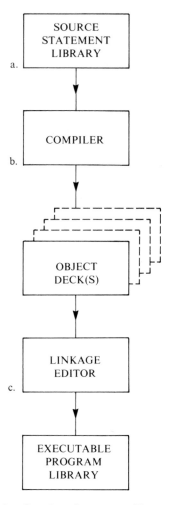

Fig. 2-3.   Creation of an executable program.

table), signed-off by the appropriate parties, and, once in the production environment, are protected from unauthorized activity.

Figure 2-3 gives a simplistic view of the libraries involved in the creation of an executable program.

1. The programmer writes the program using a language similar to English. The programmer's output is referred to as source statements and typically is written to a source statement library.
2. In order to translate these source statements into a form understandable to the computer, they are input to a compiler which produces machine language

statements (i.e., object deck) corresponding to the English language statements coded by the programmer.

3. When all the modules which make up the total program have been compiled, the various object decks are input to a utility program called the linkage editor, which creates an executable program from the various input components.

Figure 2-3 illustrates the creation of a program. However, there should be a distinction between the environment in which this program is created (i.e., the test environment) and the environment in which the program will be used to process live data (i.e., the production environment). Where control over production data files limits access to production programs, the LMS need only secure the contents of the production program libraries.

Before any program can be migrated into the production environment, it must be thoroughly tested to ensure that it does what it was designed to do and nothing more (see p. 49). After a program has been migrated into the production environment, the LMS must protect this member against unauthorized changes.

Figure 2-4 shows that it is the source statement library and the executable library members which are migrated into the production environment after they have been adequately tested.

This is a simplistic view of these procedures. In some installations there may be an intermediate set of libraries from which the user testing and data center acceptance testing would be executed. To ensure the integrity of the programs being tested, the programmers would not have access to these intermediate libraries.

The following is a list of considerations to be made in the development of an effective library management system:

- Determine what libraries require protection. If production data cannot be accessed from test libraries, the level of protection afforded to these libraries may be minimal (i.e., restricted to back-up and recovery procedures in the event of total loss). Access to protected libraries should then be restricted to authorized.personnel.
- Back-up and recovery procedures should be designed to counter a partial or total loss of the libraries.
- Changes to protected libraries (including the addition of new members) should be authorized by the user department serviced by the programs. This aspect provides for segregation of duties and prevents any programmer from submitting an unauthorized change through established channels.
- An audit trail should be made of changes to source statements in order that such changes can easily be verified to the change that was authorized.
- There should be a way of ascertaining that the most recent version of the executable program corresponds to the most recent version of the related source statements.
- After the programmer has finished testing a program in the testing environment, there should be a method of "freezing" the source and executable code while user and data center testing is carried out.

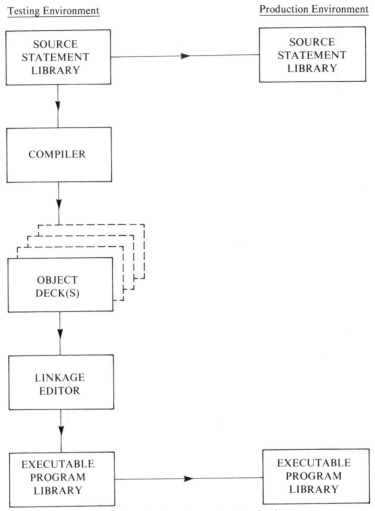

Fig. 2-4.   Migration into the production environment.

- Actual changes to the production libraries should be effected by data center personnel, thereby providing an additional level of security through enhanced segregation of duties.
- The documentation supporting any activity to these production libraries should be complete and contain provision for the appropriate sign-offs indicating that the programs may form an authorized part of the production environment.
- The archival system supported by the LMS should provide for adequate recovery facilities should a new version of a program fail to work in production.
- Management should receive reports from the LMS indicating activity against

the protected libraries and also noting any unauthorized accesses, whether they resulted in a change being made or not.

- Management should have a clearly defined policy in the event of any unauthorized activity regarding these libraries.

- Provision should be made for controlling the implementation of emergency changes. Emergency changes are usually made because of the discovery of an error in a program running in production. Time constraints usually do not allow emergency changes to go through the normal channels of authorization, testing, and sign-off. For these reasons, emergency changes must have special provisions for follow-up after the change has been implemented. On no account should emergency changes be accepted as a normal part of the operational environment. A high percentage of emergency changes indicates a lack of proper testing procedures and may even be indicative of an unstable operational environment.

THE ROLE OF THE AUDITOR

The auditor's function is to assess the adequacy, effectiveness, and efficiency of the system of internal control within an organization.

Until the introduction of computer systems on a large scale, the auditor's role in an organization was fairly well defined. In recent years however, an increasing reliance upon computer systems has forced the auditor to adjust to a new environment.

To adequately fulfill his primary function, the auditor must have access to a great deal of information not normally available to one individual. This information will include details of all the data security measures in force within an installation. An organization must, therefore, have a degree of protection against any unauthorized activities by its auditors, and the auditors, while still maintaining their independence, must be protected from unwarranted suspicion should an exposure occur.

The auditor's role in a computer environment has been the topic of a great deal of discussion and controversy. The main issue is the question of involvement and the maintenance of the auditor's independence. On the one hand is the argument that if the auditor is actively involved in the design stages of a system (whether an application system or a security system), he will not be able to present an unbiased assessment of the controls within the system and may be at a disadvantage if a weakness is subsequently highlighted. The other side of the argument is that computer systems are substantially different in their approach to security (i.e., the controls are contained within the programs and cannot be physically assessed as is the case in a manual system) and require the auditor to grow with the system if he is to attest to the adequacy of the controls built into the system.

Although this subject will not be dealt with in detail in this chapter, the following points bear mention:

- Assuming that the auditor finds the system of internal control to be adequate, he should conform to the standards and procedures governing the rest of the installation.
- All attempted violations of the system of internal control by the auditor should be documented, including what was attempted, why it was attempted, and what were the expected result and the actual result.
- More installations have gone through the exercise of identifying the various stages making up the system development life cycle. The output from this exercise is usually a checklist of tasks to be performed which is then used to chart the progress of the developing system. Similarly, it is possible for the auditor to prepare a checklist of the audit tasks which have to be performed in each of the component stages. It is recommended that the auditor prepare this checklist by component stage and issue a sign-off at the end of each stage. In this way there is no confusion between the auditor and the system development team regarding the auditor's requirements. It is also recommended that this checklist be made available to the system development department in order that they may become familiar with the criteria used by the audit department when reviewing a new system development.
- The auditor is in the position of acting as a user for any new system. Assuming that the audit department has kept abreast of all projected new system developments, it is possible for the audit department to design its own subsystem and have this programmed into the developing system at the appropriate phase.

Chapter 3

SECURITY OF STATISTICAL DATA BASES

Francis Y. Chin

University of California, San Diego, LaJolla, California

Gültekin Özsoyoğlu

Cleveland State University, Cleveland, Ohio

Computer security has always been an important issue. However, owing to the recent developments of fast and easily accessible computers with large quantities of shared data, the issue has gained far greater importance. In parallel to these changes, the problem of enhancing the security of statistical data bases has been of growing concern in recent years. A statistical data base has been defined as one which returns statistical information, such as frequency counts of records satisfying some given criteria, as opposed to a data base which returns complete details of a record, for example, name and address of an employee. Such statistical data bases have wide applicability in medical research, health planning, and political planning, to name just a few.

Essentially the security problem for a statistical data base is to limit its use so that only statistical information is available and no sequence of queries is sufficient to derive private or confidential information about any individual. When such information is obtained, the data base* is said to be *compromised*. Notice that the protected information does not necessarily reside in the data base.

In order to clarify the nature of the security problem, we present three examples. First consider an on-line system that gives information about the number of individuals having certain properties (i.e., COUNT information is revealed). The system tells us that a total of three people have the following properties; age 39, male, married, lawyer, residence in Edmonton. Suppose further that we know a particular lawyer having all of the preceding characteristics and his data are included in our data base. Now if we enquire the number of people having all of the foregoing properties and in addition with earnings over $50,000 a year, and we get an answer of 3, then we know immediately that this particular lawyer earns over $50,000 a year.

As another example, consider an off-line system, e.g., a census publication office that publishes tables of statistical information. Suppose a small county has six hardware stores and a city within the county has four of them. If retail sales are

---

* From now on, we will use the term data base for a statistical data base.

published for the county and for the city, then each of the two out-of-town stores can determine the other's sales simply by taking differences between the published county and city figures.

For our third example consider an on-line data base of employees of a company, in which salary ranges for employees are not protected. It is also known that every electrical engineer with salary < \$20,000, at least 5 years working experience, and a BS degree has had at least one "bad" rating from his manager. Suppose we know an electrical engineer with a BS degree who has worked for more than 5 years in the company. If both queries, "number of electrical engineers with BS degree and at least 5 years experience" and "number of electrical engineers with BS degree, at least 5 years experience, and salary < \$20,000" have the same answer, then that particular electrical engineer has had at least one "bad" rating from his manager.

The first two examples illustrate two different kinds of applications, an on-line and off-line application while the third example illustrates that the information deduced by the user may not be stored in the data base. For the off-line application, statistical offices traditionally examine their publications carefully to ensure that there is no disclosure. However, increasing demand for detailed information and possible use of computers for correlating several publications to disclose further information have prompted researchers to consider better (more strict) security measures, such as data perturbation techniques.[22,26,30] In the case of on-line data bases, instead of storing aggregate information, the data base contains anonymous but individual records, and returns statistical summaries of those records which satisfy the specific characteristics given in the query. Changes to the data base, such as insertions, deletions, and updates, are allowed and responses to queries are expected to reflect the current status of the data base.

Protecting statistical data bases from compromise is a difficult problem, for this situation deals with various sorts of inference mechanisms that may be employed by the users.[14,15,20] Traditional controls for off-line systems fall short for complete security for on-line systems. In the section, Review of Proposed Protection Schemes, different proposed protection schemes are reviewed and their applicability is discussed. The following section is devoted to a new approach to statistical security which employs several different types of dynamic constraints in the conceptual model level[11] in order to prevent "dangerous" inferences that may possibly lead to compromisability of the data base.

STATISTICAL DATA BASE MODELS

We will first describe a statistical data base model proposed by Denning[13,15] and then briefly discuss other models.

A *statistical data base* can be viewed as a set of n records. Each record has k attribute (property) values corresponding to attributes $A_1, A_2, \ldots, A_k$, among which some are protected attributes. Values of the protected attributes for each record are confidential, and only statistical summary information about these attributes is available. An example is a data base of employees. Each record has attributes NAME, ADDRESS, SEX, AGE, POSITION, etc. and a protected attribute SALARY.

A *query* is some statistical function, e.g., MEAN, MEDIAN, applied to some subset of the records in the data base. Every query has a *characteristic expression* C, which is a logical expression using the logical operators, conjunction (&), disjunction (v), and negation (~). The set of records satisfying the characteristic expression C of a query is called the *query set,* S(C). In order to clarify the idea of a characteristic expression, let us consider the data base of employees. C = (AGE < 40) & (POSITION = programmer)) is a characteristic expression and its query set S(C) contains all the programmers under 40 years of age employed by the company.

The most common statistical query types can be defined as follows:

$\text{COUNT}(C) = |S(C)|$, the size of $S(C)$

$\text{SUM}(C,A_i) = $ sum of the ith attribute values of those records in $S(C), 1 \leq i \leq k$

$\text{AVERAGE}(C,A_i) = $ average of the ith attribute values of those records in $S(C), 1 \leq i \leq k$

$\text{MAX}(C,A_i) = $ the maximum of the ith attribute values of those records in $S(C), 1 \leq i \leq k$

$\text{MIN}(C,A_i) = $ the minimum of the jth attribute values of those records in $S(C), 1 \leq i \leq k$

$\text{MEDIAN}(C,A_i) = $ the median of the ith attribute values of those records in $S(C), 1 \leq i \leq k$

We will use the following definition of compromisability: the data base is *compromisable* if one can deduce from the responses of the queries one or more protected attribute values of some records. This definition is more specific than the one given in the introduction since although an attribute may not be confidential, it may still be necessary to protect it if it leads to the derivation of some confidential information not necessarily in the data base.

In some models used to investigate statistical data base security, researchers have used key-specified queries to describe query sets.[17,18,31,32] Some other researchers have used binary k-bit keys to describe attribute values of records and the k-bit queries with 0's, 1's, and *'s (don't care) for the query sets.[6,29]

REVIEW OF PROPOSED PROTECTION SCHEMES

Much research has been performed on the security problem of statistical data bases and many methods have been proposed to prevent a data base from being compromised. The protection schemes may be classified into the following four categories:

1. Protection by controlling the size of the query set.
2. Protection by limiting excessive overlap between query sets.
3. Protection by partitioning the data base.
4. Protection by output perturbation or data distortion.

Below we discuss these four protection schemes. In the next section we propose a different protection scheme using a different model, namely, the use of security constraints and mechanisms described and maintained at the conceptual data model level.[9]

Criteria for the Goodness of Protection Schemes

In general, protection schemes impose restrictions on the system. In order to compare the "goodness" of these schemes, we will be considering the following factors:[42]

1. *Effectiveness.* Restrictions should guarantee security to a reasonable extent. We will also discuss the effectiveness of restrictions under dynamic data bases and users' knowledge about the real world that the data base models.
2. *Feasibility.* It is possible that some restrictions are sufficient to guarantee security but the system has no way to enforce them. The enforcement of restrictions should be feasible.
3. *Efficiency.* The implementation should be efficient. Any scheme that is virtually impossible to implement, or involves too much overhead, should be avoided.
4. *Richness.* Restrictions when applied should not conceal too much information. In other words, the data base should still be rich enough to be useful for users.

Protection Schemes

Controlling the Size of the Query Set

One of the earliest and most straightforward protection schemes suppresses queries whose query set size is small.[27,28] The examples given in the introduction illustrate that the security of the data base is endangered by allowing answers to queries with small counts. In Chin,[6] an m-response system using k-bit binary keys to describe characteristics of records is introduced. It allows only SUM and COUNT queries and prohibits answering those queries whose query sets have less than m records. Necessary and sufficient conditions to guarantee the security of a two-response system is given for a static data base (i.e., no insertions, deletions, and changes in the data base). Unfortunately this result imposes too many restrictions on the system and limits the richness of the data base. Moreover, as illustrated by the second example in the introduction, since any two users of a particular kind in a two-response system might easily know each other, it is a generally accepted practice to have an m-response system with m $\geq$ 3. However, the properties of an m-response system for m $\geq$ 3 are not well understood.

It can be shown that information can also be deduced if queries with a large query set size are answered.[13,15] Thus, the system should limit queries with very small and very large query sets. Unfortunately, this protection scheme can easily be subverted by a simple device called *tracker*.[13,33,35] A tracker is some auxiliary characteristic expression which, when added to the original characteristic expression, produces an answerable query. The user then uses this answer with some others to deduce the answer for the original unanswerable query. This idea is further extended to double trackers and general trackers, which are applied to more restricted ranges of answerable query set sizes.

The preceding results show that the technique of controlling the size of the query set is not effective (although feasible) and merely makes the intruder's job harder.

Limiting Excessive Overlap Between Query Sets

This protection scheme assumes a static data base and inhibits the responses to queries whose query sets have too much overlap with the query sets of other answered queries. When two query sets overlap completely with the exception of one record, that single record may be compromised for certain statistical queries (e.g., SUM). Even in the case when query sets overlap by no more than one record, compromise is still possible for SUM queries by solving a system of linear equations.[17] Using different statistical query types and a key-specified model, several studies have been reported on the upper and lower bounds of the number of queries needed to compromise the data base.[12,18,19,31,32] Clearly this protection scheme is very difficult to enforce. Moreover, since a previously answered query may inhibit the responses of several other more useful queries, this protection scheme may severely limit the richness of the data base.

Threat monitoring is another proposed scheme that does not guarantee security but is claimed to provide a deterrent for intruders.[15,28] The system monitors queries that have been answered and tries to detect excessively active periods of use of a data base and to detect instances of many successive and similar queries. This scheme, however, can easily be made ineffective by masking queries.[34]

Partitioning the Data Base

In this protection scheme the whole data base is *partitioned* into groups of records, each of which are in k-dimensional hypercubes defined over k attribute domains.[42] Queries are modified to report over partition boundaries. In other words, queries always involve groups of records and never subsets of groups. Thus records inside a group cannot be isolated by overlapping queries, and only information concerning whole groups can be derived. However, if the data base is dynamic (i.e., insertions, deletions and updates of records are allowed), then each change in a group can be detected and the changed record can be disclosed. It is shown by Chin[8] that if the changes are done in pairs for each group and if each group starts with an even number of records, then the system is secure for SUM and COUNT queries. Dummy records can be introduced initially to make the number of records in each partition even. Dummy records can also be used to pair with each insertion or deletion in each group such that changes to the data base can be reflected as soon as possible.

A variant of partitioning is *grouping* (or microaggregation), which is used in off-line applications such as census publications.[22,26] Records are grouped together and only aggregate statistical information is given. These two techniques, partitioning and grouping, have the same limitations of possible loss in the richness of the system, especially when the groups are ill-formed.

Output Perturbation or Data Distortion

All the protection methods discussed so far provide the user with exact statistical information from the query set. The protection schemes reviewed in this section attempt to prevent compromise by modifying the data in the data base or perturbing the responses to the queries without losing too much of the meaningfulness of the information in the data base. *Rounding*[1,26,30] is a technique commonly used in off-line cross-tabulations published by census offices. Responses to queries are rounded up and down to some multiple of a base number b. Two types of rounding functions are defined.

Let $r = m - \lfloor m/b \rfloor * b$ then

Normal rounding:

$$g_1(m) = \begin{matrix} m \\ m - r \\ m + b - r \end{matrix} \qquad \begin{matrix} \text{if } r = 0 \\ \text{if } r < \lfloor (b + 1)/2 \rfloor \\ \text{if } r \geq \lfloor (b + 1)/2 \rfloor \end{matrix}$$

Random rounding:

$$g_2(m) = \begin{matrix} m \\ m - r \\ m + b - r \end{matrix} \qquad \begin{matrix} \text{if } r = 0 \\ \text{with probability } 1 - r/b \\ \text{with probability } r/b \end{matrix}$$

Random rounding is intuitively more appealing than normal rounding. Random rounding is always unbiased in the sense that the expected value of any answer so rounded is equal to its original unrounded value. Normal rounding does not always prevent compromise due to its predictability in rounding up or down, so introducing randomization into the rounding process is expected to be more secure. Unfortunately compromise is still possible with random rounding.[1] (However, for off-line one-dimensional tables, no exact information can be derived in normal rounding with an even base b such that b/2 is odd.) Both rounding methods assume a static data base with no user knowledge of protected attribute values; thus their effectiveness is limited.

Error inoculation is another technique which trades accuracy of the revealed information for security.[2,3] Instead of perturbing the response of the query, the system distorts the record values in the data base. This approach, which results in losing the original data, may be undesirable for some applications. Several studies have been reported[10,36] about a protection technique called *multi-dimensional transformation.* This technique proposes to transform the original data base to another one in such a way that a given set of statistical properties are preserved. Part or all of the original data may be changed; however there is no known efficient method for this transformation and it is unclear whether this technique can be effectively applicable to a dynamic data base.

Sampling the data base is another technique which does not always give true answers to queries.[26] Only a small sample of the entire data base is used for answering queries. Since the set of records is no longer selected by users, the chances of compromise is small. Denning[16] proposed *random sampling* in which large samples of query sets are used for answers. It is shown that compromise risk is effectively reduced and high accuracy can be maintained. However, the data base is assumed static and users' supplementary knowledge is not considered.

Another similar protection technique is to allow the system to "lie." [12] For example, response to a query for the median of a query set may be the value of an arbitrary record in the query set. It is shown that even for such a system that lies, compromise is still possible with sufficient number of queries.

DESIGN OF A STATISTICAL DATA BASE EMPLOYING SECURITY CONSTRAINTS AT THE CONCEPTUAL LEVEL

In this section we will discuss the design of a statistical data base (SDB) which employs several dynamic constraints at the conceptual level. The details of the design are in Chin.[9]

SDB Design Features

In this section we discuss the desirable features of the SDB design in terms of the "goodness" criteria introduced previously.

1. *Effectiveness of the protection.* In order for the SDB system to be effective, the data base should be equipped with the following information.
   a. *A "good" conceptual model.* Data bases are more than collections of records; they contain a model of some portion of the real world with possibly complex relationships and inferences. Any protection scheme, in order to be effective, should be informed about all this information; that is, the security problem of SDB should be elevated to the conceptual model level.

   In the real world users may be equipped with information other than what is explicit in records. If the data base administrator (DBA) is aware of this information, effective security measures can be imposed easily. The following example illustrates this situation.

Example. Consider a data base of employees of a certain computer manufacturing company in which the sum of salaries of employees can be queried. Assume the following information (which is not represented in the data base and hence unknown to the system) exists.

   i.   Salary range of a new systems analyst with BS is $[10K,12K]$.
   ii. Salary range of a new systems analyst with MS is $[12K,14K]$.

Now assume two new systems analysts are hired and information about them is inserted into the data base. If the change in the sum of salaries of systems analysts is $27K, then users obtain the information that the new employees have MS degrees.

Most problems in SDB security can be removed with a good model of the real world environment so that the DBA can take effective measures. Thus, existing relationships and semantics of the information should always be considered in an effective SDB design.

b. *Well-defined statistical information.* Some previous studies have made assumptions like "every possible combination of record can be requested" or "all possible medians of any sets of records are queriable." [17,18,31] These types of assumptions cause an explosion in the complexity of the problem. An analysis of the real world and a definition of the statistical information will help to reduce the size of the security problem (crystallize the complex relationships that effect security, define the information to be secured, etc.).

Since the statistical information will always be about groups of objects, the intersection of these groups of objects will eventually give a set of indivisible groups of objects, and any statistical information about these indivisible groups of objects will constitute atomic statistical information. Thus we are no longer interested in giving out uncontrolled, random statistical information to users, which may be easily exploited, but rather we will give out well-defined information that can at most be reduced to atomic information.

c. *Controlled changes in the data base.* Dynamics, as well as statistics, of the real world should be revealed to users. However, this should be done in a controlled manner, and the information revealed due to changes in the environment should be recorded for auditing. (Note that the 1974 U.S. Privacy Act[40] necessitates inclusion of the changes into the data base.)

d. *Information about users' supplementary knowledge.* Some users may have had access to some protected information. This information may lead to further disclosure if it is not known by the DBA and if security measures are not applied. Thus users' supplementary knowledge should be maintained and kept up-to-date in the SDB. We assume that the DBA is correctly informed about users' supplementary knowledge of protected information.

2. *Efficiency of the protection.* Next we describe features of the SDB which may improve the efficiency of the protection.

   a. Disjoint user groups are defined because users' supplementary knowledge may be substantially different from one other, or they do not necessarily have the same access authorization to different parts of the data base.

   b. Depending on users' needs, different levels of statistical information are revealed to different users.

   c. Statistical information is classified into types such that allowable statistical queries can be defined. This leads to different security constructs and mechanisms for different types of statistical information.

3. *Richness of the information revealed to users.* Clearly investigating the security problem at the conceptual model level provides the data base designers with more control over the richness and usefulness of the SDB. Nevertheless, richness of the SDB is certainly reduced owing to the reasonably large size of atomic information. Moreover, atomic information should not be further decomposable by templates or by queries such as join, select, and project operators in the relational model. We also assume that the DBA should confirm the security and compatibility of any new view of the data base before granting access to it.

The next section briefly discusses constituents of statistical information. In the section following it we propose the design of a SDB using the generalization and aggregation hierarchies[38,39] and introduce some modifications to it. The next section defines the statistical information about each population and introduces the concept of security atom population. In the section after that, we discuss different types of security constraints, and then we introduce a statistical security management facility with three different components. Finally, the last section identifies three different inference types and briefly describes constraints which may effectively protect the data base for COUNT queries.

Constituents of Statistical Information

Statistics is the study of specific aspects of individuals in a *population.* The individuals in the population must have *something in common.* Most statistical methods can be viewed as ways of making inferences about a population. Thus, for the specific environment at hand, once the populations to be studied are found, the individuals are no longer important, and two individuals with nothing in common will never be included in the answer of any statistical query together.

Distinction should also be made between the properties of individuals and the defining characteristics of a population. For example, "sum of salaries of employees" is a quantity related with the employee population, but "sum of salaries of employees where salary > \$12K" gives information about a different population. Not distinguishing this difference may cause protection problems. Similarly, for example, "number of employees" and "number of employees convicted of felony" give information about two different populations.

Conceptual Data Model for SDB Design

Although only aggregate information is revealed to users, this does not imply that only aggregate information is stored in the data base. On the contrary, the conceptual model of the SDB should be similar to the conceptual model of any other general-purpose data base. There are several reasons for this requirement besides effectiveness of the protection and the richness of the data base.

1. For some users and at least for the DBA, the statistical data base is just a normal data base, and these users should have access to all information in the data base (not just aggregates).
2. It is necessary to have total information about the environment in order to enforce integrity and validity in the data base.

In Chin[9] the design of a secure SDB is investigated using a structured redundant conceptual model, "aggregation and generalization hierarchies," proposed by Smith and Smith.[38,39] For the SDB design, the structuredness, redundancy, and semantics of the conceptual model are important in order to (a) define nondecomposable atomic information clearly and (b) apply security measures easily and naturally without severely reducing the richness of the data base. In the rest of this chapter we will use the generalization and aggregation hierarchies as a conceptual model for the SDB design.

Smith and Smith introduce two kinds of data base abstractions. Aggregation (naming relationships) is an abstraction which turns a relationship between objects into an aggregate object. Generalization (naming classes) is an abstraction which turns a class of objects into a generic object. In the context of the relational model, generalization and aggregation hierarchies are proposed as a conceptual model.

For our SDB design purposes, the requirement of using natural language nouns to describe objects[39] is not used. Figure 3-1 illustrates one particular decomposition of Computer Scientist into lower level generic objects in a data base of employees of a certain computer manufacturing company.

Each object in the hierarchy forms a population. We call smallest nondecomposable group of individuals an *atomic population* (A-population). In forming the conceptual model we have the following rules: (1) each object in the leaves of the hierarchy forms an A-population and (2) any population corresponding to an object in the hierarchy is composed of a number of mutually exclusive A-populations.

Statistical Information Related to Each Population

For each population we define:
1. The properties of the population for which statistical information is to be revealed, e.g., SALARY or ABSENT-DAYS for the population of employees.

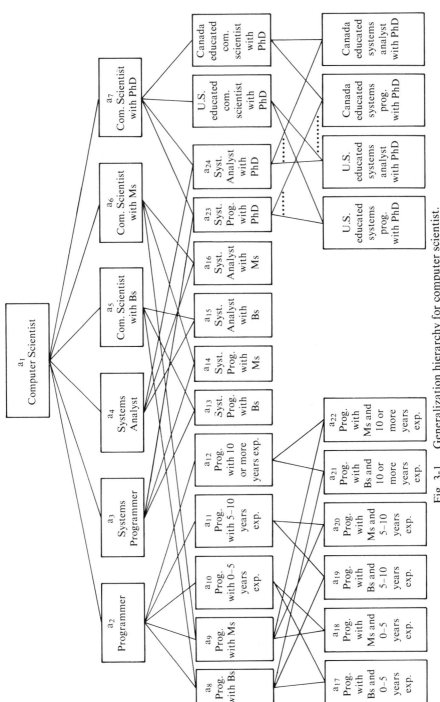

Fig. 3-1. Generalization hierarchy for computer scientist.

2. The allowable types of statistical information for each property of the population, which may be one or more of the following:

MEAN,
SUM,
MAX, MIN. MEDIAN, K-LARGEST (order statistics),
VARIANCE,
STANDARD DEVIATION,
k-MOMENT, k = 2,3, . . .

For uniformity we make the following assumptions about the type of statistical queries allowed for each population.

a. If certain statistical queries are allowed about a certain property of a population, the same statistical queries are allowed for the same property of other populations in the same cluster. (A cluster is a collection of subpopulations created by a mutually exclusive decomposition of a population in the hierarchy.)

Consider Figure 3-1. Assume that SALARY is an attribute of all the objects in the hierarchy and SUM query is allowed for SALARY of Programmer. SUM query is also allowed for SALARY of Systems Programmer and Systems Analyst.

b. Assume statistical queries Q_i, i = 1,2, . . . ,n, are allowed for the property A in some of the child populations of P. If P has the property A, then all statistical queries Q_i, i = 1,2, . . . ,n, are allowed for the property A of population P.

Consider Figure 3-1. Assume the statistical query SUM of SALARY is allowed in populations Programmer, Systems Programmer, Systems Analyst, and statistical query MEDIAN of SALARY is allowed in populations Computer Scientists with BS, MS, and PhD. Statistical queries SUM and MEDIAN of SALARY are allowed for the population of Computer Scientist.

Since COUNT queries do not directly reveal information about protected properties of populations, applying protection measures always down to A-populations may unnecessarily restrict the richness of the data base. Thus we define a *security atom population* (SA-population) to be a population such that no statistical information about any protected property of any proper subset of its individuals is revealed to users. Notice that a SA-population contains one or more A-populations. The set of values to be protected for each property in a SA-population is called a *security atom value set* (SA-value set). The following example illustrates SA-populations.

Example. Consider Figure 3-1. Assume there are *only* two protected properties SALARY and ABSENT-DAYS, and

i. For all populations, COUNT query is allowed.

ii. SUM query for SALARY and ABSENT-DAYS are allowed for populations a_1, a_2, a_3, and a_4. MEDIAN query for SALARY is allowed for populations a_1, a_5, a_6 and a_7. SUM query for ABSENT-DAYS is allowed for populations a_{10}, a_{11} and a_{12}. Clearly, smallest contiguous blocks of statistical information about

SALARY are in populations a_8, a_9, a_{13}, a_{15}, a_{16}, a_{23}, and a_{24}. Similarly the smallest contiguous blocks of statistical information about ABSENT-DAYS are in populations a_{10}, a_{11}, a_{12}, a_3, and a_4. The intersections of the populations revealing smallest contiguous blocks of information about SALARY and ABSENT-DAYS will give *SA-populations* a_{17}, a_{18}, a_{19}, a_{20}, a_{21}, a_{22}, a_{13}, a_{14}, a_{15}, a_{16}, a_{23}, and a_{24}.

Security Constraints

Dynamics of the real world or the existence of complex relationships between populations may lead the DBA to impose constraints on the security-related information in populations. The DBA should be able to state the conditions under which any statistical query about any protected property of a population may be reported to users. Since our aim is only to provide the DBA with the power to do so, we will in general distinguish three types of constraints. (Defining these constraints is very much dependent on the specific environment, and we are unable to give more detailed analysis and structural specifications of the constraints than were done by Hammer[25] for semantic integrity constraints.)

1. *Security Atom Constraints* (SA-constraints) are the constraints that apply to the SA-value set in a SA-population A and all populations that contain A. An example may be: sum salary information must not include the salary x of employee a in SA-value set w until there is another employee hired or fired.

2. *Global Constraints.* There are two types of global constraints. A type 1 global constraint applies to the individuals in a population A and individuals of all or some of the populations in the hierarchy that contain A.

Consider Figure 3-1 and the example given in the introduction. Assume user group u is allowed to access down to Systems Analyst in the hierarchy. Now the hiring of two new Systems Analysts with MS and with total salary $27K should not be incorporated into the population Systems Analyst. However if the range of salaries of Computer Scientist with MS includes $14K due to its other child populations, then the new change may be incorporated into the populations Computer Scientist with MS and Computer Scientist (if other constraints are also satisfied).

Type 2 Global Constraint applies to the individuals of a population A and individuals of another population B in a different part of the hierarchy, for example, individuals in different generic objects. Notice that if there is a relationship between individuals in A and individuals in B, then there is an aggregate object characterizing this relationship; and if protection is needed, a type 2 constraint can be imposed on this aggregate object. However, these constraints should be checked and modified together in the case of changes (i.e., insertions, deletions, and updates) affecting some or all of the populations.

A Statistical Security Management Facility

We now propose a statistical security management facility (SSMF) with three principal components.

1. A population definition construct (PDC)
2. A user knowledge construct (UKC)
3. A constraint enforcer and checker (CEC)

The PDC of a population contains information about the population, related constraints, inclusion of changes, etc., in order to achieve effective protection. The UKC of a user group is designed to record users' supplementary knowledge and to employ SA-constraints to the user group resulting from changes in the data base (i.e., feature 1c). Finally, the CEC consists of several algorithms designed to keep the PDCs and UKCs up-to-date, to enforce the security constraints, and to help the DBA in security-related decision problems.

Population Definition Construct

For each population A there is one PDC which contains the following information:

1. Definition and protected properties of A.

```
Population PROG
      description [Phrase];
      parent populations [COMP-SCI];
      child populations [PROG-BS, PROG-0-5-YEARS,
                  PROG-5-10-YEARS, PROG-10-MORE-YEARS];
      other populations in the same cluster [SYST-PROG,
                  SYST-ANALYST];
      lowest permissable user group level 2;
      allowable query COUNT;
      changes processed in PAIRS;
      protected property SALARY;
            allowable query SUM;
      protected property ABSENT-DAYS;
            allowable query MEDIAN;
      global constraints
            constraint 1
                  description [Phrase];
                  call VIOL-CS1;
            constraint 2
                  description [Phrase];
                  call VIOL-CS2;
      end.
```

Fig. 3-2.   PDC of programmer.

2. Allowable query types for each property of A.
3. Information as to how changes are included in A.
4. If A is an SA-population, the description of SA-constraints for each SA-value set of A.
5. Lowest permissible user group level.
6. Global constraints related to A.
7. Names of child populations, parent populations, and other populations in the cluster.

Items 1, 2, and 7 are self-explanatory.

In Item 3, changes due to the dynamics of the real world may be processed in many ways. How these changes are handled is described in 3 and 4.

For item 5, assume user groups are classified by numbers such that users with higher numbers have more access power to the data base than the user groups with lower numbers. Lowest permissible user group level is a number n such that user groups with number m $\geq$ n can access that population.

6. Global constraints may be static or dynamic, they may evolve and change as the DBA modifies them; e.g., a manager changes companies, thus extends his knowledge and the DBA should take necessary actions. For each global constraint, the PDC contains the description of the constraint and a call for a routine in the case of violation of the constraint. Figure 3-2 contains the PDC of Programmer in the generic hierarchy described in Figure 3-1.

User Knowledge Construct

For each user group u, the UKC records the group's lowest nondecomposable information. Figure 3-3 contains the UKC of user group u for the generic hierarchy described in Figure 3-1.

Assume user groups at third level can access all populations in the hierarchy. User group u is defined to be at third level.

The identifiable dynamics of each population containing more than one SA-population is defined in the UKC; e.g., users in user group u can identify the individuals that are updated, inserted, or deleted from the population Programmer. (There may be other variations; for example, users in group u may identify updated individuals when the update is from Systems Programmer to Systems Programmer, etc.)

Each SA-population contains the smallest nondecomposable SA-value sets, one for each protected property. Dynamics of a SA-population (i.e. inserted, deleted, updated individuals) are recorded in a list called *change sequence* in the order of occurrences of changes. (This list is kept separately if the expected number of changes is large.) Depending on the type of statistical information revealed, change sequence is used in several procedures to decide whether the security of individuals and the protected information are in danger.

For security purposes, changes may be processed in groups, say triplets. In such cases, some individuals may be waiting to be processed; these individuals are described and maintained in SA-constraint. For each SA-value set, users may know

```
USER GROUP U [user-id, user-id, . . . , user-id];
    user group level 3;
    population COMP-SCI;
            identifiable dynamics {INSERTION, DELETION, UPDATE};
    population PROG;
            identifiable dynamics {INSERTION, DELETION, UPDATE};
    population PROG-0-5-YEARS [SEC-ATOM-POPULATION];
            protected property SALARY;
                    security atom constraint: {JOHN DOE} is not
                            included;
                    change sequence parameters
                        active individuals set {(STEVE HART,
                                ROCK HO, 20), . . . , (JOHN GRAY, 3)};
                            reachability constant 0.1;
                            largest reachability set size 20;
                    known value set {(JOHN SO), . . . , (ALAN POE)};
                    known global upper bound $34K;
                    known global lower bound $8K;
                    known upper bounds list {(IAN MUNROE, $18K), . . . ,
                                (GEORGE HO, $20K)};
                    known lower bounds list {0};
                    change sequence {[(JIM JOE, INSERT),
                                (JACK YU, DELETE), (OLD MEDIAN, $15K),
                                (NEW MEDIAN, $14K)], . . . ,
                                [(PHILIP HO, DELETE), (JACK FU, DELETE),
                                (NEW MEDIAN, $18K)]};
            protected property ABSENT-DAYS;
                    security atom constraint: {STEVE HUDSON} is not
                            included;
                    change sequence parameters
                        active individuals set {(STEVE HART, 15), . . .
                                (JOHN GRAY, 7)};
                            reachability constant 0.2;
                            largest reachable set size 15;
                    known value set {0};
                    known global upper bound 90;
                    known global lower bound 0;
                    known upper bounds list {0};
                    known lower bounds list {0};
                    change sequence {[(JIM JOE, INSERT)],
                                [(JACK YU, DELETE), (CHEN TU, DELETE),
                                [(OLD SUM, 450), (NEW SUM, 345)], . . .};
    population PROG-5-10-YEARS [SEC-ATOM-POPULATION];
end.
```

Fig. 3-3.   UKC of user group u for the generic hierarchy described in Figure 3-1.

global upper and/or lower bounds of the protected property values of individuals. Some specific individuals' upper and/or lower bounds, and/or individuals' active property values may be known to users. For example, in Figure 3-3, users in user group u know that the salary of programmer Ian Munroe is less than $18K. Several parameters related to the change sequence are defined in Chin.[9]

Constraint Enforcer and Checker

The CEC is composed of several algorithms. It utilizes PDC and UKCs to perform the following two basic tasks:

1. For each query, it is evoked to check and to enforce global and SA-constraints.
2. For each change, it is evoked to modify the constraints, to decide whether to process the change for each SA-value set, and (if the change is processed) to modify the related change sequence and its parameters for each user group u.

Besides the preceding, the CEC helps the DBA in several decision problems by providing lists of individuals whose security is threatened under several events such as

1. Changes in user groups
2. Changes in A-populations
3. Giving out new views of the data (i.e., changes in the conceptual model, such as re-partitioning)
4. Detecting increased knowledge of user and retrieving the endangered protected information.

Another job of the CEC is to modify and maintain several security measures related to the change sequence of each SA-value set in order to give the DBA a measure of how secure the system really is at a particular time.

The general scheme of the SSMF is depicted in Figure 3-4.

Different Inferences and Application of Constraints for Count Queries

In this section we briefly discuss the possible security constraints for COUNT statistical queries. We distinguish three different inferences by users.

1. *Type H inferences* due to the hierarchical structure of the conceptual model.
2. *Type D inferences* due to the dynamics of the real world.
3. *Type R inferences* due to existing relationships between individuals in different populations or in the same population.

Type R inferences are dependent on the specific environment. Global constraints are defined by the DBA to prevent disclosures due to type R inferences. Chin[9] contains detailed discussions about type H and type D inferences and constraints

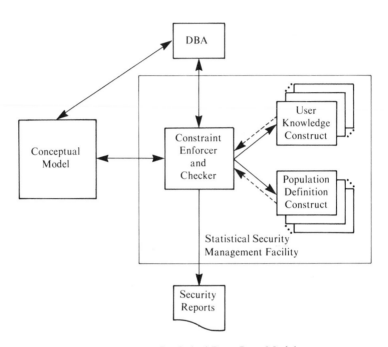

Fig. 3-4. Statistical Data Base Model.

to prevent compromise for several different statistical queries. Next we discuss only COUNT queries and the related constraints.

Assume only COUNT queries are allowed and individuals in populations are identifiable. Assume Systems Analyst with BS is decomposed into two subpopulations as "Systems Analyst with BS and convicted of felony" and "Systems Analyst with BS and not convicted of felony." It is well known[27] that

COUNT(Systems Analyst) = COUNT(Systems Analyst with BS)
        with BS   and convicted of felony
    & John Doe is a Systems Analyst with BS
        $\rightarrow^1$ John Doe is convicted of felony

---

[1] $\rightarrow$ means "implies" or "imply."

Similarly,

COUNT(Systems Analyst with BS and
 not convicted of felony) = 0   → John Doe is convicted of felony
John Doe is a Systems Analyst with BS

Thus for type H inferences we need the following global constraints.

1. in population SYST-ANALYST-BS-CONV-FELONY,
if COUNT(any superpopulation of SYST-ANALYST-BS-CONV-FELONY)
   − COUNT(SYST-ANALYST-BS-CONV-FELONY) ≤ a
     then individuals creating this difference are not
       reported in COUNT queries.
2. in population SYST-ANALYST-BS-NOT-CONV-FELONY,
if COUNT(SYST-ANALYST-BS-NOT-CONV-FELONY) ≤ a
   then COUNT(SYST-ANALYST-BS-NOT-CONV-FELONY) is not answered.

The previous disclosure type and constraint have been proposed and discussed widely in recent studies.[13,33,34] If introduced in a controlled environment, it is a viable protection procedure.

The constraints described earlier can be easily modified to consider the users' knowledge described in the UKC by changing a to (a + x) where x is the number of individuals that are known to be in the population SYST-ANALYST-BS-NOT-CONV-FELONY by the user group.

Type D inferences may be avoided likewise; e.g., only when there are $(a_1 + x)$ insertions or $(a_2 + x)$ deletions from either populations of SYST-ANALYST-BS-CONV-FELONY or SYST-ANALYST-BS-NOT-CONV-FELONY. Then changes are reported to user group u where insertion and deletion of SYST-ANALYST-BS are identifiable.

CONCLUSION

In this chapter we have examined the security problem of statistical data bases. Several proposed protection schemes have been reviewed in terms of their effectiveness, feasibility, efficiency, and richness.

In the previous section we have discussed a new approach to the security problem of statistical data bases, namely, use of dynamic constraints in the conceptual data model level. A statistical security management facility has been described, with several constructs and with a constraint enforcer and checker. Users are allowed to query the data base with different statistical queries such as COUNT, MEDIAN, or SUM. Changes in the data base are verified by the DBA. Any information involving few individuals (and therefore risking disclosure of confidential or private information) is recorded.

There are still other areas of research regarding our approach to the design of a secure SDB:

1. If the data base management system (and hence the SSMF) is not certified, there is no guarantee that it works correctly. In statistical data bases, a security kernel can be designed by having certified separate modules containing all security relevant code.

2. As large numbers of investigations have shown in Artificial Intelligence (see, for example, Winograd[41]) a static representation of knowledge is insufficient to model the real world correctly. Moreover, there is certainly no way to specify the completeness of a conceptual model in an absolute sense. Completeness can only be specified relative to (a) the ability of the designers who create the model and (b) the purpose the model serves. Thus although it may not always be needed, every aspect of the conceptual model should have dynamic capabilities; i.e., populations may be formed, deleted or decomposed, individuals may be inserted, deleted or (their properties) may be changed, relationships may be added or deleted from the conceptual model. Note that these capabilities are of utmost importance in the SDB since users do not have high-level data manipulation operators. Some means to include these capabilities within the SDB without endangering the security should be investigated.

3. Different conceptual models such as the Entity-Relationship model[4] or the extended Relational Model[5] may be investigated for their suitability in the SDB.

4. Finally, the usefulness and the efficiency of the idea of employing constraints in a conceptual model has yet to be demonstrated with an implementation.

Acknowledgment. The authors would like to thank Leo Hartman for his help in improving the readability of this chapter.

REFERENCES

1. Achugbue, J. D., and Chin, F. Y.: The effectiveness of output modification by rounding for protection of statistical databases. INFOR *17*(3): 209, 1979.
2. Beck, L. L.: A Security Mechanism for Statistical Database. Dept. of Computer Science, Southern Methodist University, 1979.
3. Boruch, R. F.: Maintaining confidentiality in educational research: a systematic analysis. Amer. Psychologist *26:* 413, 1971.
4. Chen, P. P-S.: The entity-relationship model—toward a unified view of data. ACM Trans. Database Systems, *1*(1): 1, 1976.
5. Codd, E. F.: Extending the Data Base Relational Model to Capture more Meaning. Research Report RJ2472(32359), IBM Research Laboratory, San Jose, California, 1979.
6. Chin, F. Y.: Security in Statistical Databases for Queries with Small Counts. ACM Trans. Database Syst. *3*(1): 92, 1978.
7. Chin, F. Y., and Ozsoyoglu, G.: Security in statistical databases for sum and count queries. Information Privacy, *1*(4): 148, 1979.

8. Chin, F. Y., and Ozsoyoglu, G.: Security in Partitioned Dynamic Statistical Databases. Proceedings of IEEE 3rd International Conference on Computer Software and Applications, November 1979.
9. Chin, F. Y., and Ozsoyoglu, G.: Statistical Database Design. Dept. of Computer Sciences. University of Alberta, 1979 (to appear in ACMT ODS).
10. Dalenius, T., and Reiss, S. P.: Data Swapping—A Technique for Disclosure Control. Confidentiality in Surveys, Rep. no. 31, Dept. Stat., University Stockholm, 1978.
11. Date, C. J.: An Introduction to Database Systems. Addison Wesley, 1977.
12. DeMillo, R., Dobkin, D., and Lipton, R. J.: Even databases that lie can be compromised. IEEE Trans. Software Engineering $SE-4$ 1: 13, 1978.
13. Denning, D. E., Denning, P. J., and Schwartz, M. D.: The tracker: a threat to statistical database security. ACM Trans. Database Syst. $4(1)$: 76, 1979.
14. DeMillo, R. A., and Dobkin, D.: Recent Progress in Secure Computation. Proceedings of IEEE 2nd International Conference on Computer Software and Applications, 1978, pp. 209–214.
15. Denning, D. E.: Are Statistical Databases Secure? Tech. Report, Computer Science Dept., Purdue University, 1977.
16. Denning, D. E.: Secure Database under Random Sample Queries. Computer Sciences, Purdue University, 1979.
17. Dobkin, D., Jones, A. K., and Lipton, R. J.: Secure databases: protection against user inference. ACM Trans. Database Syst. $4(1)$: 97, 1979.
18. Dobkin, D., Lipton, R. J., and Reiss, S. P.: Aspects of the Database Security Problem. Proceedings on a Conference on Theoretical Computer Science, Waterloo, Canada, 1977, pp. 262–274.
19. Davida, G., et al.: Security of Statistical Databases. TR-CS-76-14, Dept. of EECS, University of Wisconsin, Milwaukee, 1976.
20. Davida, G. I., Wells, D. L., and Kam, J. B.: Security and Privacy. Proceedings of IEEE 2nd International Conf. on Computer Software and Applications, 1978, pp. 194–203.
21. Fellegi, I. P.: On the question of statistical confidentiality. J Am. Statist. Assoc. $67(337)$: 7, 1972.
22. Fellegi, I. P., and Phillips, J. L.: Statistical confidentiality: some theory and applications to data dissemination. Ann. Econ. Social Measurement $3(2)$: 399, 1972.
23. Haq, M.: Security in a Statistical Database. Proc. Am. Information Sci. 11: 33, 1974.
24. Haq, M.: Insuring Individual's Privacy from Statistical Database Users. Proc. AFIPS NCC 14: 941, 1975.
25. Hammer, M. M., and Mcleod, D. J.: Semantic Integrity in a Relational Database System. Proceedings of VLDB 1975, pp. 25–47.
26. Hansen, M. H.: Insuring Confidentiality of Individual Records in Data Storage and Retrieval for Statistical Purposes. Proc. AFIPS FJCC, 39: 519, 1971.
27. Hoffman, L. J., and Miller, W. F.: Getting a Personnel Dossier from a Statistical Data Bank. Datamation $16(5)$: 74, 1970.
28. Hoffman, L. J.: Modern Methods for Computer Security and Privacy. Prentice-Hall, 1977.
29. Kam, J. B., and Ullman, J. D.: A model of statistical databases and their security. ACM Trans. Database Syst. $2(1)$: 1, 1977.
30. Nargundkar, M. S., and Saveland, W.: Random Rounding to Prevent Statistical Disclosure. Proc. Am. Stat. Assoc. Soc. Stat. Sec., 1972, pp. 382–385.
31. Reiss, S. P.: Security in databases: a combinatorial study. JACM $26(1)$: 45, 1979.
32. Reiss, S. P.: Medians and Database Security. Foundations of Secure Computations. New York, Academic Press, 1978, pp. 57–92.

33. Schlorer, J.: Identification and retrieval of personnel records from a statistical databank. Methods of Info. in Medicine *14*(1): 7, 975.
34. Schlorer, J.: Confidentiality of statistical records: a threat monitoring scheme for on-line dialoque. Methods of Info. in Medicine *15*(1): 36, 1976.
35. Schlorer, J.: Union Tracker and Open Statistical Databases. TB-IMSD 1/78, Inst. Med. Statist. Dok., University Giessen, 1979.
36. Schlorer, J.: Security of Statistical Databases: Multidimensional Transformation. TB-IMSD 2/78, Inst. Med. Statist. Dok., University Giessen, 1979.
37. Schwartz, M. D., Denning, D. E., and Denning, P. J.: Linear queries in statistical databases. ACM Trans. Database Syst. *4*(2): 156, 1979.
38. Smith, J. M., and Smith, D. C. P.: Database abstractions: aggregation. CACM *20*(6), 405, 1977.
39. Smith, J. M., and Smith, D. C. P.: Database abstractions: aggregation and generalization. ACM Trans. Database Syst. *2*(2): 105, 1977.
40. *Privacy Act of 1974*, Title 5, United States Code, Section 552a (Public Law 93-579), 1974.
41. Winograd, T. A.: A procedural model of language understanding. *In* Computer Models of Thought and Language. Edited by R. C. Schank and C. M. Colby. San Francisco, W. H. Freeman and Company, 1973.
42. Yu, C. T., and Chin, F. Y.: A Study on the Protection of Statistical Databases. Proc. ACM SIGMOD Int. Conf. on Management of Data, 1977, pp. 169–181.

Chapter 4

SOFTWARE SECURITY AND HOW TO HANDLE IT

Steven Cushing

Higher Order Software, Inc., Cambridge, Massachusetts

SECURITY AND RELIABILITY

When digital computers were first introduced into common usage in the 1950s, they were programmed in machine or assembly language. With the introduction of higher-order languages came a new realm of possible applications and a new set of problems. These difficulties included concepts that programmers had never had to deal with previously, such as the prevention of timing conflicts, the relationship between synchronous and asynchronous processing, and the establishment of a secure operating system. These concepts are all part of what is generally termed "software engineering." One of the most technically interesting and operationally difficult of these concepts is that of system security. How can access to the various components of a system be restricted specifically to those for whom it is intended? The requirements of security bear many similarities to those of system reliability, such as the need for modules to be clearly defined and their interaction closely controlled.[5] Given that these latter requirements are satisfied, a system can be considered secure if its modules are ordered in such a way that information flows only upward.[8]

In this chapter I will elaborate on system security in increasingly formal terms, focusing finally on the approach to system specification that has come to be known as Higher Order Software (HOS).[3,4] The HOS methodology was developed as a tool for helping to guarantee system reliability through the elimination of timing and data conflicts in the specification of large programming systems.[3] It thus contributes as well to the requirements of system security. The principles on which HOS is based also guarantee that information flows only upward in a system, again contributing to the requirements of security.[2]

PROTECTION MODELS

A general abstract characterization of system security can be given in terms of a *protection model,* in which the computer is viewed as consisting of active entities

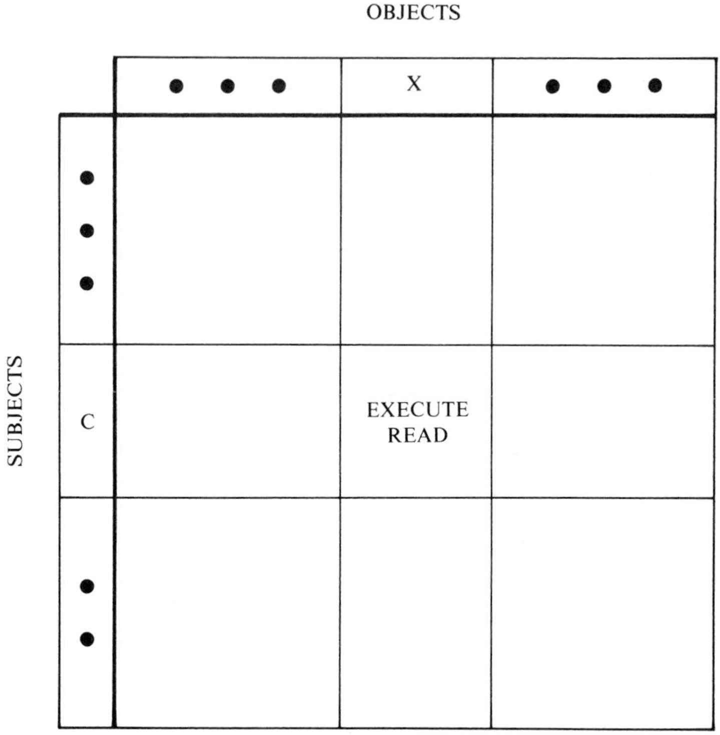

OBJECTS

Fig. 4-1.   A protection matrix.   (From Linden.[5])

called *subjects* and passive entities called *objects*.[5]   The purpose of the protection model is to define the access rights of each subject to each object.

A protection model can be represented as a protection matrix, such as the one in Figure 4-1, in which the rows are associated with the subjects of the model and the columns are associated with the objects.   The access rights of each subject to each object are represented by the entry that appears at the intersection of the corresponding row and column.   For the protection model represented by the matrix in Figure 4-1, for example, subject C may read or execute object X, because both "READ" and "EXECUTE" appear in the matrix slot that occurs at the intersection of row C and column X.

Changes to the protection matrix itself are also controlled by the access rights represented in the matrix; for example, an object can be deleted from the matrix by a subject that has "delete" access to that object.   Subjects can have access rights to each other by having subjects appear also as objects in the protection matrix; for example, an "enter" access right to one subject can permit another subject to transfer control to that subject.

A *protection environment* includes everything that a subject is allowed either to do directly for itself or to cause to be done by another subject on its behalf.   The narrower concept of *protection domain* includes access rights only to those objects that are accessible by the subject. The rows of the protection matrix represent the protection domains of the protection model.

The qualitative notion of a *small protection domain* is the minimal protection domain that still allows its subject access to everything it has to access. A protection domain may be very large in a quantitative sense, but it is a "small" protection domain if it could not be decreased in size without overly restricting the access rights of its subject. Since access to many objects is usually needed in a large program, the smallness of protection domains can be guaranteed only by having the program execute in many different protection domains. Protection domains can be kept small by having each small subunit of a program execute in its own protection domain, since these small subunits typically need access to only a small number of objects. Whether protection domains can be kept small by this approach depends primarily on the efficiency, flexibility, and ease of domain switching.

Integrating protection domain switching with the calling of a procedure permits each procedure to have its own protection domain, even though a domain switch might not be involved in every procedure. A *protected procedure* does involve a domain switch. If a procedure is protected, then it has a particular protection domain, so certain access rights may be available during, and possibly only during, executions of that procedure. Each execution of a protected procedure will possess the access rights of the procedure, whatever the calling environment may be. The procedure itself, moreover, may have a state, independent of the calling environments, that is preserved between calls to the procedure.

A protected procedure will appear both as a subject and as an object, when represented in a protection matrix. A protected procedure is an object because other subjects may have the right to call it. This right is represented in a protection matrix by the appearance of a special access right, such as the "enter" access right referred to earlier. A protected procedure also occurs as a subject in a protection matrix because it has to execute in its own protection domain.

Switching protection domains involves calling a protected procedure, the simplest case being the one in which no access rights are passed as parameters in the call. The call takes place and execution begins in the protection domain of the called procedure—if the caller has the right to call this procedure. Return to the previous protection domain, i.e., the protection domain of the caller, is triggered by a return instruction in the executing called procedure. This situation is illustrated in Figure 4-2. User A can call the editor, while executing in his own protection domain. He can also read or write files X and Y from his own domain, or he can call the editor, which is also allowed to read or write files X and Y. The user can use the dictionary, however, only by calling the editor, because the editor, but not the user himself, is allowed to read the dictionary.

A domain switch is more complex if it involves the passing of access rights to objects as parameters, with the protected procedure reentrant. This kind of call creates a new protection domain, i.e., a new row in the protection matrix. Both the permanent access rights of the protected procedure, defined by a template

OBJECTS / SUBJECTS	EDITOR	FILE X	FILE Y	DICTIONARY
• • •				
USER A	ENTER	READ WRITE	READ WRITE	
EDITOR		READ WRITE	READ WRITE	READ
• •				

Fig. 4-2.   Simple domain switch.   (From Linden.[5])

domain associated with the procedure, and the access rights passed as parameters in the call are contained in the new protection domain.   This situation is illustrated in Figure 4-3.   Figure 4-3a shows User A's own basic domain and the template domain of the editor.   User A has the same access rights as he has in Figure 4-2, but the editor is allowed only READ access to the dictionary.   It cannot read or write files X or Y, as it can in Figure 4-2.   If the user wants to use the editor to read

OBJECTS / SUBJECTS	EDITOR	FILE X	FILE Y	DICTIONARY
• • •				
USER A	ENTER	READ WRITE	READ WRITE	
EDITOR TEMPLATE				READ
• •				

Fig. 4-3a.   Protection matrix before call to editor.   (From Linden.[5])

OBJECTS / SUBJECTS	EDITOR	FILE X	FILE Y	DICTIONARY
• • •				
USER A	ENTER	READ WRITE	READ WRITE	
EDITOR TEMPLATE				READ
INSTANCE OF EDITOR		READ WRITE		READ
• •				

Fig. 4-3b.   Protection matrix during call to editor.   (From Linden.[5])

file X, however, he can pass access rights for file X to the editor in the process of calling the editor. This results in the creation of a new protection domain, labeled "INSTANCE OF EDITOR" in Figure 4-3b, in which the editor does have READ access to file X. Other instances of the same editor may also be employed by other users to edit other files.

SECURITY MODELS

A more formal characterization of system security can be given in terms of a *model for mandatory security* that prohibits unauthorized disclosure of information but allows otherwise unrestricted sharing of information.[8] This model is based on the idea of restricting access to information by giving a specific classification for each piece of information and requiring a user to have the proper clearance in order to access the information. It can be represented as an 8-tuple

$$M_0 = (R, A, C, \theta, \mu, \trianglelefteq, Cls, Clr)$$

where

        R   is a set of repositories.
        A   is a set of agents.
        C   is a set of security classes.

$\theta \subseteq A \times R$ is the "observe" relation. ($a \, \theta \, r$ means that agent a can observe the information stored in repository r.)

$\mu \subseteq A \times R$ is the "modify" relation. ($a \, \mu \, r$ means that agent a can modify the information stored in repository r.)

$\trianglelefteq \subseteq C \times C$ is a pre-ordering of the set of security classes.

Cls: $R \rightarrow C$ is the "classification" function which associates a security class with each repository. (Informally Cls(r) will be referred to as the classification of repository r.)

Clr: $A \rightarrow C$ is the "clearance" function which associates a security class with each agent. (Here again Clr(a) will be referred to as the clearance of agent a.)

Repositories correspond to objects, and *agents* correspond to subjects. The observe and modify relations correspond to two general kinds of access right that can occur in a protection matrix. The *security classes* in M_0 correspond to small protection domains; they are what determines which repositories (objects) an agent (subject) can observe or modify (access). Nothing in M_0 guarantees a null intersection of the classes of agents and repositories, so, as before, some (or all) of the entities involved may be both subjects and objects.

A basic security theorem to the effect that information flows only upward can be proved by imposing four axioms on M_0.[8] The first two axioms stipulate that the relation $\trianglelefteq$ provides a pre-ordering of the set C of security classes.

Axiom 1:   For all $c \in C$. $c \trianglelefteq c$. ($\trianglelefteq$ is reflexive.)

Axiom 2:   For all c, d, e, $\in C$, $c \trianglelefteq d$ and $d \trianglelefteq e$ implies $c \trianglelefteq e$. ($\trianglelefteq$ is transitive.)

The second two axioms impose conditions on the acquisition and dissemination, respectively, of information.

Axiom 3:   For all $a \in A$ and $r \in R$, $a \, \theta \, r$ implies Cls(r) $\trianglelefteq$ Clr(a); that is, if agent a can observe repository r, then the clearance of a must be greater than or equal to the classification of r.

Axiom 4:   For all $a \in A$ and $r \in R$, $a \, \mu \, r$ implies Clr(a) $\trianglelefteq$ Cls(r); that is, if an agent a can modify repository r, then the clearance of a is less than or equal to the classification of r. Agent a can modify only those repositories with equal or higher security class.

A fifth axiom can be that something cannot be both higher and lower in the ordering than something else, if we wish to strengthen the pre-ordering to a partial ordering.

Axiom 5:   For all c, d $\in C$, $c \trianglelefteq d$ and $d \trianglelefteq c$ implies c = d.

The security theorem itself states that information can never be transferred to a repository where it can be observed by an agent that does not have sufficient clearance to observe the originating repository, thus requiring a transfer relation $\tau \subseteq R \times R$ to the effect that an agent can transfer information from the first member of R to the second in a particular member of τ. Formally, we say that $r \tau s$ for $r \in R, s \in R$, if and only if there is an $a \in A$ such that $a \theta r$ and $a \mu s$. Also required is the reflexive, transitive closure τ^* of τ and the notion of information transfer path. The relation $r \tau^* s$ means that a finite sequence of repositories $\{r_i\}$ exists with $r = r_1, s = r_{n+1}$, and $r_i \tau r_{i+1}$ for all i, $1 \leq i \leq n$. In other words, $r \tau^*$ s if and only if information can eventually be passed from r to s through some finite string of intermediate repositories. An *information transfer path* from repository r to repository s is said to exist if $r \tau^* s$.

The basic security theorem can be stated formally in either of two ways, as follows:

Theorem: For all r, s $\in$ R, if r τ^* s, then Cls(r) $\trianglelefteq$ Cls(s). In other words, if there is an information transfer path from repository r to repository s, then Cls(r) $\trianglelefteq$ Cls(s).

Corollary: If r and s are repositories and the classification of r is not less than or equal to the classification of s, then there is *no* information transfer path from r to s.

If information flows from one repository to another, then the latter has a security class that is the same or higher than the former; in other words, information can flow only upward, so the system is, in that sense, secure.

HIERARCHICAL SECURITY MODELLING

M_0 can be viewed as the initial member of a sequence $\{M_i\}$ of models that are related in that M_{i+1} satisfies the security requirements of M_i, as well as further design requirements which make it more implementation specific. M_1, for example, might represent the security system as a system of files in a tree structure of arbitrary depth and provide a mechanism so that agents can communicate without accessing a shared file, while M_2 might provide mechanisms that can be used as discretionary controls for access to files.[8] Eventually, a model can be arrived at which satisfies all the security requirements of every earlier model but which is close to a description of an actual system as implemented.

Such a sequence of models can be characterized abstractly as a *hierarchically structured program* consisting of a sequence of ordered pairs $\{(P_0, M_0), (P_1, M_1), \ldots, (P_n, M_n)\}$, where P_i is a set of *abstract programs* that run on the *abstract machine* M_i.[6,7] In general, the pairs will occur in a tree structure, but discussion is simplified by assuming a linear ordering. Although each program runs on one machine, the collection of machines forms a hierarchy, with the primitive operations of a machine at any given level being realized by programs running on a machine at the next lower level, one program per machine operation. Only information

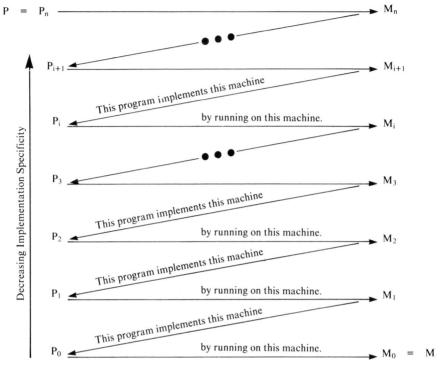

Fig. 4-4.   Hierarchical model of program P to run on machine M.   (From Cushing.[2])

about the external behavior of the machine in which it runs is available to a program, which abstracts away from the implementation details of the machine.

The general idea behind this kind of structuring is illustrated in Figure 4-4, in which the numbering scheme has been reversed to make M_0 the most primitive machine, rather than the most abstract. M_0 can thus be viewed as a higher-order language or as the instruction set of a hardware machine, with the highest-level program P_n running on machine M_n.   The direction of the arrows in the diagram represents the flow of implementation, in that for all i, $0 \leq i < n$, the set of abstract programs P_i implements the abstract machine M_{i+1}, while itself running on the abstract machine M_i.   Taken as a whole, the system amounts to a program P running on a machine M, where P_n is an abstraction of P and $M = M_0$.

Each of the abstract machines in such a hierarchy can be described in terms of two kinds of functions.   *V* (value)-*functions* return values when called.   The set of possible *V*-function values defines the *state space* (or abstract data structure) of the abstract machine, its *state* being given by a particular set of values for each *V*-function.   *O* (operation)-functions define state transformations by defining new values for *V*-functions.   Calling an *O*-function brings about a state transformation, which is described in terms of an assertion that relates new values of *V*-functions to their values before the call.   Such an assertion takes the form of a predicate that

---

integer V-function: LENGTH
        Comment: Returns the number of occupied positions in the
        register.
        Initial value: LENGTH = 0
        Exceptions: none
Integer V-function: CHAR (integer i)
        Comment: Returns the value of the ith element of the
        register.
        Initial value: $\forall i(\mathrm{CHAR}(i)$ = undefined)
        Exceptions: I_OUT_OF_BOUNDS: $i \leq 0 \lor i >$ LENGTH

O-function: INSERT (integer, i,j)
        Comment: Inserts the value j after position i, moving
        -subsequent values one position higher.
        Exceptions:
        I_OUT_OF_BOUNDS: $i < 0 \lor$ i $>$ LENGTH
        J_OUT_OF_BOUNDS: j $< 0 \lor$ j > 255
        TOO_LONG: LENGTH ≥ 1000
        Effects: LENGTH = 'LENGTH' + 1
        $\forall$k(CHAR(k) = if $k \leq$ i then 'CHAR' (k)
              else if $k = i + 1$ then j
              else 'CHAR' ($k - 1$))
O-function: DELETE (integer i)
        Comment: Deletes the ith element of the register,
        moving the subsequent values to fill in the gap.
        Exceptions: I_OUT_OF_BOUNDS: $i \leq 0 \lor i >$ LENGTH
        Effects:
        LENGTH = 'LENGTH' − 1
        $\forall k(\mathrm{CHAR}(k)$ = if $k < i$ then 'CHAR' (k)
              else 'CHAR' ($k + 1$))

Fig. 4-5.   A register as an abstract machine.   (From Robinson and Levitt.[7])

contains V-functions that make it true.   Its effect is to assert that the call results in a new state that is one of a number of possible states, thus postponing the binding of certain decisions until implementation or even run-time.   An example of such an abstract machine characterized in this way is given in Figure 4-5.

HIGHER ORDER SOFTWARE

A still more formal characterization of this hierarchical approach to system specification is provided by Higher Order Software (HOS), and some informal background discussion will be helpful as a preliminary.   HOS recognizes two modes of existence in the world, that of *being* and *doing,* and assumes that everything generally manifests both modes at once. A given thing can either be or do, and, in general, will both be and do at the same time. This dichotomy reflects the related bifurcation between *being* and *becoming.* If there is something that is doing, something (perhaps the same thing) is *being done to,* and this latter thing is therefore becoming. Again, in general, anything that is doing is also being done to and so is itself becoming as well as being.

This helps clarify the important relationship between *constancy* and *change.* If we remove the front element from a queue, for example, we still have the *same* queue, with one element removed, but we also have a *different* queue, i.e., the one that differs from the original one in exactly that element. The queue can still be the same queue, even though it has become a different queue, and we are free to choose whichever of these aspects of the situation fits our particular problems. We can also say that the queue has changed its *state,* stipulating that the queue itself has not changed, but then it is the states that are being or becoming, so the same dichotomy emerges again on a higher level of abstraction.

The distinction between being and doing is reflected in the distinction between objects and subjects, as discussed under Protection Models, and again in the distinction between repositories and agents, as discussed under Security Models. Objects are things that are done to; i.e., they are, rather than do. Subjects, in contrast, are things which do, and the objects are precisely the things they do to. Agents are things which do, and repositories are things which are and which therefore are done to by the agents. As we have observed, anything, in general, will both be and do, so anything is both an agent and a repository and both a subject and an object.

HOS formalizes the distinction between being and doing in terms of the familiar notions of *data* and *function.* Anything that can be can be represented as a member of a *data type,* and anything that can do can be represented as a function. Anything that can be, i.e., a datum, can also do, by serving as input to a function, and anything that can do, i.e., a function, can also be, since functions themselves make up a data type. In fact, this reversibility follows readily from the nature of data and functions. If datum x, for example, is mapped by functions f_1, f_2, f_3, f_4, f_5 onto data y_1, y_2, y_3, y_4, y_5, respectively, then x itself can be viewed *as a function* that maps the *data* f_1, f_2, f_3, f_4, f_5 onto y_1, y_2, y_3, y_4, y_5. Functions can themselves be data, in other words, and data can be functions, depending on the requirements of the particular problem. If FXY is the subset of data type FUNCTION whose members map data type X into data type Y, then X is the subset of FUNCTION that maps FXY into Y. Both interpretations are, in general, correct, and the one chosen reflects the specific problem.

Also in accordance with the fundamental dichotomy, although data and functions are *distinct* components of systems, given a particular choice of interpretation, they are at the same time *inseparable,* because each is characterized formally in terms of the other. A function consists of an input data type called its *domain,* an output data type called its *range,* and a correspondence, called its *mapping,* between the members of its domain and those of its range; a function can be characterized,

```
DATA TYPE:   TIME;
PRIMITIVE  OPERATIONS:
     time₃ = Advance (time₁, time₂);
     boolean = Notafter (time₁, time₂);
     time₂ = Reverse (time₁);

AXIOMS:
     WHERE t, t₁, t₂, t₃ ARE TIMES;
     WHERE Notime IS A CONSTANT TIME;
  1.    Notafter (t,t) = True;
  2.    ((Notafter (t₁, t₂) & Notafter (t₂, t₃))⊃
        Notafter (t₁, t₃)) = True;
  3.    ((Notafter (t₁, t₂) & Notafter (t₂, t₁)) ⊃
        Equal (t₁, t₂)) = True;
  4.    (Notafter (t₁, t₂) ! Notafter (t₂, t₁)) = True;
  5.    Advance (t, Notime) = t;
  6.    Advance (t₁, t₂) = Advance (t₂, t₁);
  7.    Advance (t₁, Advance (t₂, t₃)) =
        Advance (Advance (t₁, t₂), t₃);
  8.    Notafter (Advance (t₁, t₂), t₁) =
        Notafter (t₂, Notime);
  9.    Advance (Reverse (t), t) = Notime;
END  TIME:
```

Fig. 4-6.   HOS specification of one version of time.   (From Cushing.[1])

therefore, as an ordered triple (Domain, Range, Mapping). A data type consists of a set of objects, called its *members* and a set of functions, called its *primitive operations*, which are specified by giving their domains and ranges—at least one of which for each primitive operation must include the data type's own set of members—and a description of the way their mappings interact with one another and, perhaps, with those of other functions; a data type can thus also be characterized as an ordered triple, this time (Set, DR, Axioms), where Set is the set of its members, DR is a statement of the domains and ranges of its primitive operations, and Axioms is a set of constraints on the interactive behavior of the mappings of the primitive operations.[1]

An HOS data type specification for one version of time is given in Figure 4-6. Data type TIME is defined here in terms of three primitive operations. Advance is the operation of beginning at the time indicated by the first input and advancing by the amount of time indicated by the second input. Notafter is the relation, i.e., boolean-valued function, that holds between two times if the first is earlier than or simultaneous with the second. Reverse is the operation that maps each time onto its mirror image with respect to the neutral element or origin Notime. The operations ⊃, &, !, and Equal, which appear in Axioms 2, 3, and 4, are assumed to have been characterized independently, the first three on type BOOLEAN and the fourth as a universal operation on any type. The symbol "⊃" is a traditional logical symbol for material implication and has the same meaning as the English expression "if . . . then . . . ". The symbol "!" has the meaning of inclusive "or". Axions 1 to 3 characterize Notafter as a partial ordering and Axiom 4 makes that ordering linear. Axiom 5 characterizes Notime as the neutral element with respect to Advance. Axiom 6 says that Advance is commutative, and Axiom 7 says it is associative. Axiom 8 says that Advance moves upward in the ordering if the amount it advances by is above Notime in the ordering. Axiom 9 says that Reverse produces the reverse of a time with respect to Notime. Using Notafter, rather than something like Precedes, simplifies the axioms slightly, while omitting Reverse would result in a somewhat different data type corresponding to a different notion of time. On the one hand, more implementations would be allowable, because the specification would not require all of them to be capable of supporting reversal; on the other hand, fewer features of each allowed implementation could be made use of, because the specification makes no room for the *use* of reversal even in those implementations that can support it. A more realistic specification might also distinguish between moments of time and intervals of time, thus splitting this data type into two distinct though related ones, but this reasonable added complication is omitted here for the sake of simplicity. Naturally, which notion of time is chosen depends entirely on the system it is going to be used in and the capabilities it is required to have for its role in that system.

Given a system that involves certain data types, the function the system performs can be decomposed into a tree structure, called a *control map,* whose nodes are functions and whose terminal nodes, in particular, are primitive operations of the data types, where the collective effect of the functions at the terminal nodes is the same as that of the system as a whole. The domain and range of the decomposed function can be determined by the typed variables that represent inputs and outputs and by the primitive operations that appear at the terminal nodes. The tree itself is what gives the mapping of the decomposed function, by showing how that mapping is accomplished in terms of the collective behavior of the independently characterized primitive operations. Two control maps for a Regress operation on data-type time are given in Figure 4-7, where Identify$_1$[1] is just the identity function in this case.

In order to be well-formed, such a tree must satisfy the six HOS axioms listed in Figure 4-8.[3] Any software system that is specified in accordance with these axioms is thereby guaranteed to be reliable, since no data or timing conflicts can ever occur if that system is implemented strictly in accordance with the specification.[3] Formally, what the axioms tell us is that a well-formed control map is always equivalent, in terms of functional mapping, to one in which every node is occupied by one of the three *primitive control structures* shown in Figure 4-9.[3] *Abstract control structures* can be defined in terms of the primitives and used in place of them in well-formed trees; conversely, any control structure, i.e., configuration of parent and offspring nodes, can appear in a control map as long as it can be shown

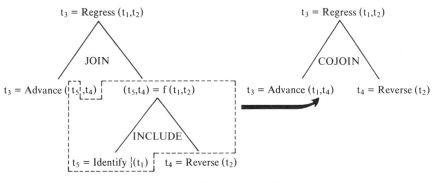

(a) Decomposition in Terms of Primitive   (b) Decomposition in Terms of the
    Control Structures   Abstract Control Structure COJOIN

Fig. 4-7.   Two control maps for operation regress on data type time.   (From Cushing.[1])

to be decomposable into the primitives.[4]   Figure 4-7b, for example, uses the abstract control structure COJOIN, which abbreviates the indicated combination of primitive control structures in Figure 4-7a.   Recursion is also allowed in control maps as long as different occurrences of the same function name are accompanied by different combinations of input and output variables.   This restriction is necessary in order to guarantee that recursion remains recursion and does not degenerate into circularity.[3]   A recursive control map for the power function on integers is given in Figure 4-10.

Control maps can be interpreted either as decomposing functions into primitive operations or as building up functions out of primitive operations.   Under either interpretation, what the tree provides is a specification of the function at its root (highest node) that is non-procedural, non-algorithmic, and entirely free of implementation considerations.   The tree provides a complete and explicit account of the functional mapping the function performs and shows how that mapping is carried out collectively by the primitive operations on the relevant data types.   Everything is spelled out clearly in terms of the hierarchical organization of functional mappings, with no need for abstract programs, i.e., procedural sequences of abstract calls to the primitive operations of abstract machines.

In particular, HOS does not require a general distinction between O-functions and V-functions, though the distinction can always be introduced in the implementations or specifications of specific systems for which it is useful.   Functions are things that can do, as opposed to be, and which different *kinds* of functions need to be sorted out depends on the particular problem.   This point is illustrated by the example in Figure 4-5.   There is a big difference between an implemented register and the integers it contains and thus between changing the state of the register and taking one of those integers as a value.   From the point of view of specification, however, a register is every bit as much of an abstraction as is an integer, and the two abstractions differ only in the interactive behavior of the

DEFINITION: Invocation *provides for the ability to perform a function.*

> AXIOM 1:   A given module controls the invocation of the set of functions on its immediate, and only its immediate, lower level.

DEFINITION: Responsibility *provides for the ability of a module to produce correct output values.*

> AXIOM 2:   A given module controls the responsibility for elements of its own, and only its own, output space.

DEFINITION: *An* output access right *provides for the ability to locate a variable, and once it is located, the ability to give a value to the located variable.*

> AXIOM 3:   A given module controls the output access rights to each set of variables whose values define the elements of the output space for each immediate, and only each immediate, lower-level function.

DEFINITION: *An* input access right *provides for the ability to locate a variable, and once it is located, the ability to reference the value of that variable.*

> AXIOM 4:   A given module controls the input access rights to each set of variables whose values define the elements of the input space for each immediate, and only each immediate, lower-level function.

DEFINITION: Rejection *provides for the ability to recognize an improper input element in that, if a given input element is not acceptable, null output is produced.*

> AXIOM 5:   A given module controls the rejection of invalid elements of its own, and only its own, input set.

DEFINITION: Ordering *provides for the ability to establish a relation in a set of functions so that any two function elements are comparable in that one of the said elements precedes the other said element.*

> AXIOM 6:   A given module controls the ordering of each tree for its immediate, and only its immediate, lower level.

Fig. 4-8.   The HOS control axioms and associated definitions.   (From Hamilton and Zeldin.[3])

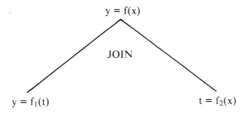

COMPOSITION

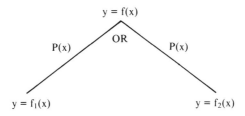

SET PARTITION

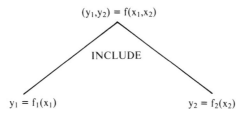

CLASS PARTITION

Fig. 4-9.   The three primitive control structures of HOS.   (From Hamilton and
Zeldin.[3,4])

primitive operations that are needed to characterize their data types, as this behavior
is specified in the axioms of the respective types.   Changing the state of an implemented register in a system really amounts, in the specification of the system,
to producing a new abstract register as a value.   Taking a register and removing
its last element, for example, produces a new register that is identical to the original
register except that it lacks the latter's last element.   *O*-functions *are V*-functions,
in other words, if we view systems at a high enough level of abstraction.

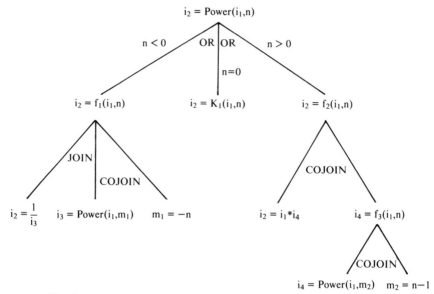

Fig. 4-10. Recursive control map for the power function on integers.

Since abstract programs serve as the characterizations of functions, they correspond in HOS to control map trees. Since abstract machines provide the primitive operations that abstract programs are allowed to call, they correspond in HOS to data-type specifications. Formally, therefore, each pair (P, M) in a hierarchically structured program corresponds, in general, to an ordered pair (D, T), called a *data level* of HOS, in which D is a set of data types for the abstract machine M and T is a set of control maps for the set of abstract programs P.[2]

Because of the simplifying assumption we made in connection with Figure 4-4, data levels end up, through this correspondence, being linearly ordered, but only a partial ordering is necessary as long as there is a maximal data level in the ordering that contains only one tree.

Higher data levels are related to lower data levels in that the control maps of *each* data level decompose the primitive operations of the next higher data level in terms of the primitive operations of the lower data level. In fact, a more general framework is possible, as will be discussed in the next section. For every primitive operation f of a member of D_{i+1} ($i \geq 0$), in other words, there will be a control map in T_i whose root is f and whose leaf notes are primitive operations of a member of D_i. The primitive operations of the *lowest*-data level data types D_0 are the primitive operations *of the system,* because these are not decomposed at all, but are characterized solely in terms of their axiomatic interaction. The simplest case, in which each D_i contains a single data type and in which T_n contains only one decomposed function f, corresponding to the single program P in Figure 4-4, is illustrated in Figure 4-11.

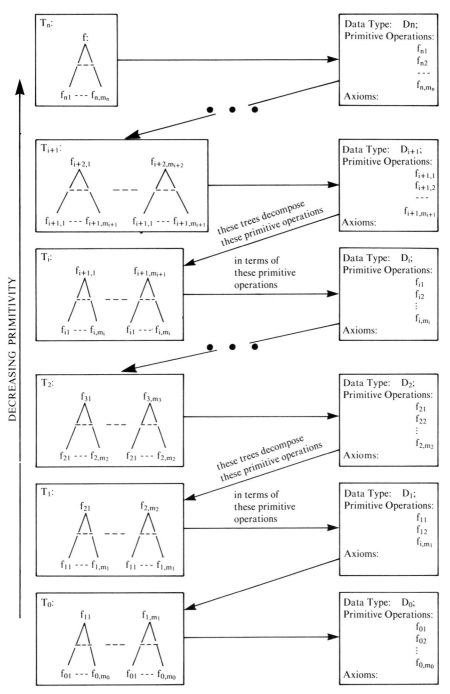

Fig. 4-11.   HOS decomposition of function f in terms of primitive operations of data type D_0. (From Cushing.[2])

SECURITY IN HOS

The first thing one notices when trying to specify the security model M_0 in terms of HOS is that the data types are not of equal status.[2] An agent can be viewed as anything that can observe or modify a repository, or a repository can be viewed as anything that can be observed or modified by an agent; in each case the other of the two data types can be viewed as consisting of anything at all that can be partially (or pre-) ordered. In either case, the only real effect of security classes is to measure the relative sensitivity of one of the two data types, and that effect can be achieved just as well by ordering that data type itself. For the purposes of discussion, the first of the two alternatives has been chosen, characterizing repositories first (as a data type independent of agents) and agents second (as a data type in relation to repositories). Security classes will thus be eliminated from the model altogether by imposing their ordering directly on data type REPOSITORY and assigning each agent a minimal repository it can observe and a maximal repository it can modify.

An HOS specification of data type REPOSITORY is given in Figure 4-12. As just noted, the only primitive operation needed in this data type, other than equality, which is assumed to be available for every data type, is a (partial) ordering, here called Atmost. Whereas the ordering is treated in the description of M_0, in the section on security models, as a general relation, i.e., a general subset of $C \times C$ or,

---

DATA TYPE: REPOSITORY;

PRIMITIVE OPERATIONS:

$\qquad$ boolean = Atmost (repository$_1$, repository$_2$);

AXIOMS:

$\qquad$ WHERE r, r_1, r_2, r_3 ARE REPOSITORIES;

Atmost (r,r) = True;
((Atmost (r_1, r_2) & Atmost (r_2, r_3)) $\supset$ Atmost (r_1, r_3)) = True;
((Atmost (r_1, r_2) & Atmost (r_2, r_1)) $\supset$ Equal (r_1, r_2)) = True;

END REPOSITORY;

Fig. 4-12.　HOS specification of data type REPOSITORY. (From Cushing.[2])

equivalently, a general set of ordering pairs (C_1, C_2), it is treated here as a function, i.e., a subset of REPOSITORY $\times$ REPOSITORY $\times$ BOOLEAN in which the first two components of (R_1, R_2, b) uniquely determine the third. The fact that any relation can be treated in this way as a BOOLEAN-valued function is taken full advantage of in HOS and makes it possible to integrate relations that might not normally be viewed as functions into the general functional-decomposition framework of HOS and thus to see how such "non-functional" relations fit into the system as a whole of which they are a part.

An HOS specification of data type AGENT is given in Figure 4-13. One primitive operation, Observeclearance, assigns to each agent a maximal repository it can observe, and a second one, Modifyclearance, assigns to each agent a minimal repository it can modify. The remaining two primitive operations, Observes and Modifies, correspond respectively, to the θ ("observe") and μ ("modify") relations in the way discussed in the previous paragraph.

The three axioms of data type AGENT together provide the intended effect of the earlier Axioms 3 and 4 (see Security Models) without the use of security classes. The first axiom says that if an agent can observe a repository, then that repository must be lower (but not strictly lower) in the ordering of repositories than the maximal repository the agent can observe. The axiom functions, in other words, as a mutual definition of "can observe" and "maximal observable repository" in terms of each other and the ordering. The second axiom says that if an agent can modify a repository, then that repository must be higher (though perhaps not strictly higher) in the ordering of repositories than the minimal repository the agent can

---

```
DATA TYPE: AGENT;
PRIMITIVE OPERATIONS:
        repository = Observeclearance (agent);
        repository = Modifyclearance (agent);
        boolean = Observes (agent, repository);
        boolean = Modifies (agent, repository);


AXIOMS:
        WHERE a IS AN AGENT;
        WHERE r IS A REPOSITORY;
(Observes (a,r) ⊃ Atmost (r, Observeclearance (a)) = True;
(Modifies (a,r) ⊃ Atmost (Modifyclearance (a),r)) = True;
Atmost (Observeclearance (a), Modifyclearance (a)) = True;


END AGENT;
```

Fig. 4-13.   HOS specification of data type AGENT.   (From Cushing.[2])

modify. This functions, again, as a mutual definition of "can modify" and "minimal modifiable repository" in terms of each other and the ordering.

Given the first two axioms, the third axiom provides the desired effect of security classes by guaranteeing that the maximal observable repository is always lower in the ordering than the minimal modifiable repository. This means that, for a given agent, the lattice of repositories can be divided into an "upper half" and a "lower half" such that the agent can observe only repositories in the lower half and modify only repositories in the upper half. Since this is really the only purpose that security classes serve in M_0, they can thus be dispensed with entirely.

In fact, to attempt to define a separate data type "SECURITY CLASS" would lead to substantive technical complications. Such a data type could be defined in terms of the ordering, but it would be impossible to write axioms on the data types AGENT and REPOSITORY for the "primitive operations" Cls and Clr that map these types into that one without introducing a host of other "primitive operations" with which they could interact. Similarly, there would be no non-arbitrary way to decide whether θ and μ, which take both agents and repositories as inputs, should be primitive operations on AGENT or on REPOSITORY. Recognizing that the only function of "SECURITY CLASS" in M_0 is to provide an appropriate ordering for REPOSITORY makes it clear that the latter is a more basic data type than the former and that the ordering should be defined directly on REPOSITORY. In other words, "SECURITY CLASS" *is* REPOSITORY, at the level of abstraction at which M_0 is defined.

The 8-tuple

$$(R, A, C, \theta, \mu, \trianglelefteq, Cls, Clr)$$

thus reduces to the 7-tuple,

(REPOSITORY, Atmost, AGENT, Observes, Modifies,

Observeclearance, Modifyclearance)

in which one of its data types has disappeared and primitive operations that map into that type are replaced by different primitive operations that have only the two remaining data types as domains and ranges. A parallel argument could be made for agents, rather than repositories, as noted at the beginning of this section. The earlier observation that repositories correspond to data types in HOS and agents correspond to functions is thus further confirmed, since functions with domain and range data types are partially ordered, in systems specified in HOS, by their occurrence in control-map trees, with no further mechanism, such as security classes, needed to provide an ordering for them.

The significance of this result becomes clearer if one focuses on the direction of information flow. Observe first, however, that HOS is considerably more general than the model in Figure 4-11, which inherited the simplifying assumption of linear ordering used in constructing Figure 4-4. In particular, there is no reason for the relationship between successive data levels to be as direct as Figure 4-11 suggests. In the figure, the primitive operations of one data level are decomposed directly into the primitive operations of the next lower data level. In general, however, there can be intermediate operations on the lower data level that mediate this decomposition.

As mentioned earlier, a data level of HOS is an ordered pair (D, T), where D is a set of abstract data types and T is a set of control maps. The data types are ordered and are related in that the control maps of each data level decompose the primitive operations of the next higher data level in terms of the primitive operations of the lower data level. In the most general case, however, the control maps on one data level also use the primitive operations of that data level at their terminal nodes to define operations that do *not* appear as primitive operations of the next higher data level. In this case, there will be further control maps between the data levels whose roots are primitive operations of higher data levels and whose leaves are primitive *or non*-primitive operations of next lower data levels.

To put the point a little differently, a data level of HOS, from the most abstract point of view, is nothing more than an ordered pair (D, T), where D is a collection of sets and T is a collection of mappings, i.e., mathematical functions. Each such ordered pair, however, is subject to a set of constraints imposed by the HOS axioms. Every member of D is not only a set, but a set whose members behave toward each other in a way specified in an HOS data-type specification. Every member of T is not only a mapping, but a mapping that is decomposed in a well-formed HOS tree.

The mappings in T can represent completely general functions and do not have to be *primitive* operations on either their own or any other data level. If a mapping f is non-primitive on its own data level, then a control map connects it to the primitive operations of that data level. Such a tree can be said to be *horizontal,* because it relates primitive and non-primitive operations on a single data level. There is also, however, a *vertical* control map that relates f to the primitive operations of the next higher data level. In this tree f is one of the leaves and the root is one of the primitive operations of the higher data level.

What appears instead of the arrows in Figure 4-11, in other words, is the retroflex step structure in Figure 4-14. Each line segment in Figure 4-14 represents a set of control maps, some of which are horizontal (on a data level) and some of which are vertical (between two data levels). The arrows point away from the root nodes and toward the leaf nodes of the trees they represent. Filled circles represent primitive operations of a data level, while filled squares represent non-primitive operations of a data level. Movement away from f produces increasingly decomposed operations (functions, mappings, etc.), i.e., an increasing degree of primitivity. Movement toward f produces increasingly abstract or complex (decompos*able*) operations, culminating in f itself.

In Figure 4-15, this is elaborated somewhat for a system with three data levels. As in Figure 4-14, filled circles in Figure 4-15 represent the primitive operations of a data level, while filled squares represent non-primitive operations of a data level. Open circles denote non-primitive operations that are needed in the intermediate *levels* of a control map, distinct levels being defined relative to controllers

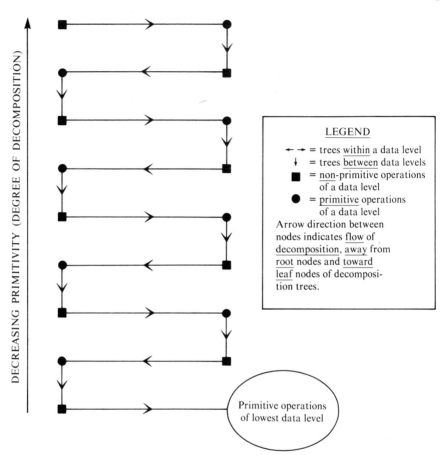

Fig. 4-14.   Retroflexed step structure of HOS data levels. (From Cushing.[2])

or parent nodes. These are described in terms of three primitive HOS control structures or in terms of abstract control structures that are definable in terms of the primitives, as noted in the section, Higher Order Software. Trees with solid branches are horizontal control maps, which decompose non-primitive operations of a data level in terms of primitive operations of the same data level. Trees with dashed branches are vertical control maps, which decompose primitive operations of a data level in terms of non-primitive operations of the next lower data level. Primitivity of operations, therefore, is a relative notion, defined with respect to the data level on which an operation is defined.

    Clearly, if one is not interested in the data-level structure of a particular f that has been decomposed as in Figures 4-14 and 4-15, then he can "fix" f in space, as it were, and "pull the rug out" from under the lowest data level, so the filled nodes act as pivots and the entire system stretches out into one gigantic tree structure, as shown in Figure 4-16. Consider what the HOS axioms say about the information

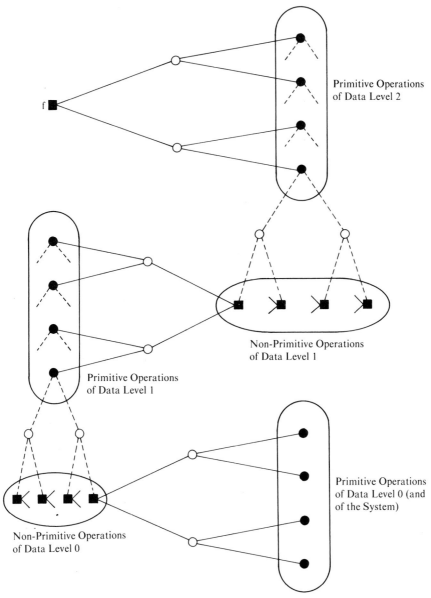

Fig. 4-15.   HOS decomposition of function f with three data levels.   (From Cushing.[2])

flow in such a structure, however (Fig. 4-8).   Axiom 3 states that the access rights to the output of a function in a tree like that of Figure 4-16 are controlled by, and only by, its parent node ("module", in the axiom), i.e., the node immediately above it.   Axiom 4 similarly states that the access rights to the input of a function in such

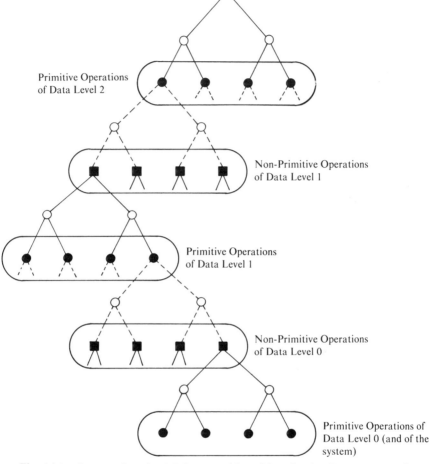

Fig. 4-16.　De-retroflexed HOS decomposition of function f.　(From Cushing.[2])

a tree is also controlled by, and only by, its parent node. A given function can look at data only if its parent allows it to, and it must dispose of its results, again, only as its parent allows it to. The flow of control in an HOS system, therefore, is always from the top down.

The flow of *information,* however, is always from the *bottom up.* A given node performs its function by having its offspring nodes, i.e., those on the immediately lower level, perform the function for it. This is precisely what decomposition is all about. Decomposing a function is just a formalized version of *delegating responsibility.* If someone can perform a task all by himself, then there is no point in delegating that task to subordinates. If responsibility *is* delegated, he performs his task precisely by guaranteeing (via control) that his subordinates perform theirs.

Formally, the offspring nodes *observe* the data that the parent allows them to (Axiom 4), *modify* those data by performing their functions on them, and then dispose of those data as the parent requires, i.e., either by reporting them directly to the parent or by passing them on to an appropriate sibling (Fig. 4-9). In particular, a given function has no idea what higher-level functions are doing. It just chugs along, turning input into output, disposing of that output as its parent tells it to. It *is* aware, however, of what its own offspring are doing, because that is where it gets its input in the first place.

The distinction between variables and values becomes very important here. Control is defined in terms of variables, but information is defined in terms of values. A node controls the access rights of its offspring to variables, telling them what variables they can look at and what variables they must report back about. The offspring thus get their variables from the parent. This is the sense in which control flows downward. The parent node has no idea, however, what the values of those variables are, until it gets those values from its offspring. The parent tells an offspring what variable to look at, and the offspring looks at the variable to find its value, operates on that value as input to change it into a value of an output variable, and reports that value (either to a sibling or) back to the parent. Thus, while parents tell offspring what variables they can look at and assign, it is the offspring that tell the parents what the values of those variables are. Information flows upward, in other words, precisely because control flows downward, as stated in Axioms 3 and 4.

Since Figure 4-16 is functionally equivalent to Figure 4-15, differing, in fact, only in its physical arrangement on the page, our proof of upward information flow is also valid for Figure 4-15, which includes the internal data-level structure of the system. The de-retroflexed tree in Figure 4-16 was used in the proof because the HOS axioms refer to "higher" and "lower" levels of a system, and what these terms mean is not as clear in connection with a retroflex structure like the one in Figure 4-15. The same effect could have been achieved, though less dramatically, by simply pointing out that "higher" and "lower" refer to the parent/offspring relation in decomposition, and not to the physical geometry of the diagram.

Quite aside from the contribution it makes to security through the contribution it makes to reliability, HOS contributes to security also by guaranteeing upward information flow. As noted in connection with M_0, a system can be considered secure if its repositories (data) and agents (functions) are ordered in such a way, and the access rights of the agents (functions) to the repositories (data) are assigned in such a way, that information can flow only upward in the ordering. If a system is specified according to HOS, however, its functions (agents) and data (repositories) are so ordered, and the access rights of the functions (agents) and data (repositories) are so assigned, that information always flows upward in the ordering.

This result makes it possible to refine this discussion of HOS somewhat, and it would be worthwhile to pursue this opportunity a bit. It was shown earlier that systems have a dual character in two distinct senses. On the one hand, a system is a function, in that it performs a function, and it is also a member of a data type, in that it exists at all. On the other hand, a system consists of both data and functions, and these two components are inseparable. What emerges from our proof of upward information flow is that each of these components has a dual character as well, and again, in two senses, when actually put together in a system.

A function in a system decomposition is a *controller,* because it controls the behavior of its offspring, in accordance with the axioms of HOS. It is also a *performer,* however, because it helps carry out the mapping of its parent. Every function plays both roles, and the fact that it plays one role is the reason it must also play the other. Even primitive operations are controllers, potentially, because a lower data level can always be added in which they, too, are decomposed; highest-level functions are also performers, potentially, because any system can always be used as a subsystem of some other system.

Data types also serve in two capacities in system decomposition. Every data type in a control map provides both the *input* of one function and the *output* of another. "In" and "out" are as diametrically opposed as any two things can be, but again, one cannot exist without the other.

The components are dual-natured also in a second way. On the one hand, data have a *constant* aspect, as individual entities that can serve as inputs or outputs of functions, but, on the other hand, they have a *variable* aspect, because they exist as the members of data types. A given datum is an *individual* entity itself, but it is also a *representative* member of a data type that can serve as a value of a variable of that type. This dichotomy enables functions as well to play a dual role in systems in a second sense. In the terminology of M_0, a function can *observe* functions at a lower level of its control map by receiving data values from output variables of those functions and can *modify* functions at a higher level of its control map by providing data values to input variables of those functions.

On the one hand, therefore, functions act as agents, since they can observe lower-level functions and modify higher-level functions. What really gets observed and modified by these agents, however, are the output variables of the respective functions with the modification occurring via the use of the input variables, so it is the output variables that serve as the repositories of the system. On the other hand, the input variables also function as agents, because they receive values from (observe) other functions and give those values to their functions to use in modifying the values of the output variables. In general, in other words, it is the complete functions themselves—mappings, domains, and ranges, with the latter two represented by variables—that act as *both* agents and repositories in an HOS system.

It follows that one not only does not have to distinguish between repositories (or agents) and security classes, as shown earlier, but also does not really have to distinguish even between *repositories* and *agents* either. Since a function by itself inherently has a dual character, being made up of a mapping *and* two data types, functions themselves can play both roles. When functions occur in a control map, they can observe and modify other functions and they can also *be* observed and modified *by* other functions, and they, and the "agents" and "repositories" that they are, are ordered. A function in a system *is* both an agent and a repository and, since it occurs in a tree structure in any system, can also serve as its own security class.

The stipulation made in the section on higher order software in connection with recursion now takes on an added significance. If a system does not involve recursion, then security classes can be identified with function names (mappings) alone, since each one occurs only once in the control map. If some function is called recursively, however, then its name will occur more than once when the control map is fully expanded for a given set of values for the input variables of the system. The stipulation that different occurrences of a function name must occur with different variables, while needed independently to avoid circularity, also makes it possible to preserve the ordering in the tree that is needed for the proof of upward information flow. In other words, security classes in a non-recursive system can be identified with individual function names, but security classes in a recursive system must be identified with function names together with the degrees of recursion (embedding in the tree) with which they occur. Since every function occurs both with its name *and* with its input and output variables, the distinctness of these variables guarantees that of the functions themselves and thus identifies their degrees of recursion. Again, it is the entire function—mapping (name), domain, and range—that determines its security class, receiving information from below and then passing it on up the tree.

REFERENCES

1. Cushing, S.: Algebraic Specification of Data Types in Higher Order Software (HOS). Proceedings, Eleventh Annual Hawaii International Conference on System Sciences, Honolulu, January 1978, p. 124.
2. Cushing, S.: Security Aspects of Higher Order Software. Proceedings, Second International Computer Software and Applications Conference (IEEE Computer Society COMPSAC), Chicago, Illinois, November 1978, p. 481.
3. Hamilton, M., and Zeldin, S.: Higher Order Software—A Methodology for Defining Software. IEEE Transactions on Software Engineering, SE-2, 1.9-32, March 1976.
4. Hamilton, M., and Zeldin, S.: The Relationship Between Design and Verification. Journal of Systems and Software I, 1.29-56, 1979.
5. Linden, T. A.: Operating System Structures to Support Security and Reliable Software. ACM Computing Surveys, VIII, 4.409-445, December 1976.
6. Robinson, L., et al.: On Attaining Reliable Software for a Secure Operating System. Proceedings, International Conference on Reliable Software, Los Angeles, April 21-23, 1975, p. 267.
7. Robinson, L., and Levitt, K. N.: Proof Techniques for Hierarchically Structured Programs. Communications of the ACM, XX, 4.271-283, April 1977.
8. Walter, K. G., et al.: Structured Specification of a Security Kernel. Proceedings, International Conference on Reliable Software, 285-293, Los Angeles, April 21-23, 1975.
9. This chapter is based on work done under Contract No. DAAG29-76-C-0061, sponsored by the Army Research Office, Research Triangle Park, North Carolina.

Chapter 5

DESIGNING FOR PRIVACY: THE DATA VAULT

Richard M. McConnell

Diagnostics Inc., Oakland, California

The public's demand for more information about the workings of government, coupled with their desire to have government know less about them, has produced two strong and conflicting demands on the data processing industry. The topical focal points of this twofold and divergent impulse are security and privacy.

Access to information is the functional area of stress. While on the surface security and privacy may appear to be two sides of the same coin and are often discussed in the same context, they differ dramatically in the origin of concern. Corporate and public officials want more security (defined as less or controlled access), while the general public wants more privacy (also defined as less or controlled access).

It is, however, the selectivity of the application of these constraints in the self-interest of each group that has enabled enactment of both freedom of information legislation, as well as privacy legislation. We want to be able to find out everything about the operations of government and corporations, while at the same time not allowing them to know more than they need to about us.

The computer designer's dilemma is that design's basic tool, logic, is too crude to cope with conflicting human desires. Logic permits only more or less access. Part of the reason for this inability to respond technically to these conflicting demands lies in the basic computer system architectural design, as shown in Figure 5-1.

While there have been vast technological advances since this design was originally implemented, the most significant variation in architectural theme has been adding "windows and telephones" to the house, i.e., multiple limited and subordinate control terminal ports for on-line development and inquiry. Through this approach, shown in Figure 5-2, it is possible to observe and change, in process, the process itself.

Most of the dramatic breakthroughs of the past 25 years have been the product of increases in volume or velocity. Put simply, the house has bigger rooms and shorter halls, but nevertheless the same basic floor plan. To satisfy the demands placed upon data processing systems, it is necessary to rethink this floor plan and develop one that can accommodate these differing access requirements.

Computers were born of the wartime need to calculate in quantities and speeds never known before. In retrospect, considering the current use of these systems,

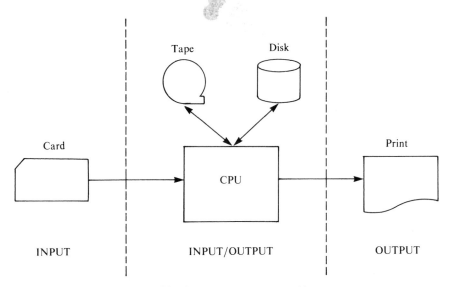

Fig. 5-1.   Classic computer system architecture.

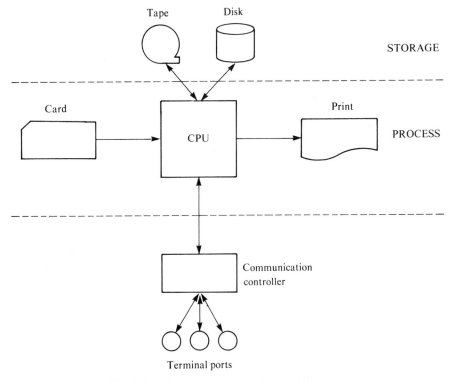

Fig. 5-2.   Communication system architecture.

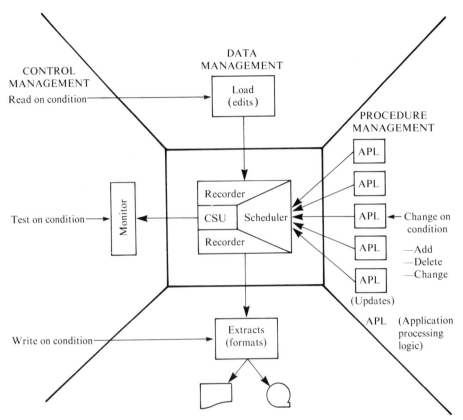

Fig. 5-3.   Data Vault System: central storage unit concept.

it would probably have been wiser to focus on the filing cabinet rather than on the calculator as the key element to automate.

This chapter deals with a different kind of architecture designed around a central storage unit (CSU) rather than a central processing unit (CPU).   Figure 5-3 shows the basic elements of the Data Vault architecture.   This approach functionally holds data in a central location and processes against them, instead of forcing all data to be physically freighted to the logic factories for processing.

DATA VAULT SYSTEM COMPONENTS

The key concept of the Data Vault System is the central storage unit (CSU). The CSU can be thought of as a core memory although in fact it could physically be engineered as micro-chip memory.   Consider a core with the dimensions of 80 bytes width, 100 bytes length, and 10 bytes depth.   Eighty bytes width is chosen only for the ease of considering the core storage to be the same as the familiar

80-column card image record input.   Core itself can then be considered as a file block containing 1000 (100 × 10) 80-byte records.

Now an immediate thought is: Core is expensive, so don't store data permanently in core.   This thought can be put aside for the moment because it deals with the economics of the system not the inherent characteristics of the system.   The possibilities of the design will be explored before the cost justification of any given application.

So in CSU architecture, core becomes the permanent residence of stored *data,* not the temporary residence of stored programs as has been the traditional situation in CPU architecture.   Now in the CSU, since the data have permanent residence in core, one benefit is that the logical record layout can be mapped one-to-one to the physical data position.   Addresses become permanent and known.   There is an immediate operational benefit.   Just as scientific notation is helpful in working with very large and very small numbers because it eliminates the tedious task of writing strings of zeros for correct positional significance, so positional significance is helpful and most used in dealing with numbers that cluster near the zero point on the real number line (numbers generally from 10,000 to 1/10,000) because the numeric value is known immediately from the position.   In other words, it is easier to add $29 + 101 = 130$ than to add $2.9 \times 10^1 + 1.01 \times 10^2 = 1.3 \times 10^2$.   The positioning near zero on the real number line is self-identifying, thereby eliminating the need to index the correct power of the tens multiplier.

In the same way permanently positioning data at known physical addresses eliminates the majority of processing necessary for address resolution in any computer system.

The second and major step forward in processing efficiency in a Data Vault CSU architecture is the gain in reduced programming required because data do not have to be moved.   Data are no longer like transients in a hotel with different room numbers every night, that is, if they have been checked in.   Data have a permanent fixed room number so data can always be fetched from or examined at their known address.

Think of this in light of data processing history.   In the beginning programmers had to write every instruction for every system action.   It soon became apparent that the majority of programming effort was going into the tedious and redundant handling of I/O operations from the peripherals to the mainframe CPU.   The solution to this growing and onerous housekeeping chore was the introduction of operating systems with the advent of second generation hardware equipment.   Now the system itself could handle I/O exchanges from mainframe to peripherals.   The next step forward came with awareness of the problem of redundancy and its need for coordination.   The data processing manager's classic nightmare is that social security numbers will be lengthened.   Since data definitions in COBOL programs are physically resident with the procedure divisions, every program using social security numbers would have to be inspected, its data definition changed, the program recompiled, and tested.   This herculean and thankless task not only would have to be managed transparent to data processing users, but also would provide users no benefit. It would also impact user's current data processing service request backlog adversely by expending scarce programming talent. Data processing management daily is confronted with similar if less dramatic or massive maintenance "must do" tasks. The solution to the problem has been the growth of data base systems that divorce the data characteristics from the procedures processing against the data bases and copylib members.

Data Vault System's CSU offers the next step forward by eliminating the application programmers' need to move data. The CSU system assumes all data movement tasks. Before examining how the CSU system handles data movement, the APL module must be described.

APPLICATION PROCESSING LOGIC

The application programmer works through Application Processing Logic (APL) modules that contain the stored program. The APL modules need not be concerned with data movement since the data reside in fixed locations with known addresses. This means the elimination of reads, writes, and moves from APL code. The application programmer will be concerned only with data availability to a program; that is, is the data file open or closed to the program? The program is limited to the procedural logic of file maintenance activities, such as add, delete, or change records based on specific conditional application logic.

An example of an APL procedure statement would be:

If Statement Balance equal zero, delete record.

for a file of current AR or AP data. If the AR or AP data file were to contain both current and historical records, then the following statements would be examples of APL procedure statements;

If Statement Balance equal zero, set Paid Flag.

If Paid Flag not set, add Service Charge.

Naturally, Statement Balance and Paid Flag would be predefined fields in the record layout. So would Service Charge if it were a field unto itself. The amount of Service Charge could be predefined in a table accessible by the CSU through the Data Loader Device or provided as a literal in the APL code. Both methods would be easy to update. Changing APL code would be less cumbersome than changing present COBOL source code because without all the data movement and data manipulation logic in the procedure, program listings would be less complex and compiles shorter and less costly because there would be less code to compile.

DATA MOVEMENT

In considering the CSU, the storage unit was portrayed as a memory core 80 characters by 100 by 10. A central storage unit of these dimensions could physically contain and logically represent 1000 80-column cards of data information. This information was received from the Data Loader Device and will be sent to the Data Extractor Device. Before discussing the Data Loader Device and the Data Extractor Device, one should reconsider the size of the central storage unit core itself. Now certainly many data files are larger than 1000 records. So two of many alternatives are (1) to increase the size of the core or (2) to pass data through the core. Picking the right size of core for some applications would be difficult so for those cases, one can consider passing data through the core. At first it may seem that to pass data through the core violates the whole concept of fixed data in a central storage unit. This does not have to be the case. Data can reside in different media and still be self contained if the design only allows for limited access. In other words, a dedicated direct access storage device can page data into core and out of core similar to the way in which it happens now but in a manner that allows for the system to control all movement and the design to retain the advantage of programming logic freed from moves, reads, and writes. This constraint would maintain the severe limitations of the APL programmer to manipulate data. It is this limitation that provides the major security gain in the CSU architecture over present CPU architecture.

In picturing how paging works, consider two analogies. In the first case, where 1000 records is sufficient, core needs no backup storage. This situation is analogous to a suburb where every family has a permanent home. As in the suburb every record in this case has a permanent address. In the second situation there are more records than permanent addresses. This is analogous to the previously mentioned hotel where every permanent room may have different occupants. In a CPU system, rooms are allocated on a random (called dynamic) basis. Any record's data may, in subsequent job executions, find itself anywhere in core. In a CSU system, room is predetermined to coincide with the logic mapping of record field position; that is, everytime record 1001 comes in, record 1 goes out and record 1001 is located at address 1. This situation could be compared to that of a hotel guest always staying in the same room and always checking in on Monday and out on Tuesday.

If this is difficult to imagine, consider a manual rotary file such as is often used for desktop address and telephone lists. As the file is rotated, certain records come into view and others go out of view. Regardless of what is in view or out of view, the relative sequence of the records remains unchanged and the format of each record remains constant. Rotating data through the CSU core is a more apt phrase than "passing" data because of confusion of terminology with that of CPU architecture. In fact, rotating cores could be constructed so as to be physically similar to the abandoned memory drums of second generation equipment. This is not a design necessity, however, for a CSU system. The point is that a CSU system can allow for interchange among different storage media without violating the functional design separation because only the CSU is permitted access or paging through the secondary storage media.

It is important also to consider the parallel processing possibilities in this discussion of CSU and APL interaction. In the dimensions of the 1000 80-byte core, the depth of the core was 10; i.e., the first plane of the core contains 10 records in their entirety. If instead of the present CPU register architecture, CSU registers mirror all 10 records, in other words a register bank of 80 by 10 or 800 bytes representing the 10 records, then these 10 records could all be processed simultaneously in one master clock cycle time. This situation is true of parallel processing and represents a very large gain over the present system of factoring out and overlapping, in one cycle time, different processing functions based on the sequence string of events necessary to move data through I/O in a CPU.

Carrying this parallel processing to its logical and costly conclusion, the entire core could be register mirrored so that the whole file could be processed in one cycle time. Interleaving of one physical column of data and one physical column of register input would keep the travel time to arithmetic logic constant. If paging is the bringing in of one page of data at a time, then the register mirror imaging of the complete core would be akin to updating whole chapters or even books of data simultaneously. While certain applications for such a technique would be those characterized by high-volume information floods and ultra-rapid response necessary to justify instantaneous total update, one paging problem would be eliminated in such a design. Since the whole data file resides in core, there would be no thrashing.

MONITOR

The monitoring device controls the entire operation of the Data Vault CSU system. As such, it is akin to the CPU operator console. Also similar to the CPU console, the monitor can start, stop, suspend, and status check all system actions. Unlike a CPU console, the monitor cannot be an alternative data entry input device for either data or programs. It is a passive device in regard to any possible application and only an active device in regard to systems operation. Like a traffic cop it can control traffic but it cannot create traffic or change the contents of any specific vehicle although it can inspect them.

Physically the monitor would be a video display terminal. Multiple monitors not only would be desirable but would be necessary for any inquiry capabilities of the system. As with present networks of terminal inquiry systems, it would be prudent to have a master terminal to control data communications. Actually both the phrase data communications and teleprocessing are somewhat misleading when applied to CSU architecture, for data communications often connotes data entry. In a CPU system with its non-specific functionally generalized use, this represents no problem in either application or use. In like manner, teleprocessing most often connotes the execution and returned program results of programs submitted through or initiated from remote devices. In the CSU concept, data communications that involved data entry would be routed through the Data Loader Device. Teleprocessing that initiated program execution would be routed through the APL modules.

The monitor would not be capable of either data entry or processing initiation. The monitor is limited strictly to monitoring, that is, inspecting, viewing, inquiring into the data file, the schedule of authorized initiated updates, the current actions of both the data loader device and data extractor device, and all resident logs of past activities. In this sense, the monitor is a tele-inquiry or data inquiry function, not a teleprocessing or data communications function.

Oddly enough, for the ever-growing number of existing inquiry systems using CPU architecture, only a rare design (system, software, or hardware) takes into account the unique requirements of different types of questions. Certainly present inquiry systems are capable of answering a multitude of different questions, but no system to my knowledge has been designed to handle different types of questions with precision and efficiency. To compensate for this, CSU architecture through its monitor(s) has a system facility called LASAR (Limited Access Search And Retrieval). The benefit of this facility can be illustrated by considering a situation that occurred a few years ago at one of the nation's largest multinational banks.

During the 1974/75 recession a very large East Coast bank was on the verge of collapse. As the news spread and the banking system moved to stabilize itself, the burning question of the West Coast bank (all banks, for that matter) was: What is our position in terms of the failing bank? Do they owe us? Do we owe them? If so, how much? The West Coast bank for all its tens of millions of dollars invested in data processing equipment and systems, for all its hordes of analysts, programmers, operators, and managers, could not get a ready answer without combing through dozens of reports and checking with its stock and financial fund traders, loan officers, credit card division, and the clearing house. All the king's horses and all the king's men could not give the king's question an answer in a time frame necessary for immediate protective and supportive action based on factual information. The theoretical problem was that while the CPU architecture could churn millions of checks daily and handle other predefined systems processing, it could only answer immediately questions that had been pre-established even though the total system environment could juggle hundreds of files, subfiles, and varying versions daily. A CSU system by predefining data formats *and* locations and disallowing multiple locations and versions of data information can rapidly answer questions such as the one posed.

Present CPU architecture is built to expedite the processing of item question handling only, i.e., transaction processing. While this capability is certainly necessary, it is also quite limited. There are other types of questions, specifically, in addition to item questions, unit questions, feature questions, and field questions. The West Coast bank president's question, though easily phrased in a few words, is really a bit more complex than originally perceived. Regardless of its complexity it is a frequent, necessary, and obvious question asked tens of thousands of times daily in business, albeit usually under less stressful circumstances: "What is our position with XYZ Corp.?" What is really being asked is a unit question based on a comparison of two fields of features which are resident in item data vehicles distributed throughout the possible full extent of files. The two fields are credits and debits. To rephrase that into a somewhat meaningful English language example would be to restate the president's question as: Are there more redheads or blondes in that traffic jam? To get an answer, the two features (redheads and blondes) would have to be ascertained from the field (all cars in the traffic jam) by examining every item (each car), tallying the counts and then performing a unit test (comparing the totals of each feature to determine which was "more"). In a traffic jam, cars are not easy to get to, do change position, are inclined to get away if possible, and do not tend to cooperate with census takers. The same is unfortunately true of CPU data. Data are contained in data vehicles called records that are passed all over the system with many temporary residences in multiple versions and subsets of files. Furthermore, the features or contents of the record fields often vary in the differing versions of the files depending on processing that has been executed in sometimes multitudes of job streams. Trying to answer questions such as the one posed in a CPU environment is like trying to catch all the ants at a picnic. It's hopeless. If the question has not been predefined, the CPU system cannot respond on an urgent or command basis. To make any real progress in this area, data processing as a profession and computer science as a science must engineer an answer to this rather basic need in information theory.

LASAR, as a CSU facility, first of all recognizes that there are item questions, feature questions, unit questions, and field questions. It further recognizes and provides for the fact that data vehicles (records) can have either item or feature characteristics and be arranged (sequenced) in different types of indices. The amount of processing necessary to satisfy any given inquiry is determined by the characteristics of all these factors. Present techniques of both file and even data base design are of necessity geared toward the severe streamlining of record sizes because the inherent design of a CPU system forces records to be nomadic. A CSU system with permanent residence is under no such size limitation for mobility's sake. It's the cattlemen versus the settlers all over again. The settlers build towns, fence off the land, and support a larger population. So too does a CSU system collect in proximity; data, while separating and limiting functions by speciality, erect permanent positional data location ownership, and thereby gain the capacity to answer not only more but different types of inquiries.

DATA LOADER DEVICE

The data loader device can be thought of as a family of intelligent data entry devices. This family consists of card readers, key-to-disc equipment, CRT terminals, and any other device that collects input data, converts data from one media to another, and prepares media for storage.

In terms of the CSU concept, all data editing is done on the data loader devices. This editing requires what is normally called "intelligence" in each and every data loader device. Intelligence in the data loader devices performs more than the present functions of providing prompts to input operators and handling data communications message packaging. All actual system edit programs are executed in the data loader device itself. The data loader device can be thought of as a single limited-purpose computer with the sole job of filtering all input to the CSU. The data loader device(s) edit program execution assures that alpha characters are in alpha fields, that numbers are in numeric fields, that coded fields contain valid codes, that new records have all critical fields filled, etc.

Working as a filter, the data loader device has the functional responsibility of providing reject information for output error report processing. Error report generation can be handled by incorporating a print mechanism into the data loader device or by linking to the data extractor device for formatting and report writing. This latter case would be the only instance of a "passed" data file in the CSU system. This instance is limited to input rejects that are "flushed" out of the system before polluting the integrity of the stored data residing in the CSU.

The information flow of the data loader device is a read only from external sources regardless of media (cards, tape, disks, teleprocessed terminal input) and a write only to the CSU. The data loader device cannot make inquiry of the CSU. There are no interactive capabilities for this device. The data loader device is strictly limited to putting accurate data into the CSU. This strict limitation of input extends to all CSU input devices the inherent security in the unchallenged claim, "No one ever stole a report from a card reader."

DATA EXTRACTOR DEVICE

The data extractor device, like the data loader device, can be thought of as a family of intelligent report writing devices. This family consists of printers, punches, tapes, disk packs, and any other device that creates output records on any tangible medium, such as paper, cards, tape, disks, and diskettes.

In terms of the CSU concept, all report formatting and generation are done on the data extractor device, so it must be an intelligent device. This intelligence goes a step further than present spool handling of enqueued formatted reports waiting for printer time. All report programs would actually be executed on the data extractor device. The data extractor device, once again like the data loader device, can be thought of as a single limited-purpose computer. The data extractor device's sole job is to pick data from the CSU, package the data in accordance with user formatting requirements, and ship the reports out of the system on the predefined medium.

All present programming considerations dealing with packed or unpacked fields, data compression or expansion, display formats, etc. are handled solely by the data extractor device's programs. With this system work being done on the data extractor device, the APL modules are free to deal exclusively with file update, the

Monitor to deal exclusively with inquiry, and the data loader device to deal exclusively with edits.

The information flow in the data extractor device is read only from the CSU and write only to the output media. The data extractor device cannot make inquiry of the CSU. It only handles those jobs pre-established, scheduled, and operator released. There is no interactive capability in the data extractor device. It can only get from the CSU. It cannot put anything into the CSU. In this manner, the strict limitation to output extends, to all data extractor devices and their programs, the inherent security gained from the fact that, "No printer ever wrote over the only master file copy."

SCHEDULER

The scheduler in CSU architecture performs the same function as an operating system scheduler in CPU architecture. The makeup of the schedule itself is different because, instead of a single program being able to read, edit, update, format, and write records or reports as in a CPU system, these functions are split up and parceled out to different components in the CSU system. This creates the need for more consideration and coordination to the sequence of processes taking place in the CSU system. The trade-off is the reduced consideration and coordination that have to be given various files, versions, and their sequences that presently cause a headache with JCL and make tape libraries (along with their management) necessary in CPU architecture.

Present CPU scheduling is handled by the operating system supervisor, which always gives highest priority to I/O operations because I/O is the slowest operation and therefore the principal cause of any system log jam. Since the CPU is a throughput machine, it, like a manufacturing plant assembly line, can be shut down if there is a parts, i.e., data, shortage.

The CSU concept is analogous to a warehousing function. Highest scheduling priority goes to the monitor inquiries, which are akin to inventory taking: second, to data extractor device requests, which are queued based on update requirement condition codes being met; then to APL module file update logic, which applies all enqueued Data Loader Device input which has successfully passed all editing checks.

In any given master clock cycle time, any of the four types of peripheral devices can be accessing the CSU, but only the Data Loader Device can write to the CSU and only if authorized from an APL module. While there is input in to the CSU through the Data Loader Device and output from the CSU to either the Monitor or the Data Extractor Device, there is no I/O operation in the sense that any device can both input and output from the CSU. Like traffic in an urban center, everything in a CSU Data Vault System travels down one-way streets with many stop points for control.

RECORDER

The function of the recorder in CSU architecture is to log all entries and exits from the CSU as a permanent record of change to the CSU on a chronological basis. The recorder's logging function provides a complete audit trail capability and the necessary data for backup in case CSU data are lost during system failure or physical equipment damage.

The manner in which the recorder logs changes is a matter of engineering and cost justification. Of the many alternatives, one is a variation of the PROM (Programmable Read Only Memory) concept. Instead of a PROM, a PWOM (Programmable Write Only Memory) card is interfaced between the Data Loader Device and the CSU and also between the CSU and the Data Extractor Device. As the contents of PWOM's fill up, they are removed and new PWOM boards are inserted. The removed PWOMs can be kept by auditors for reference. In this way, auditors for the first time in computer data processing have permanent physical records of all systems activities.

The recorders are designed to log many things beyond basic input and output. All monitor inquiries are also logged by source, time, and response. Statistical information on types of inquiries and the data's dynamic characteristics may also be maintained. Oddly enough, present-day CPU data processing has no capacity to measure the dynamic behavior of the data that pour through its resources. One only knows indirectly of data through their impact on program structure. Typically this knowledge is negative as when an "OC7" data exception blows up a program and ruins a whole run in a CPU job stream because alpha characters were in a numeric field.

In CSU architecture, the job stream is radically different from the CPU job stream concept. In CSU architecture the stream is the flow of data through the system, not the flow of programs through the CPU. In terms of programs and program code, the CSU Data Vault System recorders also track the operational characteristics of the APL module code. Statistical spreads show which code is most used, seldom used, and never used. This code performance checking function provides visibility into program structure and utility. Program and therefore programmer productivity can be measured.

DATA SECURITY IN THE DATA VAULT SYSTEM

Having identified the need and sketched the basic design of a Data Vault System, one can consider the issue of security more closely. First of all, in comparing a classic CPU design to a Data Vault System, a Data Vault System is a throughput machine turned inside out. In a Data Vault System the data reside centrally in core or at the core of the system and programs are passed. In a CPU throughput system, the program logic is in core and external data are passed. In a CPU throughput system the unavoidable security risk is that the data are physically located external to the heart of the system, the CPU, except when they are being processed. In a Data Vault System, the data reside secure in the heart of the system and are only vulnerable when being processed against.

The basic concept of the throughput machine is the stored program and the formula, input, process, output. This formula, elaborated by Von Neumann as an analogy to the stimulus response passage of information in a nerve cell, has been the foundation of all computer science to date. Now, however, with the capabilities of micro-chip technology, the theoretical concepts of parallel processing, and the pioneering efforts of establishing new computer architectures based on other than throughput considerations, such as Tandem's reliability architecture, it is possible to design automated digital equipment based on criteria other than the sole needs of financial or scientific numerical transaction handling. Security as shown here is just one of a universe of possible criteria.

How well do we handle security now?

Security of the Past

In terms of the past, I prefer to think of the Data Vault System more as an automated icebox than as an automated filing cabinet. Like food the value of data perishes as it ages. Old data though have one peculiar characteristic unlike old food. While the probability of any set of information retaining value diminishes over time, the likelihood of any particular piece of information searched for being of value, increases over time. For example, most old stock certificates are worthless, but a few are worth enormous sums of money today. The whole field of dealing with history files and archives is woefully underdeveloped.

Regarding this problem, today's present CPU architecture is much more likely to yield better libraries of program code to future generations than collected information sets of data for research. So present computer architecture is not adept at preserving the past. Like last summer's flowers, last summer's transactions are lost as expired generation tapes are scratched for today's use. The past is not secure because it is not accessible.

Security of the Present

Most security concerns focus on limiting the dissemination of current file contents. Reasons for secrecy or confidentiality are many. On an individual basis the right to privacy, the right to a good name, a reputation, freedom from slander, libel, malicious gossip, misinformation affecting one's life; on a corporate basis, the right to trade secrets, the security of business plans being kept from competitors. Courts, banks, and health care facilities all share the need for security of information while having unique requirements for information use. So do police departments, lawyers, pharmacists, buyers soliciting competitive bids. All these are ever-present data security needs in a time when information processing equipment is built on the principle of producing reports and displaying information as fast and cost effectively as possible. CPU methodology is entirely geared to produce information, not to contain information.

Security of the Future

This area has been totally untouched by present CPU computer architecture. What can it possibly even mean? One idea is the ability to project future occurrences based on present known data. Some statistical forecasting applications now exist but they are invariably based on the shaky premise of continuation of present trends. Perhaps a more fruitful endeavor would be the generation of multiple scenarios based on known or possible limitations. Concerning the future, today's CPU architecture is entirely passive, being content to meet today's messenger today. Tomorrow's output is based on tomorrow's input and that is accepted as unknown. In that input, process, output is based on the nerve cell metaphor of stimulus response, today's computer architecture can be accurately described as reactive.

So how secure can CPU architecture be, with no design features for history, when it is assembly line report production geared, and ultimately reactive to its daily input? The answer is, as secure as any manufacturing plant with a full retinue of guards and gates, badges and passes. All CPU security is based on password protection as all data communications security is presently based on data encryption. Password protection beats having no protection at all, but not by much. It does have its limitations. The primary problem is that password protection is a manual, therefore, erratic, and fallible system.

An example is the situation that occurred when a bank using a time sharing system had the entire parts manual of a new proprietary product of a major space contractor printed out in its office because, being near Christmas, both the bank's terminal operator and the manufacturer's terminal operator, in changing passwords daily and both being rushed, chose SANTA as the password on the same day. When the bank's terminal operator mistakenly keyed in the identification number of the manufacturer's terminal operator simply by mis-keying her own identification number, she gained full access to the manufacturer's cataloged data. The point is not that this coincidence is likely to happen often, but that it did happen and is possible. A more likely situation than SANTA at Christmas or BUNNY at Easter is the coincidence of boyfriend or girlfriend's names. Passwords are not foolproof.

Data Vault Security

Granted the problem with CPU security and given the Data Vault components described and the CSU design, where is the additional security? The major security gain in the Data Vault System lies in the limitation of each component and its programming. These limitations make it more difficult to breach the system's security. APL modules and Data Loader Devices programming can pollute the CSU data, one by improper file maintenance and the other by improper input editing. Both would be breaches of data integrity; that is, they would adversely affect data accuracy. Neither though has the capacity to generate system output, and both have transaction logs for audit and data reconstruction. Misuse of Monitors and Data Extractor Devices programming can be the cause of data theft, one by unauthorized use of inquiry capabilities and the other by unauthorized generation of reports. Both would be breaches of data security; that is, data confidentiality would be violated. However, neither has the capacity to change system data. While these vulnerabilities are serious enough, this is still a gain over present CPU architecture where a single program can establish a false record, change amounts in real records, generate reports that mask illegal transactions, and print checks or reports of vital information leaving no trace. To accomplish this same series of security violations in a Data Vault CSU System, three, usually four programs would have to be written or modified, compiled, executed, and purged. While that is not impossible, it is far less likely to occur in a Data Vault CSU System than in a CPU mainframe today.

Additionally, in a CSU system the data are always machine resident. In a CPU system, theft of a master file is as simple as getting an excuse to go into the tape library. If the tape librarian can be avoided, evaded, confused, or seduced, all the CPU hardware system checks and passwords in the world are to no avail. Finally, the accounting profession, which has in its long history been satisfied for more than 500 years with its present double-entry bookkeeping system for proper checks of arithmetic accuracy and the organizational separation of functions of the treasurer and the controller for financial integrity, is content with two checks or safeguards in each area. Data processing in its 50 plus years' experience with automated equipment (tab equipment included) can no longer rest content with a CPU design that is, ultimately, despite its operating system maze, a single string machine concept for any given transaction. The Data Vault CSU with its fourfold functional separation is an improvement from a security viewpoint.

EFFECTS OF DATA VAULT ARCHITECTURE

Since in this system the storage unit becomes the central location of activity and its functional requirements the controlling factors of processing, there would be no more libraries of fading snapshot data, only user libraries of provisional procedural logic. In that most code has a half-life of 6 to 12 months and many file formats have survived from the wire-plug days, this may be a design more tailored to the facts of systems life. Logic could be completely user controlled, if not generated, and would have to pass through a code inspection and scheduler before entry to a permanent physically removable PWOM access recorder.

Software would change in that present instructions would be grouped and subdivided to meet the control separation possible by factoring and logically packaging Edits on a Data Loader Device accepting write-only programs, and Formats on a Data Extractor Device accepting read-only programs. The major security gain would be that no one program could be capable of the one shot, hit and run, no trace data grab now possible in present architecture.

Operations major function would be the proper running of the equipment and the monitoring of who puts what in and who takes what out. Applications would primarily have concern with their functional responsibilities: work scheduling and procedural change. Systems would be responsible for file structure design that would become hardware constants. The Controller or MIS Director would have the responsibility of setting collection, editing, formatting, and distribution policies. The Auditor would be able to take physical possession of add, delete, and change access histories for permanent off-site retention.

In terms of an operating system, the scheduling function would be critical to coordinate the sequence of edited new data loads triggered by processing change orders and extracts to be formatted into tapes or printed reports. An interrupt system giving highest priority probably to the passive monitor would be required. Another factor would be that all accepted reads would be written to the permanent recorder as well as all writes to the extractor. An interesting aspect would be that, since files would not be passed, there would be no sorts or merges. For this gain in reduced processing (that is, machine activity) the trade-off would probably be in the advanced planning and possibly variable key construction required for index schemes and subset identification. File reorganization would become the system generation since the system is based on the file, not the instruction set logic. Interface between two unique Data Vault Central Storage Units would be possible by matching extracts to loads of common data fields. Naturally there would be the desire to minimize this occurrence, but not at the cost of an overly complex file structure with its attendant scheduling problems and search times.

Applications for such a Data Vault scheme would be any Master File/Data Base collection of information fields characterized by high retention and security requirements and low calculation complexity. This is not the design of an interactive system. It could be used that way but it would be cumbersome on the input side. This is a design whose primary criteria are security and change tracking or audit trailing. It is amenable, however, to on-line inquiry capabilities through an extension of the monitor. Applications such as bank check posting, with its requirement for security against manipulation and need for real time inquiry, would be a good fit of architecture to tenant.

Such a hardware architecture as proposed is just an initial concept, the fruition of which will require monumental rethinking in terms of consequences on methodology, skill development and retention, and interface of CSU to CPU technology, if possible. This Data Vault may offer a better approach to the security/privacy demands than the reliance on complexity and apathy to generate enough ignorance and inertia to deter data thieves. One thing is clear. This design will not solve the tug-of-war of freedom of access versus limitation of access. It can, however, improve our control of access (there is no I/O operation)—a control without which the other questions may never be resolved.

Chapter 6

SECURITY PROBLEMS IN A DATA BASE ENVIRONMENT

Joseph J. Rodriguez and Paul S. Fisher

Department of Computer Science, Kansas State University, Manhattan, Kansas

SECURITY CONCERNS OF THE MANAGER

As a manager, one fundamental responsibility will always involve the security of assets and resources, as that is a functional goal of any organization. In the field of computing, business and government have increasingly recognized the large price tag attached to the data processing operation. Consequently, any manager who takes the requirements of security lightly is likely to have a rude and painful awakening when disaster strikes. Therefore, a data processing manager's goals should include increasing his personal knowledge and awareness of the broad area of computer security requirements, in addition to recognizing the current status and technology demands needed to accomplish thorough security.

Normally, the organization's data processing environment may present special requirements, however; whether it is a single site or one of several in a distributed processing system, safeguarding computer operations requires a systematic approach. Ordinarily, this methodology will include considerations of policy, cost/benefit analysis, as well as audit and evaluation of security measures implemented.

In the literature, it is generally agreed that two broad categories of computer security requirements exist: (1) the individual's right of privacy, and (2) security of the entire system. Aside from providing some general background concerning these categories, the primary focus of this section will be on general methods used in the penetration of a system, the way in which it is done, and the corresponding planning measures required to counteract such potential compromise.

General Background

When the privacy category is evaluated, the primary goal is to safeguard the personal privacy inherent in the information possessed within the data base. Typically, a set of recommendations and guidelines are developed, including compliance with current laws, which encompass identifying actual and potential threats to privacy. Information privacy may be further defined as the right of individuals to know that the recorded personal information is accurate, pertinent, complete, up-to-date, and reasonably secure from unauthorized access—either accidental or intentional. More important, the concept of information privacy should include the right of the individual to influence the kind, quantity, and quality of information about him contained in information systems. Regardless of whether this information is open to the view of the general public, or specifically required by law to be confidential, these privacy concepts should be acknowledged by all operators and users of information systems. In addition, privacy guidelines should be observed from the time that data are collected, through processing and use, to final disposition.

The concept of privacy also consists of two basic principles. First, there will be some disclosure of personal identifying information. Second, there must be some provision for the individual to participate in determining the amount, nature, and extent of data collection and disclosure. An important implication of these two principles is that privacy is not necessarily inconsistent with disclosure and the use of personally identifying data. A recognition of the important role of the individual in the collection and use of that information is self-evident.

The security category also requires being able to identify threats to, and vulnerabilities of, a computer system. In addition, the development of (1) a methodology for auditing and evaluating a secure environment, (2) methods for determining security exposure, (3) step-by-step cost-effective security measures, and (4) a security policy are critical to achieving security goals. The intent is simply better protection for the data, the mechanisms and resources used in processing data, and the security mechanisms themselves.

Data security involves the protection of information against accidental or unauthorized destruction, modification or disclosure using both physical security measures and controlled accessibility techniques. Physical security means the protection of computer facilities against all physical threats, i.e., damage or loss from accident, theft, malicious actions, fire, flood, and other hazards. Controlled accessibility is the term applied to the protection provided to data and computing resources by software and hardware mechanisms of the computer itself, for example, the use of a software password package for user identification and of a hardware protection scheme for the operating system.

The Vulnerable Facility

The following weaknesses, discussed by Parker in "The New Criminal," [11] provide a description of characteristics, in descending order of importance, which leave an organization most vulnerable to criminal activity.

1. The computer operator performs financial processing applications such as:
   a. Input and output of negotiable documents
   b. Inventory of goods
   c. Valuable mailing lists being maintained

2. Employee dissatisfaction and staff self-interest exist.
   a. There is frequent employee rationalization.
   b. Little organizational loyalty is shown.
   c. Low morale is evident.
   d. Individual defensiveness and the potential for collusion exists.
3. There is a lack of dual controls or separation of sensitive job functions. Consequently, there is no separation of tasks and responsibilities, especially in the area of applications programming, program testing, system programming, data handling, input and output, materials storage, and computer operations.
4. System services and physical facilities are readily available without supervision.
5. The operating system and program security controls are weak.
6. Personnel control policies are virtually nonexistent.

Penetration

The design of a secure computer system, in order to be reasonably successful, must realistically take into account the methods which can be expected to be used to penetrate it. Only in this fashion can a manager expect to develop countermeasures to foil intruders. Penetration can be described as the act of gaining unauthorized access to the data, procedures, or system hardware resources. In itself, unauthorized access does not necessarily mean a compromise; however, according to Lackey,[8] it can often be expected to lead to any or all of the following: (1) observation—reading of data; (2) extraction—copying or withdrawal of information; (3) alteration—the changing or modifying of data, procedures, or hardware; (4) addition—the adding of extraneous information; and (5) utilization—the usage of the system's hardware or software resources.

The extent and level of penetration of a system are affected by two major factors. First is the degree of control loss which the system allows; second is the knowledge of the penetrator combined with the extent to which he exploits each intrusion.

Threats to a system are primarily in communication associated areas, that is, the operating system, the access controls, and the storage protector hardware. Clearly, since the operating system controls almost all main functions (the allocation of system resources, input/output management, etc.), it can be instrumental in gaining control of the whole system. Likewise, discovery of (or weakness in) access controls readily allows the system and its checking mechanism to be circumvented.

The six major categories of system penetration, discussed in "Penetration of Computer Systems: An Overview," [9] are: (1) Browsing-(B)—the searching of residue or storage for unauthorized information which may aid in system penetration and compromise; (2) Foible-(F)—an accidental or unintentional opening which permits unauthorized control of the system or access to information; (3) Artifice-(A)—the intentional introduction of devious program code into a system to be used later for subversion from within; (4) Impersonation-(I)—masquerading as a legitimate user or device, eventually expected to introduce unauthorized code, perform unauthorized acts, or obtain unauthorized information; (5) Tapping-(T)—gaining direct access via direct connection to a communication line or a part of the central system; and (6) Radiation-(R)—a passive eavesdropping without direct connection to a line. Some specific examples of the penetration techniques presented by Lackey, with the respective category letter-code shown in parentheses, follow.

Penetration Techniques

1. Test & Diagnostics personnel looking through core dumps could find passwords or other confidential information. (B)
2. Illegal viewing of the system I/O buffers is allowed as a result of asynchronous processing and I/O. (B,F)
3. Unauthorized system activity is allowed by incomplete parameter checking, such as an improper return from a system service. (F)
4. Clandestine code is placed in an intelligent terminal device for the theft of user ID's and passwords. (A)
5. Intelligent terminal software simulates the host computer (using clandestine software) to collect information. (A,I)
6. Someone can be using the system resources while a user is logged on but inactive ("known as between the lines entry"). (I,T)
7. "Piggybacking" an entry into a system can be done by the selective interception of communications between a legitimate user and a system, then releasing, with a modification or substitution, an entirely new message while returning an error message to the user. (I,T)
8. It is possible to record information going to and from a terminal via magnetic or acoustical coupling. (R)
9. Information is siphoned from a multiplexed communications line via "cross-talk." (R)

Planning for Security

When proper attention is given to system security and protection, specific countermeasures must consider the amount of effort and resources which have to be expended to gain unauthorized access. Improving the system mechanisms and procedures can make penetration too costly to the perpetrator. This is the type of security for which an organization should strive.

One type of sytematic evaluation involves the use of a questionnaire. As an initial step, it offers several sound advantages. Cost is moderate, approximately 10 to 20% of the monthly operations cost of an average data processing facility, depending upon size and complexity of the functions performed. Also, outside assistance is not normally required. A team with the skills required to perform a credible survey is normally drawn from within the organization. The increased staff awareness in the area of security is a positive by-product of a survey and a definite advantage. According to Jacobson,[8] however, a questionnaire approach has two significant drawbacks. First and foremost is that one or more of the questions may be faulty. A poorly constructed question may confuse the problem and foil its solution. As a result, a particular solution may be endorsed by implication, and in other cases it may not be clear how to answer a question or interpret the answer. Finally, it may be difficult to interpret overall results. At best, any questionnaire can only evaluate specific security requirements against some arbitrary standard. Unless designed continuously over time for a particular environment and a specific facility, it does not normally reflect the loss exposure and threat environment of that organization.

A primary consideration in developing a secure system, as Lackey[9] indicates, is to include security and penetration prevention ideas in the system design, in addition to the use or creation of hardware and software security checklists. The next step is to plan for detection of a violation in security by the use of both hardware and software monitors to track file and data base accesses by user identification and time. In the same fashion, utilization profiles can also be developed. A security console which displays all security messages is an additional deterrent which can be considered. In the final analysis, it is far better "to know that you have been HAD than not to know at all."

Lackey further states that specific countermeasures should address increasing the number of levels of privilege available for system implementation, in effect, creating several barriers which must be penetrated by distributing the operating system over several levels. As a matter of procedure, the method of changing these levels of privilege should also be tightly controlled. Particular advantages of a multi-level privileged system include forcing undebugged programs to execute in a low privilege area.

In addition, the unifying of batch and time-sharing systems allows the use of a common checking mechanism. This technique eliminates such inconsistencies as differing error messages and diagnostics, controls the work load level, and allows for more efficient use of system resources.

Another systemwise scheme, outlined in "Penetration of Computer Systems: An Overview," [9] which should be devised as a part of the design of a system, is a process of unique identification between hardware components and software modules. The use of the identification mechanism would be a standard requirement. Information about the type of device options and the revision level of the hardware would be especially useful for test and diagnostic programs. The operating system could also use this information to limit the functions performed according to the capability of the installation. Software identification would be used by both the called and calling modules, including information about assembly date and parameters. Through the use of tailored enforced rules, greater protection of both hardware and software interfaces would be possible.

Summary

In determining the specific needs for security required in an organization, it is strongly recommended that a risk assessment be undertaken. Three benefits can be derived:

1. It can be used as a basis for deciding what additional security, if any, is required.
2. It will ensure that additional safeguards do help in countering serious risks.
3. It saves money that might have otherwise been wasted. The primary goal becomes to identify and prioritize those risks. The makeup of the team should include an experienced representative of the organization, the ADP manager, a system's programmer, a security auditor, and the person responsible for physical security.

In "Risk Analysis and Computer Security," [8] Jacobson states that the basis for a Quantitative Risk Analysis (QRA) can best be shown by the equation: Expected Loss = Expected rate of occurrence × single occurrence loss. Since organization budgets, operating reports, etc., are usually in annual terms, the equation can also be modified to express loss in the same fashion: Annual expected loss = Expected occurrences per annum × single occurrence loss.

A QRA has many powerful advantages, the first of which is identifying the real issues, that is, the significant loss exposures and the threats which can cause them. Choice of security measures is based on determining which ones will yield the greatest reduction in expected loss per dollar of cost. Contingency planning can also be done more wisely in that the day-to-day cost of maintaining or implementing a particular security measure can be balanced against the potential cost of not having it. By accurately identifying the truly dangerous and major loss exposures, a security training program can be structured to assure effective responses to emergencies. In addition, inspections and audits can be directed toward the areas of greatest concern. Finally, the impact of a major system change can be fully evaluated during a decision-making process rather than after the fact.

For several reasons, a QRA technique is not widely used, however. First, it is quite expensive, as it requires a skilled analyst with a broad, detailed understanding of the organization and its function. Second, a well understood and generally accepted methodology is not available. Furthermore, business managers are instinctively wary of quantitative predictions, not recognizing that many other business decisions are also based on just such predictions. Often a manager finds it difficult to substitute the abstract finding of a QRA for his own practical experience.

A general consensus, though, is that a need exists for a practical methodology to satisfy the following requirements: (1) a simple procedure to minimize costs, (2) effort expended in proportion to the expected loss, (3) results that are easy to understand and use, and (4) a methodology that accounts for all threats and all potential losses.

One proposal is to classify threats and loss potentials into groups and accumulate all of these into manageable sets, each employing the same estimating technique. Threats would be classified into four types: (1) acts of nature, (2) sabotage, (3) theft, and (4) internal breakdown, while loss potential would represent three other categories: (1) processing delay, (2) tangible data processing assets, and (3) other organization assets.

In the process of structuring the best estimates possible, two useful discoveries are generally made. First, certain threat-loss combinations can be dismissed from further consideration. Second, as the loss potential estimates are developed, the analyst and others will be forced to think seriously about the realities of the loss controls that exist. An exposure imagined to be grave may be discovered to be minor or proved to be so by the evaluation. After the combinations have been rank ordered, further attention can be given to any refinement deemed necessary for estimates on major exposures.

At this stage the analyst can proceed confidently to the payoff phase, the selection of optimum countermeasures, the development of realistic contingency plans, and the beginning of a sharply focused security audit program.

In conclusion, though the most important resource of an organization and its manager is people, it is extremely important that he KNOW each individual thoroughly. Even though great success can be achieved, so can ruination when a worker becomes a threat. Establish a well-known and explicitly detailed policy, use checklists, and review/revise plans periodically. Attempt to stay current in security measures available and, above all, keep the company management involved and informed.

A DATA BASE NEMESIS

The value of information in any system is determined to a great extent by some process of subjective evaluation and must take into account certain perceptions held by different groups. Different types of data may have different value for each group within an organization. For example, critical operating information, like current weekly sales orders and production requirements, will have a much higher value to an organization than to its source, i.e., the customers, or to potential intruders. Personal information, on the other hand, may have a higher value to the individual, as with medical information in a personnel file, than to either the organization or an intruder. Proprietary information, like marketing forecast data belonging to the company, would be much more valuable to an intruder, such as a competing company, than to either the sample customers or the organization which has finished analyzing the data.

According to the authors of Computer Security,[7] information has four levels of importance: (1) vital—irreplaceable data crucial to the operation of the organization; (2) important—data that could be replaced but at a great cost and difficulty; (3) useful—data which is useful and would be difficult to replace although the organization could operate effectively without it; and (4) nonessential—data no longer needed by the organization. Characterizing information in this way can be quite difficult, however, because the data may be used and evaluated differently by the groups within a company. In addition, the importance rating, which is time-varying, requires careful periodic review for currency.

Security mechanisms, a combination of software techniques and procedures, must be employed to provide a meaningful information security plan. In doing so, it is important to consider the objectives to be accomplished and the specific organizational responsibilities necessary to carry it out. Security violations by authorized insiders may greatly outnumber those likely to occur from external intruders. Effective security requires the cooperation and planning of many people in an organization and should address at least the following three types of issues.

1. *Policy*—This area, which covers the use and types of procedures, requires the active participation, formulation, and backing of top management.
2. *Operational decisions*—This area involves the active implementing of those policy decisions into practice through systems programming and operations.
3. *Economics*—Cost overhead is an important consideration, and must be carefully evaluated to ascertain the level of risk which the organization can withstand. The role of a risk manager is critical to ensure that decisions do not involve extensive uncertainty or incomplete information and risks. Such decisions should be made on a continuing basis, to allow for the changing environment and contents of the data base.

Specific security measures should include: (1) identification, the process of uniquely recognizing each user of the system; (2) verification, or authentication, the process wherein the user establishes that he is the person identified by the system and not an impostor; and (3) access control, which, implemented at the data level, limits access to data base contents according to declarations that have been made in the data definition process.

Research

In "A Model of Statistical Databases and Their Security," [24] the authors examine the problem of information about an individual being inferred from a data base from which only statistical queries may be made. In this paper, Kam and Ullman use a simple and abstract model in an attempt to establish how specific the queries may be before individual information is obtained. They show that when the data base contains arbitrary integers, nothing can really be inferred. When the numbers in the data base lie in some fixed range though, it is shown that the value of individual records can often be determined. They studied the security of a class of

key-matching sum queries: each key is a bit-string of b bits, and there are 2 **
b data elements. To initiate a query, the user specifies the values of some set of
a bits, where a $<=$ b; the query program then returns the sum of the data elements
whose keys match in the given a positions. Whenever users have no information,
the data base is secure if a $<$ b and if the ranges of values of the data elements are
unknown. Otherwise, compromise is possible.

The article, "Even Data Bases That Lie Can Be Compromised," [3] takes the
approach that a selection query of the form: What is P for the following list of k
records?, where P selects a value from one of the records, can determine an element
from an unknown class. P might be maximum, medium, or a random value. The
authors show that a sequence of such selection queries, even when the penetrater
has no prior knowledge, can always be used to determine the value of a particular
record. Although naive strategies are used for delivering responses to queries, the
authors conclude that a determined user does not need any understanding of the
manner in which responses to his queries are actually selected to compromise the
data base.

In "Security in Statistical Databases for Queries with Small Counts," [17] the
problem addressed concerns a data base which allows queries for sums and averages
under the following assumptions: a protection policy prohibits answering queries
with small record counts (except for classes containing at least two records), the
system will always return true answers to all legal queries, the user may know some
information about the records stored, the user also has some knowledge of the query
language operation, and the database contains error-free information. It is shown
that if a key of one record is known, then the keys of all records can be determined.
It is also demonstrated that if the value of a record with a known key is determined,
then the values of all the records can be determined. Studies undertaken on
counting queries have indicated that the danger of compromise is greatest when
the system responds for small query sets; estimates of the number of queries needed
are also provided.

In "Secure Data Bases: Protection Against User Influence," [6] the authors
address the problem of users inferring the content of a specific record from earlier
responses to queries. The queries computed simple (unweighted) sums of elements
in the query set, which also requires no initial knowledge. Upper and lower bounds
were developed on the number of sum queries sufficient for compromise, with the
restriction that no two query sets can overlap by more than one element. A model
with which to study this problem is presented in the paper. The authors then an-
alyzed and made a determination of the smallest amount of data necessary to permit
statistical inference of information contained in the same record. With this
knowledge and in order to stop any compromising, they were able to demonstrate,
only for queries about averages and medians, how to control the queries a user could
make. They note, however, that their work is only an introduction to many related
problems in this area which remain open for research.

In "Linear Queries in Statistical Databases," [13] the argument is that a data base
can be compromised if a user is able to determine the data elements associated with

keys which he did not know previously. With the use of initial information, a resulting system of key-specified queries is solved by posing a finite set of linear queries (weighted sums) over sets of data elements. Seemingly harmless summaries contain vestiges of the original data. Through correlating enough summaries, an intruder may infer privileged data. One striking aspect of the results is that a user who knows as little as the value associated with a single key can often achieve a full compromise of the entire data base—and with a query sequence whose length is not much longer than the number of stored data elements. It is assumed that data from known classes are functionally independent of data in unknown classes. As a result, the unknown classes are secure. In a partitioned data base, this is true only if at least two of the weights or classes are kept secret. The unmistakable conclusion, however, is that security depends on denying the enquirer any information about the data base, for example, by restricting access to records. Unfortunately, there is no way to be absolutely sure that this can be done effectively.

The Inference Problem

To illustrate the strategy used in effecting a data base compromise, certain techniques will be discussed and summarized from "The Tracker: A Threat to Statistical Database Security." [5] Denning studies data bases in the context of the following two properties: each person's record contains one or more confidential values and is uniquely identified by a set of characteristics; second, the query program examines a query set (a collection of records and characteristics which match those of a given characteristic formula).

According to Schlorer, a questioner knows from external sources that a specific individual, I, is uniquely identified by a formula C. Known as isolating the record, this *individual tracker* uses the following method to determine whether I also has a particular characteristic: a raw statistic is computed by the query, usually sums of values from records of the query set. Through the responses of several queries, additional unknown characteristics of I can be derived. When necessary, this tracker can pad small query sets (known as masking) with enough extra records to obtain a compromised answer. This method places the individual in a group with a given property and determines, by the responses, whether he has the same characteristic. Another slant on this method is to place the individual outside a group with a given property. The questioner can continue to use this information to "track down" additional characteristics of an individual.

A *general tracker* requires no prior knowledge and employs a single formula that works for the entire data base. The power of a general tracker is in its ability to answer every query applicable to any record in the data base without changing the basic formula. The authors state that almost all data bases have a General Tracker, so there is little point in determining the existence of an individual tracker.

A *double tracker* is a pair of characteristic formulas employed for a query set with a size restriction so strong that no general tracker exists. A double tracker is ruled out only when less than one third of the possible query set sizes are observable. The single and double tracker define sufficient conditions so that it is almost always possible for one to calculate any unanswerable query, even if no general tracker exists.

Schlorer states that over 99% of data base trackers will be general trackers, and that a questioner is likely to find one simply by guessing. Denning indicates that the corresponding effort required to retrieve the desired information is usually quite low.

Four principal results of the study, according to the authors, were: (1) the discovery of a general tracker, which permits arbitrary queries without any pre-knowledge of the data base; (2) the presentation of a simple structured condition which guarantees existence, and specifies the form, of a general tracker; (3) a demonstration that tracker compromises apply to any statistical query, not just counts; and (4) the way to find a tracker.

Specific models reviewed previously from the literature, regardless of the structure of the data base and its protection policy, arrive at the same general conclusion: the problem that remains is not whether a database can be compromised, but how easy it is and when it is most likely to occur. In light of this nagging question, current controls that can be effective are reviewed next.

Inference Controls

In a timely article, "Data Security," Denning outlines current inference controls for the protection of statistical data bases. By preventing leakage of confidential information through query language manipulation, the risk of an intruder correlating responses from summaries is reduced. The primary objective, which is also known as the work factor, is to make the cost of getting privileged information prohibitive to an intruder. Since most compromises are based on isolating a desired record at the intersection of a set of interlocking queries, the authors propose three main defenses.

1. Controls on Query Set Sizes and Overlaps: withholding a response for improper queries by the use of a partitioned data base. By storing predetermined records in groups, queries will not apply to subsets of records within any group, although they will for any set of groups. Consequently, attacks based on inclusion and exclusion can only isolate and query one of the groups. The two practical limitations, however, can be quite severe. First, excessively large or ill-considered groupings can inhibit the legitimate free flow of statistical summaries. Second, the forming and reforming of groups, as records are inserted, updated, and deleted from the data base, leads to excessive bookkeeping.

2. Rounding and Error Inoculation: distorting the responses by either rounding or falsifying data in such a way that the exact answer is confused by a small amount before it is returned to the user. Using a pseudo-random value based

on the data is preferred since a given query always returns the same reply. Although fairly effective, this method can be subverted by trackers with dummy records or by comparison with previous responses. With error inoculation, the same effect can be achieved by replacing one value in a record with another before it is used to compute a statistic. Both of these methods reduce the quality of the statistics released by introducing large errors into the data in an attempt to prevent compromise. An alternative suggested by the authors is data swapping. As a result, the enquirer would have no way of knowing with which record the value is associated. Finding the sets of records for swapping, however, is the difficulty. In addition, the increased cost may not warrant its use.

3. Random Samples: applying queries to a subset of records chosen at random. Although it is potentially the most effective method, the user sacrifices control over the size of query sets. Current systems which constantly change from update activity would render this technique useless. The results would not be statistically significant, since they would not represent the current state of the data base.

In summary, Denning states that without proper controls, data bases subject to simple or routine compromises will be the rule rather than the exception. Extraordinary measures, at expected cost, will be required for tight security when the circumstances warrant. Final defenses included in this category will involve threat monitoring—the use of inspection logs or audit trails for unusual patterns of queries on the same record. Although it is impossible to control the flow of information in a query system, monitoring directly threatens to expose the illegal activity of an intruder.

SUMMARY

Surveillance

By the use of an audit trail and/or monitoring methods, the capability for detecting security violations is expanded. An audit trail (log) is a permanent record of every significant action taken by the system. In principle, log records are accumulated and never change. They serve several important purposes:

1. As an aid in discovering violations.
2. As a traditional audit for tracing transactions through the system.
3. For minor and massive recovery from malfunctions caused by software and hardware during normal operations (making it possible to reconstruct information that may have been destroyed or made invalid by the malfunction).
4. For correction of errors which alter or destroy data.
5. As a deterrent to insiders who might otherwise contemplate a security violation.

A careful management study should determine what information to log and how it can be organized most effectively. Several types of periodic reports to be produced can include, but should not necessarily be limited to, Unsuccessful Log-On Attempts, Sensitive Data Access, System Operator Privileged Command Usage, and User-Time Access (if available). A plan for examination should be able to detect security violations in a timely manner. Ideally, the logs should be systematically reviewed as standard reports and transactions should be randomly selected for examination by the checking programs. In addition, on-line access to the logs for management personnel or the security officer can be considered.

Monitoring is a more active form of surveillance since, while the system is in operation, various forms of information and statistics can be accumulated and displayed on a special monitor. It can be used for both security and non-security purposes. Many of the previous points made about an audit trail apply to a monitoring facility. In addition, it can also be highly educational for both new and current managers to see the system in operation. System designers can explore and discover potential areas of improvement by monitoring system performance and utilization.

Surveillance techniques must keep in mind two additional security considerations. First, the audit trail and monitoring capability also requires that the backup and audit tapes be secure against theft or subversion. Second, both facilities must also be audited to guard against the possibility of a dishonest security officer or someone who discovers how to gain access to these facilities. Careful consideration should be given to their arrangement and purpose, as well as to the knowledge of their existence. Finally, threat monitoring of all requests to the system for detecting excessive access of the data base, such as asking too many queries that are quite similar, is not necessarily a favorable alternative if it conceals too much information from the user and limits access.

Enforcing Security Policies

Security policies define generally who may use what information in a computer system, whereas protection mechanisms are designed to enforce them. The problem which surfaces is the question of what policies an enterprise can and does enforce. The concept of soundness for bridging this gap is addressed by Jones and Lipton[23] in determining the completeness of any protection mechanism.

The distinct problem of controlling information dissemination is primarily one of security. Techniques are developed for controlling who can obtain certain information, when they can obtain it, to what uses they may put it, and even who can produce it. A precise and complete understanding of this security requirement is mandatory. For example, when a security error occurs, the violator does not disclose the system flaw which allowed unauthorized actions. Too frequently, no trace remains when confidential information has been compromised. For these types of reasons, precision and proofs are a necessity. In addition, in order to be credible, the basic framework used must be simple and clear.

The basic elements to be considered are precise security policies, protection mechanisms, and definitions of programs. A security policy can be described as the specific definition of what information is to be protected; it is non-procedural. A protection mechanism, by contrast, defines explicitly how information is to be protected and is of a procedural form. Soundness, as the key relationship between the two, is determined when the mechanism enforces the policy through program implementation.

Security policies most commonly supplied in real systems are characterized by whether they allow a user some, all, or no information about some input. Security enforcement, consequently, involves restrictions on the behavior of the computer program. It involves determination of whether the output of a program encodes the proper information. This result clearly will depend on the program's functional behavior. If it is a view function, the classic confinement question arises: Does the value of the program's output contain any information that it should not? As an operation function, a data security question is appropriate: Has the function of the program altered any information that it should not?

In this discussion, the *view function* is the security question being considered. The security model example given by Jones and Lipton is restricted to checking carefully that the value of the program's view function is all the pertinent information that is available about its inputs. In an Observability Postulate presented by the authors, no proof that this restriction holds can ever be given, however. One example of a program output (which is sometimes overlooked) is its execution time, an unquestionable output that is often available for interactive programs.

The contribution, by way of a general framework of Jones and Lipton, is in the isolation and precise statement of key questions and concepts needed in any theory of security. The following questions are proposed as being central to any such theory, and are also expressed precisely (in parentheses) according to the authors' theory.

1. What is to be enforced? (What is the security policy?)
2. What is to do the enforcing? (What is the protection mechanism?)
3. Does it do the enforcing? (Is the protection mechanism sound?)
4. If it does, then how well does it do the enforcing? (How complete is the protection mechanism?)
5. What assumptions, if any, are made in answer to #3? (Does the Observability Postulate hold?)

Goals for Security

A key concern in any computer system is that of multiple use; consequently, some scheme is needed to ensure a desired authority structure. Martin succinctly identifies seven requirements for data base security: the data should be protected, reconstructable, and auditable; the system should be tamperproof, able to make positive identification of the user, and to verify that his actions are authorized; finally, a user's actions should be monitored.[25] A common controlled sharing of information among multiple users is therefore a fundamental consideration in designing for security. As presented in Saltzer,[12] three broad categories of potential security violations are: (1) unauthorized information release, (2) unauthorized information modification, and (3) unauthorized denial of system use. The biggest complication today is that the intruder may be an otherwise legitimate user of the system.

System design principles which have emerged since the early 1970s are addressed by Saltzer[12] and Hoffman[21] as the most important principles to be followed in undertaking the design of both computer and non-computer systems. Hoffman categorizes the first five as directly concerned with security and the last three as system design oriented.

1. Default to access denial: An access decision which is correctly based on the permission required, making users justify their need for access before it is granted. It is a safe method which allows for immediate detection of unknown design or implementation flaws.
2. Non-secret design: Although not universally accepted, the concept of an open system design relies upon the probable exposure of system deficiencies through published information and communication during the planning stages. The underlying belief is that early discovery of any security flaws is preferred to the later exploitation of it by an intruder.
3. User acceptability: The ease of use is fundamental to ensuring the proper, routine, and automatic application of a protection mechanism by users. If it is not, users will bypass it, making it an ineffective security feature.
4. Complete meditation: Every individual access to every object must be checked for authorization. This process ensures that current changes in authority are protected and forces a systemwide view of access control.
5. Least privilege: The "need to know" of a user should correspond to the privilege necessary to complete a job, thereby reducing the number of potential interactions among privileged programs to a minimum.
6. Economy of mechanism: Simply stated, keep the design as simple and small as possible. This practice further facilitates the successful use of software techniques like line-by-line inspection.
7. Separation of privilege: A principle often used in bank safe-deposit boxes; i.e., a protection mechanism which uses two keys to unlock is inherently more flexible and robust. The keys can be separate and distinct persons, programs, or organizations made responsible for them.
8. Least common mechanism: Since every shared mechanism represents a potential information path between users, this sharing should be minimized. It is also easier to satisfy one or a few users of a shared resource than all of them.

In addition, Saltzer stresses two further design principles which can best serve as warnings, instead of absolute rules, of potential trouble. The design should then be carefully reviewed to account for the system violation and any appropriate action required.

9. Work factor: Compare the cost of circumventing a protection mechanism to the resources of a potential intruder. Direct costs in time, effort, and money to carry out a plan may be too high and may consequently serve as a substantial deterrent. Certain security mechanisms, however, cannot be determined by a direct work factor calculation. Indirect strategies by a perpetrator to defeat a security mechanism must also be considered.

10. Compromise recording: The reliable recording that a compromise has occurred is just as valuable, although it must be recognized that guaranteeing discovery when security is broken may be difficult.

Conclusions

While a wide variety of protection mechanisms and techniques exist for the implementation of system security, Gaines and Shapiro have properly emphasized the need for qualitative judgments in assessing all interrelated factors.[19] By balancing the effectiveness of the available protection mechanism with the constant or changing value of the resource to be guarded, a better measure of the security requirement is attainable. In essence, the use of several features consistently guarantees a better security posture.

A principal problem in computer security, as described earlier, is in the access control area. Valid users who are not allowed full access to data, nevertheless, normally possess direct access to computer resources. Consequently, the concept of degrees of security, as presented by Gaines, is of particular merit. In this regard, the enhancement of security should explore protection mechanisms for the active detection of violations. In this category, it is well recognized that such "white-collar" intruders strongly fear unexpected detection and exposure because it would cause tremendous embarrassment and a loss of prestige with one's peers.

Detection features, designed with flexibility in mind, can be placed anywhere and periodically moved. In addition, parameters which describe tolerances and patterns of detection can be frequently changed so as to keep any potential intruder, who may know of the method, off guard. Since discovery of an unauthorized entry is often accidental or by casual observation, additional methods can reinforce this possibility and also act as a deterrent. One example is the technique used in remote access terminal systems, wherein the user receives a report at each log-in of his previous session. This procedure fosters security consciousness on the part of authorized users and allows subsequent detection of unauthorized usage of the account.

Current research must continue to explore new operating system designs, specifically with security in mind. Since most present and future computer systems will not be explicitly designed with a thorough use of security principles, other effective means for achieving critical security requirements are still badly needed. Many important problems still exist, however, aside from those of a secure operating system. The correct functioning of the system's hardware is another prime example. Its exact characteristics must be accurately matched and taken into account to ensure the correctness of software written for implementation of protection schemes.

SELECTED BIBLIOGRAPHY

Primary Sources

1. Browne, P. S.: Computer Security—A Survey. National Computer Conference, 1976, pp. 53–63.
2. Browne, P. S., and Brandstad, D. K.: Planning for Computer Security, p. 1-1, Data Base/Applications Security, p. 3-1, Physical and Administrative Controls, p. 4-1. Tutorial on Computer Security and Integrity, 1977.
3. Demillo, R. A., Dobkin, D., and Lipton, R. J.: Even Data Bases That Lie Can Be Compromised. IEEE Transactions on Software Engineering, January 1978.
4. Denning, P. J., and Denning, D. E.: Data security. Computing Surveys, September 1979.
5. Denning, P. J., Denning, D. E., and Schwartz, M. D.: The Tracker: A Threat to Statistical Database Security. ACM TODS, 1 March 1979.
6. Dobkin, D., Jones, A. K., and Lipton, R. J.: Secure Databases: Protection Against User Influence. ACM TODS, 1 March 1979.
7. Hsiao, D. K., Kerr, D. S., and Madnick, S. E.: Computer Security ACM Monograph Series, Copyright 1979.
8. Jacobson, R. V.: Risk Analysis and Computer Security. Electro 76, paper 22-2.
9. Lackey, R. D.: Penetration of computer systems: an overview. Honeywell Computer Journal, 8/2 1974, pp. 81–85.
10. Los Angeles Chapter, ACM: Privacy, Security and the Information Processing Industry. Association for Computing Machinery, 1976.
11. Parker and Nycum: The new criminal. Datamation, January 1974, pp. 56–58.
12. Saltzer, J. H., and Schroeder, M. D.: The Protection of Information in Computer Systems. Proceedings of the IEEE, September 1975.
13. Schwartz, M. D., Denning, D. E., and Denning, P. J.: Linear Queries in Statistical Databases. ACM TODS, 2 June 1979.
14. U.S. Department of Commerce, National Bureau of Standards: Guidelines for Automatic Data Processing Physical Security and Risk Management. FIPS Pub. 31 (Excerpts).
15. U.S. Department of Commerce, National Bureau of Standards. Computer Security Guidelines for Implementing the Privacy Act of 1974. FIPS Pub. 41, 20 pages.

Secondary Sources

16. Beardsley, C. W.: Is your computer insecure? IEEE Spectrum, January 1972, pp. 67–78.
17. Chin, F. Y.: Security in Statistical Databases for Queries with Small Counts. ACM TODS, 1 March 1978.
18. Datapro Research Corp.: Data Security and Protection Structures. Operations Management: CS40-750-101, June 1979.
19. Gaines, R. S., and Shapiro, N. Z.: Some security principles and their application to computer security. Operating Systems Review, July 1978.

20. Gallagher, T. L., et al.: Security, Privacy and Accessibility. A Discussion/Workshop, August 1976.
21. Hoffman, L. J.: Modern methods for computer security and privacy. *In* Statistical Data Banks, 1977.
22. Institute for Computer Sciences and Technology, National Bureau of Standards: The necessity for computer security (A handbook).
23. Jones, A. K., and Lipton, R. J.: The Enforcement of Security Policies for Computation. Operating Systems Review, 1975.
24. Kam, J. B., and Ullman, J. D.: A Model of Statistical Databases and Their Security. ACM TODS, 1 March 1977.
25. Martin, J.: Computer data-base organization. *In* Objectives of a Data-Base Organization, 2d ed., 1977.
26. U.S. Department of Commerce, National Bureau of Standards: Glossary of Terminology for Computer Systems Security. FIPS Pub. 39, 1976.
27. Wasserman, J. J.: Plugging the leaks in computer security. Harvard Business Review, Sep/Oct 1969.

Chapter 7

A SURVEY OF COMPUTER-BASED PASSWORD TECHNIQUES*

Helen M. Wood

National Bureau of Standards, Washington, D.C.

With the growth of timesharing and other forms of computer networking, the use of remotely accessed computers has become widespread. However, with this ease of access have come increased operational risks. Systems without adequate access controls are more vulnerable to a variety of threats including theft, fraud, and vandalism. Potential losses range from unauthorized use of computing time to the unauthorized accessing, modification, or destruction of valuable data. Perpetrators of such abuse may be otherwise honest individuals wishing to play a few computer games, or sophisticated corporate spies, hoping to learn trade secrets or acquire the list of a competitor's top ten accounts. (See references 68 through 71 for a discussion of computer crime.)

Current privacy legislation and increased public concern with the integrity and protection of data in such computer systems have made the problem of controlling access to computer resources most urgent. An example of such legislation is the Privacy Act of 1974 (5 U.S.C. 552a). This Act imposes numerous requirements upon Federal agencies to prevent the misuse of information about individuals and assure its integrity and security. Guidelines for implementing this Act may be found in reference 26.

An essential component of access control is user authentication. The technique of using passwords to authenticate a terminal user to a resource-sharing computer system is well known. Nearly all systems in use in the Government, and all of the commercial timesharing systems, use this technique.[2] However, passwords alone are not sufficient to guarantee system security. Rather, the use of passwords is one of many technical and procedural controls that can be used in concert with

---

* This work is a contribution of the National Bureau of Standards and as such is not subject to copyright. Certain commercial products are identified in this report in order to specify the procedure being described. In no case does such identification imply recommendation or endorsement by the National Bureau of Standards, nor does it imply that the product identified is necessarily the best available for the purpose.

others to provide an adequate level of security for a given system and its environment.

This chapter surveys the generation of passwords and their effective application to the problem of controlling access to computer resources. After describing the need for and uses of passwords, the features of password schemes are categorized according to

- selection technique
- lifetime
- physical characteristics
- information content.

Password protection, in both storage and transmission, is dealt with in the next section, followed by brief sections on current implementations and cost considerations. Security-related terminology used in this report is defined in reference 25 and much of the networking and communications terminology may be found in reference 64.

It is not the intent of this chapter to provide formal guidelines for the effective utilization of passwords, but rather to bring together descriptions of the various techniques and their capabilities and limitations. Such a survey is a necessary first step in generating appropriate guidelines for the effective use of passwords in controlling access to computer resources.

AUTHENTICATION

Typically when a user wishes to access resources on a remote computer system, he or she states a claimed identity, perhaps through typing a user name or identification number. The user is then required to verify the claimed identity. This latter process is referred to as personal authentication.

There are three basic methods by which a person's identity may be authenticated for the purpose of controlling access to a remote computer system:

- something the person *knows*
- something the person *has*
- something the person *is*.

The first category includes passwords and lock combinations. Badges, ID cards, and keys fall into the second category; while "something a person *is*" includes characteristics such as one's appearance, voice, fingerprints, signature, and hand geometry. The advantages and limitations of these types of authentication techniques has been discussed extensively.[11,18,28,62] Techniques for dynamic signature verification are described in references 19 and 35.

Personal authentication may be required at any number of points along the path to accessing data. Such points include:

- entry to building
- entry to terminal room
- enabling terminal
- encryption interface unit
- login
- file access
- data item access.

Physical devices (e.g., cards, keys) are commonly used at the first three access points; while passwords, alone or in conjunction with other techniques, are commonly used at login, file access, or data item access time.

The authentication techniques selected for a given system should be determined by a cost/risk analysis, which considers potential threats, the probability of these threats occurring, and the expected losses resulting from a successful penetration of the system, versus the cost of providing data protection. General guidelines for performing risk analyses have recently become available.[29]

Password systems cost less at present than most of the other techniques for personal authentication. Consequently, it appears that passwords, perhaps in combination with other techniques such as badges or keys, will continue to be heavily utilized.

In addition to authenticating users to systems, password schemes may provide some protection against other types of threats. In their report on information privacy, Petersen and Turn describe types of threats against which passwords may be effective:[73]

1. browsing—using legitimate access to a part of the system to access unauthorized files.
2. masquerading—claiming the identity of an authorized user after obtaining passwords or other authentication items through wiretapping or other means.
3. between-lines entry—penetration of the system when a legitimate user is on a communications channel but not using his terminal.
4. piggy-back infiltration—interception of user-processor communications and the returning of messages that appear to the user to be from the computer system.

The degree to which passwords are effective against such threats varies greatly. They provide good protection against browsing when implemented at the file or data level. However, passwords are ineffective against the threats of between-lines entry and piggy-back infiltration unless used for every message (in the former case), or when used as a means of reverse (e.g., processor-to-user) authentication (in the latter case).

Carroll and McLelland also discuss these threats as well as some counter-measures.[16] Lientz and Weiss consider costs of implementing these counter-measures and levels of sophistication of the threats.[58]

Data encryption keys and the banking community's Personal Identification Number (PIN) are forms of passwords when used as a means of verifying identity. An encryption key controls the algorithmic transformation (encryption) performed on data to render the data unintelligible. The PIN is typically a four- to six-digit number assigned by the bank or selected by the cardholder. It is typically used in conjunction with a magnetically encoded card. Throughout this report analogies will be drawn among encryption keys, PIN's, and passwords.

The following sections discuss password-related techniques and mechanisms which can be combined to create the appropriate password scheme for a given system.

PASSWORD SCHEMES

Password schemes differ according to

- selection technique
- lifetime
- physical characteristics
- information content.

In this section the types of password systems are discussed along with the threats against which they are most effective. Examples are also presented. (See references 88 and 89 for another discussion of password techniques.)

Selection

A password may be chosen by the system user or assigned. User-selected passwords are far from secure since people tend to pick words or numbers that have some personal meaning (e.g., birthday, child's name, street address) and consequently are easy to guess.[5] The primary advantage of a user-chosen password is ease of recall, alleviating the need for writing the word down.

Passwords may be assigned to users by the system security officer or by the computer system itself. Although assigned passwords are generally more secure than user-selected codes, their benefits may be nullified if they are written down by the user, taken from a master list which is discovered,[87] or generated by an algorithm that is deducible.[52]

In his investigation of the latter problem, Johnson examined the use of pseudo-random numbers as passwords and discovered that various "logistically attractive" periodic password generation systems are in fact vulnerable to simple number-theoretic analysis.[52] The generating systems he considered were of the type

$$x_{n+1} = ax_n + b(\text{mod } 2^u), u = 40,$$

where a and b are selected constants and x_n is the nth password generated. This type of generating system would be considered attractive, for example, in a large system in which it is not practical to use complex password schemes. To reduce vulnerabilities of such schemes, Johnson proposes new password generation and distribution strategies that would help to ensure a higher degree of security, without significantly increasing the system costs.

An example of a computer-generated password scheme is the random word generator developed to run on Honeywell's Multiplexed Information and Computer System (Multics).[32] The random word generator forms pronounceable syllables and concatenates them to create words. A table of pronounciation rules is used to determine the validity of each construct. This system was developed to enhance the security of some Multics installations, such as the Air Force Data Services Center (AFDSC).

The motivation for a pronounceable password generator is to make the assigned words easier to remember, thus lessening the temptation to write the words down. However, what is deemed pronounceable by one person may be considered gibberish by another, even though the rules of grammar for the particular language are followed.

In order to enhance pronounceability, generated words may be presented to the user in hyphenated form. Examples of the words generated are:

> qua-vu
> ri-ja-cas
> te-nort
> oi-boay
> fleck-y.

Besides being easy to remember, the generated words must be difficult to guess. This requirement is satisfied by giving the program the ability to generate a very large set of possible words in a random fashion.

The random word generator is capable of generating words of any length. However, words of five to eight characters are recommended. Longer words tend to be less pronounceable, while shorter words result in too few available passwords for a given system and its user population.

At the AFDSC the use of the password generator is not mandatory. To help lessen the problem of being given a password that to them is unpronounceable, users can reject the assigned password and try again. Under the current implementation they can also elect to provide their own passwords. After nearly 18 months of operation of the password generator, it was observed that about 50% of the system users allow the system to assign their passwords.

In recognition of the need for password schemes that are secure against penetration attempts based on guessing, Bushkin states the following principle of computer security:

No passwords or other user authentication data shall have been or shall be created or generated either by the human user who will use them or by a non-human agent (e.g., a program) of his creation or under his control . . .

The intent of such a rule is to thwart attempts at guessing the password. Furthermore, Bushkin indicates that nonhuman (automated) generation of passwords is the preferred method for enhanced system security.[12]

To assist users in remembering numeric passwords, portions of the password (e.g., groups of two digits each) could be associated with easily visualized objects. For example, the user could be assigned the number 2356, where the 23rd item on a list is a basketball and the 56th is a tire. Then the user could form a mental image of the two objects and use that image to more easily recall the true password. A list of ordered objects could be posted at each terminal, and by recalling the image the user could, if necessary, easily determine the password. Thus if, in the preceding example, 100 items were contained on the list, the total number of passwords possible would be 10,000. Of course in such a scheme the list would have to contain enough items to discourage trial-and-error attempts at determining passwords.

A consideration in password generation systems is the number of duplicate passwords assigned. If the user space is large and very few users have the same password, then assuming that one password for one user is known, the likelihood of determining which other users have that password is small. For example, if five users out of 1,000 had identical passwords, the probability of a penetrator determining the other four users of the known password would be 4/999. Duplicate passwords need not be a problem, then, unless the number of duplicate passwords at any one time is large. However, the probability of successful penetration of a system with even a small number of duplicate passwords assigned increases when the encrypted (i.e., algorithmically transformed) password table is available to the users. This latter case will be discussed in the section on password protection.

Lifetime

Current password schemes allow password assignments to be used for an indefinite period of time, for fixed intervals of time (e.g., one month), or for a single time only (one-time passwords). The length of time that a password remains in effect is called the password lifetime or period.

Passwords that remain in effect indefinitely (often called "fixed" passwords) are the most susceptible to compromise. Due to the length of time available, these passwords are especially vulnerable to exhaustive testing. Making the length of the password appropriately long, locking-out log-on attempts after several (e.g., three) tries,[34] and enforcing time delays between log-on attempts provide some defense against exhaustive password enumeration attempts.[85]

Another shortcoming of passwords with indefinite lifetimes is the difficulty in detecting a successful compromise of the password. Some systems prohibit a user from being logged onto the system from more than one terminal at a time.[5] Others, such as the Monitor operating system for the DECSYSTEM-10, inform the user at log-on and log-off of the presence of other users with the same user name or identification number, and hence the same password. However, even if such system constraints are present, the odds of a system penetrator and the legitimate user attempting to use the same account at the same time depend upon the frequency and duration of access of each. To lessen the probability of detection in this manner, the penetrator may elect to use the system late at night when the legitimate user is presumably asleep.

As a deterrent against such threats, some systems (e.g., Multics at the Massachusetts Institute of Technology and TENEX at Bolt, Beranek and Newman, Inc.) include the last time logged on as a part of the banner (i.e., the informative messages displayed by the system whenever a user logs on). This presumably informs someone if such successful penetration has taken place.

An example of a system penetration that was successful over a period of 3 1/2 months was recounted in an August 1976 article in the *Washington Post*. This article detailed the successful penetration of a small computer firm's system by a former employee. In this case, the employee continued to use his old account and password after he ceased to be employed by the firm.[74]

Frequent password changes are desirable.[1,87] An example of a system which requires password updates at fixed intervals of time is the AFDSC. In this system, users are required to change their passwords every 6 months. The enforcing mechanism is the operating system.

One-time passwords are recognized as generally providing a higher level of protection.[1,10,72,85] Successive passwords may be selected by the system from an internal list,[85] generated by a program,[4,32,52] or selected from lists or cards previously distributed to authorized users.[5,72]

Anderson advocates the use of one-time password schemes.[1,2] He contends that if passwords are changed each time they are used, there is "no more risk in writing down the password than in carrying a key to a locked room." Should loss or theft occur, prompt reporting would minimize the risks involved. Nonetheless, the legitimate user would have to access the system frequently in order to ensure the timely discovery of a successful system penetration.

As a means of further reducing the risk of carrying a password openly, Anderson suggests that the system could print a list of passwords for each user. Only one of the words on the list would be the actual password, and the exact location of the valid password could vary from user to user. He also mentions the possibility of encoding the new password on a magnetic card.[1]

The feasibility of using one-time passwords in conjunction with magnetically encoded cards was investigated by Richardson and Potter.[77] In their design of a prototype system, the cardholder was required to key-in a secret password in addition to that read from the card. As has been noted previously, combinations of authentication techniques may provide a higher degree of security than systems incorporating only one such technique. Here, the use of a manually entered password is necessary to prohibit unauthorized use of a lost or stolen card before the loss has been reported. Likewise, the password is of no use to a would-be penetrator without the card. It was noted in references 1 and 77 that the major disadvantage of such a technique is the cost of the magnetic card reader/writer.

Lawrence Livermore Laboratory's OCTOPUS network uses a password scheme, similar to one-time passwords, incorporating a changing counter. A computer generates and authenticates all combinations (passwords). At each terminal session a counter associated with the combination is incremented and this new value is communicated to the user. Thus, the skipping of a value would imply that the combination had been used by someone else.[3]

One-time passwords were adopted for use in SWIFT (Society for Worldwide Interbank Financial Telecommunications), the worldwide banking system developed by the Burroughs Corporation. When a terminal is connected, the operator uses a four-digit, one-time password taken from a list which is supplied in two lists sent separately. For example, with the following lists:

LIST 1	LIST 2
1 2	4 5
3 7	9 8
4 6	3 5
.	.
.	.

the first password would be 1245. Additional security features in SWIFT include message sequence numbers and the generation of a four hexadecimal digit authenticator result. This latter number is generated by running the entire message text through the SWIFT authenticator algorithm. In addition, at log-out time the operator specifies the next log-in time. SWIFT will refuse any earlier log-in attempts.

Major drawbacks to the use of one-time passwords are the cost and difficulty associated with the distribution of lists to large numbers of users[2] and with the support of users who get "out of step" in a system with a heavy workload.[5] Beardsley illustrates this latter point by describing a heavily used administrative system with nearly 6,000 users, 1,300 terminals, and a half-million transactions on a given day. However, in the previous two examples, which incorporated counters or incremented passwords, the distribution problem is minimized.

Petersen and Turn have noted that one-time password schemes alone are not effective against the threat of between-lines or piggyback entry. For protection against these threats, message authentication via attachment of one-time passwords to each message would be required. Encryption at the terminal level is also an effective protection mechanism in this situation.[73]

Physical Characteristics

A password's physical characteristics include its size and makeup (i.e., the "alphabet" or set of characters from which it is made). The number of different passwords possible in a given scheme is called the password space.

The Personal Identification Number (PIN) used in conjunction with banking transaction cards is typically a four- to six-digit number; while some computer systems accept passwords eight or more characters in length, with numbers, letters, and special characters (e.g., backspace, '@', vertical tab) being permitted.

Given a password of length L that is formed using any of the 26 letters in the English alphabet, there are 26^L possible words of length L that could be generated. For example, the number N of all possible words of length 8 that can be formed from the English alphabet is 26^8, or approximately 2.1×10^{11}. The password space may, however, be somewhat larger if passwords of lengths *up to* L are permitted. Then the password space S becomes

$$S = \sum_{i=1}^{L} N^i,$$

where N equals the number of characters in the alphabet.[34] When conditions such as pronounceability are added to the scheme, then a fraction f of the total number of possible words would comprise the password space. Once we know f, then for a given length L, we can calculate the number of pronounceable words n by

$$n = fN.$$

In the previously described pronounceable password system,[32] an estimate for f of 0.02653 was found for words of eight letters. The resulting value for n was thus

$$n = 0.02653N = 5.540 \times 10^9.$$

Meissner emphasizes that, in order to adequately assess the security of a given password scheme, one must consider the number of *allowable* combinations for valid passwords, rather than simply the theoretical number of combinations based upon the size of the alphabet and the generated password.[28]

Anderson[1] considers passwords generated as random strings of letters or numbers. He presents a formula for determining the random password length required to provide a given degree of protection against systematic testing. The assumption is that tests occur at the maximum line transmission rate, as would be the case if another computer were attempting penetration by exhaustive enumeration. In his formula, the password size is found by solving:

$$(R/E)4.39 \times 10^4 \, (M/P) \leq A^S \qquad (1)$$

for S, where S is the password size in characters. Here, R is the transmission rate of the line in characters per minute, E is the number of characters exchanged in a log-on attempt, P is the probability that a proper password will be found, M is the period over which the systematic testing is to take place (in months of 24 hours per day operation), and A is the size of the alphabet from which the password is made.

As an example, Anderson determines the password size drawn from the English alphabet that gives a probability of no more than 0.001 of recovery after 3 months of systematic testing. He assumes a line speed of 300 characters/minute, and an exchange of 100 characters during a log-on attempt. The computation is as follows:

$$\frac{300}{100} \times 4.39 \times 10^4 \times 3 \times 10^3 \le 26^S \tag{2}$$

$$3.951 \times 10^8 \le 26^S \tag{3}$$

$$26^S = 3.089 \times 10^8 \text{ for } S = 6 \tag{4}$$

$$26^S = 8.03 \times 10^9 \text{ for } S = 7 \tag{5}$$

Therefore, in this example $S = 7$ is the reasonable choice. Note that increasing the alphabet to 128 characters (e.g., for 7-bit ASCII) reduces S to 5.

Although encryption keys can be considered authenticating mechanisms analogous to passwords, a determination of adequate key size is based upon additional considerations. For example, Shannon notes that the size of the key space should be as large as possible, not only to discourage trial-and-error approaches, but to permit the assignment of unique keys to large numbers of users and to allow frequent key changes.[78]

It should also be noted that the effectiveness of encryption as a protection mechanism does not depend solely upon the encryption key chosen, but rather upon:

1. the algorithm employed.
2. the implementation of the algorithm (e.g., when does encryption take place).
3. the criteria used in selecting the key (e.g., if an algorithm supports a key space of 2^{56}, but encryption keys of only four digits are used, then the effective key space is drastically reduced).

Information Content

The password may provide information in addition to personal authentication. The University of Western Ontario's generalized information retrieval system (GIRS) incorporates the use of assigned, functional passwords whose contents reveal the users' authorization levels.[14] In particular, these passwords determine:

1. which subset of available processing functions can be exercised
2. which portions of records can be operated upon by these functions
3. which records the user is privileged to work with, or conversely, which records the user is prohibited from using.

Note that in this system an additional password is needed for authentication; the functional password is used by the information retrieval system to assess a user's authorization level or capabilities. This arrangement is not intended to indicate, however, that both functions could not be provided by one password, used only at logon time.

Besides imparting authorization information, it has been suggested that passwords could be constructed to contain check digits or some other sort of self-checking code. "Check digitry" is already being successfully used in other environments, as discussed in a series of articles by Alan Taylor.[79,80,81] In one example reported by Taylor:[79]

The Pennsylvania Bureau of Sales and Use Tax adopted a Modulo-10 check digit to safeguard a seven-digit number. The technique selected was to multiply the first digit by 7, the second by 6 and so forth until the last digit was multiplied by 1. It then used the Modulo-10 complement of the answer as the check digit and placed it after the seventh number.

The computation would appear as follows:

Account Number:	1	9	3	4	2	6	7
Multipliers:	7	6	5	4	3	2	1

Check Digit Computation:
$1 \times 7 = 7$
$9 \times 6 = 54$
$3 \times 5 = 15$
$4 \times 4 = 16$
$2 \times 3 = 6$
$6 \times 2 = 12$
$7 \times 1 = 7$
Total $= 117$
Mod-10 $= 7$
10 Complement $= 3$

Thus, the resulting check digit for 1934267 is 3.

Techniques such as this, combined with some elementary analysis, could help more sophisticated password systems discriminate between entry errors (such as transpositions of digits) and actual penetration attempts, especially attempts via exhaustive testing.

This idea is similar to that embodied in Kaufman and Auerbach's general model of an electronic funds transfer system. This system incorporates the use of cryptographic check digits derived *from* the PIN.[55]

HANDSHAKING SCHEMES

Other types of authentication schemes which may provide a higher degree of security than lower-level schemes such as fixed passwords are those incorporating the execution of an algorithm for authentication. Such procedures are often referred to as "handshaking" or "extended handshakes." [5,13] Some of these procedures directly involve the use of passwords; others can only marginally be considered password schemes.

The ADEPT-50 time-sharing system incorporates a handshaking scheme.[85] In order to gain admittance to the system, the user must supply information items including user identification, password, and accounting data. The terminal identification is also compared against the terminal ID list for which the user ID was franchised.

Although not a password scheme, Hoffman's formulary model is also considered an example of an extended handshake access procedure.[37] Formularies are sets of access control procedures which grant or deny access to data at data-access time, rather than at file-creation time. This approach is the opposite of control provided by most password schemes in which passwords are associated with files.

In several systems, handshaking is accomplished by a dialog between the system and the user. In such procedures the user may be required to answer questions (e.g., cat's name, astrological sign) asked in a semi-random fashion, or to supply additional passwords and/or account information.[59] This is analogous to having several passwords, any number of which may be requested in any order. It is even conceivable that the questions themselves could be chosen by the system user.

In another variation, credited to Les Earnest by Hoffman,[36] the handshaking is accomplished by both the system and user performing a transformation on a given number and comparing the results. The system presents the user with a pseudo-random number and requires that the user perform a specified mental transformation T on that number. The result is then sent back to the computer, which performs an appropriate transformation and compares the results. Thus, the user has performed T on a number x and transmitted $y = T(x)$. Consequently, an eavesdropper monitoring the transmission would at most see x and y. Note that the latter transformation need not be the inverse of the former transformation, but may be any suitable (e.g., non-degenerate) calculation whose results are dependent upon the user-transformed value.

Hoffman asserts that even "simple" T's such as

$$T(x) = \left[\left(\sum_{i \text{ odd}} \text{digit } i \text{ of } x\right)^{3/2}\right] + (\text{hour of the day})$$

raise the work factor in breaking the scheme significantly. In such a system the transformation itself would still have to be kept secret by each user.

PASSWORD PROTECTION

The previous section has been concerned with the selection of a password scheme that, in addition to being convenient to use, is secure from discovery through guessing or exhaustive enumeration. However, regardless of the password scheme implemented, protection of the password (or authenticating algorithm) is vital.

Let us assume that authentication algorithms or handshaking procedures are guarded by the system's full array of protection mechanisms. (Note that if a penetrator succeeds in gaining access to the algorithm under these conditions, he could just as easily access any other files in the system!) Accordingly, emphasis shall be on protection requirements for passwords.

The three times during which the password must be protected are

- initial distribution
- storage
- entry and transmission.

This section considers the requirements for guarding the passwords against potential threats that might occur at such times.

Initial Distribution

The initial distribution of passwords to users is one aspect of password assignment, selection, and transmission. Two items must be considered in this situation:

- user identification
- distribution method.

Ordinarily, first-time users of a system make application in person for authorization to use the system resources. At that time a temporary password can be assigned. The user then has the responsibility for logging onto the system and changing the password to one known only to him.

In another form of password distribution, more useful when users are great distances from the computing facility, the password is transmitted by mail to the user. PIN's are normally distributed in this manner. If more assurance of receipt is required, registered mail or special messengers can be used.

Initial distribution of encryption keys could be handled in a similar manner, with the magnetic card bearing the first key being sent via registered mail.

Password Storage

Most password schemes use tables or lists which contain the current password for each authorized system user. (A notable exception would be the user-transformation scheme described previously.[36]) As these tables and lists are perhaps the most vulnerable part of a password system, efforts should be taken to protect them.

In recognition of the vulnerability of tables and lists associated with authentication techniques, Bushkin[12] includes the following principle in his set of design requirements:

All passwords and authentication data shall be stored in an irreversibly transformed state.

R. M. Needham is credited with being the first to recognize the vulnerability of password lists. An encipherment algorithm attributed to him has been implemented at Cambridge, England. As opposed to ordinary communications ciphers in which the enciphering and deciphering algorithms are of nearly equal complexity, the cipher produced by this algorithm is a "one-way cipher." This is a cipher for which no simple deciphering algorithm exists. In such a scheme, the user's password is encrypted as soon as it is received by the system, and the transformed password is then compared with the encoded table entry.[86]

A discussion of Needham's system and the merits of various others can be found in reference 23. Purdy[75] also describes the Needham scheme, discusses the selection of good one-way ciphers, and suggests the use of polynomials over a prime modulus.

Lawrence Livermore Laboratory's OCTOPUS network also incorporates password table encryption. Fletcher notes that if an encrypting algorithm is chosen so that attempts to break it by cryptanalysis would be as time-consuming as by trial-and-error methods, then there would be no real need to protect the encrypted password table. However, in the OCTOPUS network, the password table is protected.[31]

There are still potential threats involved in such schemes. One is the interception of passwords prior to encryption, and another is the selection of a poor cipher. The former problem will be dealt with in the next section.

An example of a poor cipher would be one that is highly degenerate (i.e., one in which many combinations encrypt to the same value).[31] Under such a scheme the simple exposure of the encrypted list could give enough information to a would-be penetrator to allow him to, if not break the algorithm, at least access the files of any users whose passwords in their encrypted form were identical to his. Note that this is also the case when several users of a system have identical passwords.

As a part of their Multics vulnerability analysis, the Air Force considered the threat of exposure of password files.[53] Their report suggests that accessing the system password file could be of minimal value to a system penetrator. Assuming that the password file is the most highly protected file in the system, anyone who succeeded in accessing this file could conceivably penetrate *any* other file in the system!

For completeness the Air Force study did analyze the "non-invertible" encipherment scheme used at that time by the Multics system. A report soon to be published, will detail their successful penetration of that scheme.[22] Basically, the approach was to assume that although Multics would accept passwords up to eight characters in length, most individuals would use words less than six characters long. Proceeding with the assumption of trailing blanks, the scheme was broken for passwords of this size. After developing a solution for this special case, they then succeeded in developing a general solution. As a result of this study, the Air Force has provided a "better" password scrambler for Multics.

Not all operating systems read-protect encrypted password tables. Bell Laboratories' UNIX* timesharing system, for example, allowed users to read the

---

* "UNIX" is a Bell System Trade/Service Mark.

password table in which user passwords are stored in encrypted form, under the assumption that password encryption alone provides adequate protection.

This protection, however, is not entirely dependent upon the algorithm used. If both the password table and the encryption algorithm are available, then even if the passwords are difficult to decrypt (i.e., a "one-way" cipher is used), one could reasonably hope to derive them by exhaustive enumeration. For example, the encrypted password table could be copied to another computer system and compared against the outputs of the same algorithm when run against all words of five or less alphabetic characters. The use of larger, more frequently changed passwords could thwart such attempts.

Note that if key-oriented algorithms (such as the Federal Data Encryption Standard[27]) are used, access to the password table and knowledge of the encryption algorithm alone are not sufficient to obtain the passwords. Either the key itself would have to be exposed, or an unencrypted password and its encrypted form would have to be obtained. In this latter case, the encryption key would still have to be derived, and a larger sample of encrypted and unencrypted text would probably be needed.

In some systems using magnetically encoded cards, the PIN itself is stored on the card in an encrypted form. Currently two methods exist for protecting these PIN's:

1. The PIN and other account-related data are encrypted and encoded on the card. In off-line systems using this scheme, the terminal is then responsible for decrypting the data and comparing the customer-entered number with the PIN.
2. In other systems, the PIN is not encoded at all, but instead has a predetermined arithmetic relationship to such data as the account number which is encoded on the magnetic card.

In an article discussing the threats to bank card systems,[67] Industrial National Bank Vice President Ernest Northup describes the components of a card-based electronic funds transfer system (EFTS) and notes that the "use of a standard PIN scrambling technique or algorithm for bank interchange would require that its elements be widely known, at least among equipment vendors. This increases its vulnerability." He categorizes a secure PIN system as one utilizing a technique that

1. demonstrates its resistance to cryptanalysis mathematically.
2. does not require direct exposure of the PIN during transmission.
3. can be physically protected from analysis within the device in which it is contained.

Kaufman and Auerbach present a comprehensive set of EFTS security principles. Concerning the storage of PIN's, they state that "there should be no way to derive the PIN from information on the card," although they observe that many current schemes are based upon techniques for deriving the PIN from information on the card. PIN storage on the card does reduce the need for storage in the system; however, it is extremely risky. With such a scheme, the incentive for theft of the algorithm for deriving the PIN is high since, once the algorithm is obtained, all PIN's can be derived for the entire system![55]

Password Transmission

As with any other transmitted data, passwords are vulnerable to several threats during their transmission from terminal to computer. These threats include wire-tapping, electronic eavesdropping, and piggyback infiltration. The password may also be discovered later in the trash if a hardcopy terminal was used, or observed on a CRT screen immediately after entry. These latter two problems are usually dealt with by masking (the over-printing or under-printing of a series of characters) or echo suppression. However, as pointed out by Carroll and McLelland,[16] in general the "use of a mask affords no protection to users on CRT visual display terminals." Furthermore, echo suppression is meaningless when the keyboard input is printed directly, as in half-duplex mode, rather than echoed. Another method sometimes used as a countermeasure against such forms of password detection is the use of non-printing characters as a part or all of the password.[28,34] In some half-duplex systems there exist print/display suppress keys which can be used at the terminal to locally inhibit the display of the password.

In a discussion of piggyback infiltration, Carroll and Reeves described a situation in which unsuspecting terminal users could be "exploited by a process which mimics the real system long enough to obtain a password . . ."[17] Echo suppression and masking are of no help in countering this type of threat. Furthermore, if a more intelligent device than a conventional (i.e., non-intelligent) terminal is used to intercept the conversation, then non-printing characters also lose their effectiveness.

The user-transformation schemes described by Hoffman[36] and Carroll and McLelland[15] are one way of effectively shielding the password in transit. Here the user, when presented with a random number, performs a predetermined transformation on it and transmits the result back to the computer for verification. The incorporation of a date-time group into this transformation is recommended to provide additional protection against piggyback infiltration.[15] User-transformation schemes, however, would seem to be costly, particularly if there is to be some variability among the users.

Another method for password transmission can be found in Babcock's description of the RUSH timesharing system.[3] Here mention is made of a "dial-up and call-back" system in which the user is directed to telephone the password to the computer system operator when access is requested to very sensitive files. Although this technique might afford a degree of protection for the password, it would not be appropriate for a large, heavily used system.

A similar technique involves the computer breaking the communications link, and then placing a call to the terminal. This procedure ("call back") is useful for verifying that an authorized terminal is being used; however, this alone is not sufficient to verify user identity.

Optimal protection of the transmitted password can be realized by encryption of the communications link during the entire conversation.[4,6] (The Federal Data Encryption Standard would be suitable for this purpose.[27]) Communications systems incorporating the use of encryption are currently in use in the non-military environment. In one such system, a banking institution uses hardware code scramblers to protect customer passwords in transit. In this application, the customer selects a 16-character password, which is then scrambled twice before reaching the computer where it is filed as a six-digit code. The scrambling, which is claimed to be irreversible, is handled by integrated circuits built into relay boxes at the terminals and computer center.[65]

Branstad notes that encryption keys and authentication codes may be in effect the same item. In his proposed network access control machine, these keys are never transmitted through the network, but rather are loaded simultaneously by interface units into a primary encryption device. Thus, authentication can be considered complete at that level (at least) if a message can be encrypted, transmitted, and correctly decrypted.[6,7]

In a master's thesis on encryption-based protection protocols, Stephen Kent considers encryption key distribution.[56] He identifies two basic transmission techniques:

- chained key changes
- two-level key distribution systems.

Under the chained key system, each new key is enciphered using the last key issued. This new key is then used until another change occurs. Under the two-level distribution system, a special key is used solely for transmitting new keys to remote users. Kent describes protocols for using these two schemes and considers the use of magnetically encoded cards for distribution of keys. He presents the following example of a login sequence incorporating two-way authentication:

1. The user enables the terminal and establishes a connection to the host.
2. The host responds in cleartext confirming the connection by sending the host name.
3. The user transmits in cleartext the login identifier, and then inserts a magnetic striped plastic card containing his (primary) key and enables the encryption module.
4. The host locates the user's primary key using the login identifier presented in cleartext. A new (secondary) key to be used during this session is then created and transmitted using the standard key change protocol.
5. The terminal deciphers the key change messages and loads this secondary key. The host switches simultaneously to this new key. The terminal then transmits a message confirming key receipt and the host, upon receipt of the confirmation, is ready to engage in secure communication with the user. All communication from this point on will be carried out using the new key.

Additional steps involve transmission of the current time and date, enciphered using the new key, to the user. Such a login protocol not only succeeds in authenticating the user's identity to the system, but also confirms the system's identity to the user, thus providing an effective means of protection against such threats as piggyback infiltration and between-lines entry. More observations on good key protection practices may be found in reference 8.

Again considering the EFT environment, Kaufman and Auerbach present the security principle that the "exposure of PIN's should be minimized during a transaction." [55] In their general design for a local EFT system, they include a provision for one-way PIN transformations. The PIN in clear form is neither transmitted nor stored anywhere in the system.

It should be noted that this study accords only cursory treatment to encryption techniques and key management concerns. Those desiring more complete information on the topic of encryption are advised to begin with Diffie and Hellman's excellent introductory paper.[21] Encryption is considered in concert with other security techniques in reference 38.

EXAMPLE IMPLEMENTATIONS

Computer hardware and software vendors are responding to the demand for enhanced system security.[33,39-45,51,60] Their efforts in the software area can be categorized as those involving operating system modifications or add-on packages.

Current implementations of password systems have been described in references 12, 14, 16, 30, and others. Several of these are discussed in this report and their features are summarized in Table 7-1. In all of these systems, the password facility was built into the operating system or data base management system.

Recently, in response to the demand for more secure computer systems, vendors have made available add-on security packages. Examples of such systems are those marketed by IBM Corporation and Tesseract Corporation. Other manufacturers and software vendors may offer similar packages.

IBM markets a package called the Resource Access Control Facility (RACF), which is supported by their MVS operating system. The purpose of RACF is to assist computer installations in controlling user access to data sets on direct access storage devices. It performs three major functions:

1. User identification and verification—identifies and verifies a RACF-defined user to the system during TSO logon and batch job initialization.
2. Authorization checking—determines whether a user is permitted to access a RACF-protected data set.
3. Logging—writes records to SMF (System Management Facilities) and routes messages to the security console following the detection of (1) unauthorized attempts to enter the system, and (2) authorized or unauthorized accesses to RACF-protected data sets.

TABLE 7-1
Password implementations

		Password Features			
System	Selection Technique	Size (charac- ters)	Alphabet	Lifetime	Comments
ADEPT-50	System	12	Alphanu- meric	One-time	Internal list of 64 passwords for each user.
Multics at AFDSC	System (word generator)	5–8	A–Z	Fixed (max. 6 months)	Users can currently reject assigned passwords for each user.
Bank card transaction systems using PIN	Assigned to user	4–6	Usually numeric	—	PIN may be stored on card.
GIRS	Assigned to user	9–23	Numbers	Indefinite	Additional password used to logon to system.
OCTOPUS	System	6	Alphanu- meric	Fixed number of uses or fixed interval of time	A counter, associated with the password, records password uses.
RACF	User selects	1–8	Alphanu- meric	Fixed	User selects expiration date of password.
SWIFT	Assigned to user	4	Numerics	One-time	Passwords taken from list mailed to user in two separate parts.
TSO/Codes Update	Assigned to user	5	2 Alphabetic, 3 Numeric	Fixed	

Descriptions of RACF, ranging from a product announcement to technical description, may be found in references 46 through 48.

IBM also offers an installed user program called the TSO/Codes Update System.[49,50] This package features

1. fully automated password update.
2. date-oriented construction of passwords utilizing randomizing routines which should not create duplicate passwords in a 100-year period.
3. facility for initial distribution of passwords using mailer-type forms.

Tesseract Corporation has developed the Data Access Security System (DAS), versions I and II. DAS I operates on all versions of the IBM Operating Systems OS MFT/MVT, VS1 and VS2 (SVS/MVS), including HASP, ASP and TSO. It is described as an improvement upon IBM's password facility that "makes the facility more generally usable and prevents the unauthorized disclosure of passwords." [82] In contrast to DAS I, which built passwords from components of the Job Control Language and then provided them to the existing password facility, DAS II is a rewrite of IBM's password facility.[82] Its features include the support of shared password data sets and the ability to restrict

1. the number of accesses to a protected data set
2. accesses to a particular period of time
3. access to batch jobs only, or TSO users only
4. access to specific jobs, TSO users, programs, and job accounting parameters.

These are only a few examples of the types of add-on security packages available. With the ever-increasing emphasis on computer security and data integrity, packages such as these are appearing more and more frequently, and no doubt will continue to do so until more operating systems, designed with security in mind from the beginning, are developed.

Although not a commercial system, the Experimental Network Operating System (XNOS),[57] designed and implemented at the National Bureau of Standards, provides an example of password use in a distributed processing environment. In that system, a minicomputer was logically placed between network users and the systems providing them services. This minicomputer acted as an intermediary, providing data and command translation services.

Wood and Kimbleton have investigated the implications of providing access control mechanisms in such an environment.[90] Issues addressed included maintaining separate accounts on every supported network system for every user versus a single, common account on each supported system. To facilitate implementation, the latter approach was adopted in the XNOS application, thus minimizing the effort involved in managing account names, corresponding passwords, and file spaces.

Password management is only one concern in the area of secure distributed processing. A number of the issues arising in a distributed environment are considered in reference 54. Also, Denning examines a situation that may be typical for personal computing applications, wherein personal computer users must exchange information with or through untrusted remote systems.[20]

COST CONSIDERATIONS

The costs of a given password scheme are those incurred by the intruder as well as by the protector. These costs must be considered in conjunction with the value of the information to be protected. (See reference 84 for a discussion of the value of personal information in qualitative terms.)

The costs to the protector include not only those for the hardware and software, but also the effect on overall system performance. For example, the amount of processing time required and the degree of communications channel loading may result in severely degraded system response time.

Lientz and Weiss consider the implementation costs of various security measures in a computer networking environment.[58] For costs related specifically to password schemes, they include the following:

1. Simple password for identification: cost of software, systems performance, storage.
2. Changeable passwords: cost of software, updating lists and storage, systems performance.
3. Password transformations: cost of software, cost of random lists and storage, systems performance, computational cost.
4. Magnetically encoded cards with constant or changeable passwords: cost of terminal to read/write, cost of software, systems performance.

Nielsen et al. also consider password-related costs in a comprehensive report which focuses on the identification and analysis of computer system integrity safeguards.[66]   Among the password-related controls addressed are password protection, change, amplification, generation, penetration detection, compromise detection, and print suppress. The annual costs (e.g., implementation, operation, and overall) of each safeguard are indicated as being small, moderate, or large; and the effectiveness of each in the prevention, detection, and reduction of computer system integrity violations is judged.

Password schemes which involve authentication to the file or data item level are more costly than systems employing passwords only at log-on. In a report on the principles and costs of privacy protection in data banks, Turn observes that the "costs of access control operations reflect themselves in increased processing time and storage space requirements." He relates the results of a study of these costs which revealed a 22% to 140% processing time increase in file access operations, depending upon when access controls are applied (e.g., at file open time, or data item access time).[83]

Since add-on security packages are becoming available, cost of such "retrofit" techniques must be considered. The total cost of such systems includes not only the purchase or lease price, but also the cost of any additional hardware and programmer time needed to install and support the system.

The cost to the system intruder includes the investment in time and equipment (i.e., the work factor) necessary to, in this case, determine the password or password-generating algorithm. Risk can also be considered part of the penetration cost.

As an example, consider the intruder's costs of acquiring passwords through wiretapping. These could range from the cost of recording equipment (a few dollars), to the cost of a minicomputer and associated software development (several thousand dollars). Risks include possible legal prosecution.[84]

As aptly stated by Petersen and Turn, "the level of work factor which is critical for a given information system depends, of course, on an estimate of the magnitude of threats and of the value of the information." [73] They suggest that a work factor of one day of continuous computation required to break a single encryption key might be adequate against low-level threats.

Then, the cost of the system utilized in the penetration effort must also be considered in order to better estimate the work factor required; that is, one day of continuous effort by a person with a hand calculator is hardly comparable with a day's effort by a large-scale computer system. For example, at an NBS workshop[61] the following problem was chosen: the design of a large-scale digital machine which could be used for recovering the key used for encrypting data under the [at that time] proposed Federal Data Encryption Standard (DES). The results of that study indicated that to achieve key exhaustion time on the order of one day, the estimated cost would be several tens of millions of dollars, and that such a machine could not be placed in operation before 1990.

Thus it would appear that with the encryption key for the DES taking the place of the traditional password as a means of personal authentication, nearly optimal protection against exhaustive enumeration attempts can be achieved.

CONCLUSIONS

Although automated personal authentication techniques such as fingerprint, voice, and signature recognition are becoming less expensive and more accurate, it is apparent that the majority of commercial and Government timesharing systems are continuing to rely upon passwords. We have shown that passwords can be an effective form of personal authentication when care is taken in their selection and protection. The features of password schemes have been categorized, their capabilities and limitations identified, and points at which password protection mechanisms are needed have been indicated.

Table 7-2 briefly summarizes some of the advantages and disadvantages of the various types of password schemes which have been examined here. Generally speaking, an ideal password scheme is difficult to guess, easy for the authorized user to recall, frequently changed, well-protected, and inexpensive. But to be more specific, based upon these and other considerations presented in this report, a fairly strong password scheme would be characterized as follows:

- one-time
- computer generated or otherwise assigned to a user
- highly unique over the supported user population
- at least six characters long
- randomly generated
- encrypted when stored
- encrypted in transmission
- not displayed when entered.

TABLE 7-2
Password characteristics

Password Scheme	Some Advantages	Some Disadvantages
Selection Process:		
User-selected	Easy to remember	Often easy to guess
System generated	Difficult to guess	More difficult to remember; generating algorithm may be deducible
Lifetime:		
Indefinite	Easy to remember	Most vulnerable to exhaustive enumeration and guessing attempts; difficult to tell if password stolen
Fixed	Easy to remember if time interval is fairly long (e.g., week or month); more secure than indefinite (shorter the time interval, better the security provided)	Vulnerability depends upon time interval
One-time	Useful for detecting successful penetration of system; short lifetime prohibits exhaustive testing	Difficult to remember unless written down; valid user locked out if successful penetration occurs
Size and alphabet:	Larger the password and alphabet, the more difficult to guess; less need for duplication of passwords	Larger the word, more difficult to remember and more storage required
Information Contents: (e.g., authorization information and check digits)	Could aid detection of penetration attempts if penetrator unaware of valid password structure	May cause passwords to be long and thus more likely to be written down; if scheme becomes known, passwords could be easy to deduce
Handshaking Schemes: (e.g., dialogs, user transformations)	Resistant to exhaustive enumeration attempts; provides some protection during transmission	May be time consuming; requires more storage space than single passwords

Additional safeguards include the use of techniques such as banner lines to inform users of previous attempts (both successful and unsuccessful) at logging onto their accounts.

The exact password scheme appropriate for a given system depends upon the required level of security as determined by cost/risk analysis. It may well be the case that for most non-military systems, the cost of supporting the preceding example password scheme would be prohibitive. Formal guidelines for the selection of appropriate password schemes and for the use of passwords in conjunction with other authentication techniques are needed.

In addition, emphasis on personal authentication should not result in the neglect of other technical and procedural controls such as logging, journaling, and authorization checking.[9] For example, the certainty that there is a record of activities of a user's terminal session may often prove to be more of a deterrent to computer abuse than would system-imposed restrictions on what a user is authorized to do.

Until other forms of personal authentication become more cost-effective, the password will no doubt remain the most widely used means of controlling access to remote computing systems and services. With careful selection of appropriate password schemes and attention to password protection, in both transit and storage, it can be a most effective personal authentication mechanism.

REFERENCES

1. Anderson, J. P.: Information security in a multi-user computer environment. Advances in Computers, Vol. 12. New York, Academic Press, 1972, p. 1–36.
2. Anderson, J. P.: On Centralized Distribution of One-Time Passwords in Resource Sharing Systems. Fort Washington, PA, James P. Anderson and Co., August 1971, 8 pp.
3. Babcock, J. D.: A Brief Description of Privacy Measures in the RUSH Time-sharing System. Proceedings of the Spring Joint Computer Conference, Vol. 30, 1967, p. 301.
4. Baran, P.: On Distributed Communications: IX. Security, Secrecy, and Tamper-free Considerations. Rand Corporation, August 1964, AD-444 839, 39 pp.
5. Beardsley, C. W.: Is your computer insecure? IEEE Spectrum (January 1972), p. 67, 16 refs.
6. Branstad, D. K.: Encryption Protection in Computer Data Communications. Proceedings of the Fourth Data Communications Symposium. IEEE Computer Society, October 1975, p. 8-1 to 8-7, 2 refs.
7. Branstad, D. K.: Security Aspects of Computer Networks. Proceedings of AIAA Computer Network Systems Conference. New York, American Institute of Aeronautics and Astronautics, April 1973, 8 p.
8. Branstad, D. (Ed.): Computer Security and the Data Encryption Standard. National Bureau of Standards, Special Publication 500-27, February 1978.
9. Broadman, I. S.: Protection Techniques in Data Processing Systems to Meet User Data Security Needs. (IBM Corporation, Gaithersburg, MD), Proceedings of the Second International Conference on Computer Communication (Stockholm, Sweden, August 12–14, 1974), 1974, p. 485, 2 refs.
10. Browne, P. S.: Security in Computer Networks. Approaches to Privacy and Security in Computer Systems (Proceedings of conference held at National Bureau of Standards, March 1974), September 1974, NBS Spec. Pub. 404, p. 32.
11. Browne, P. S.: Computer Security—A Survey. Proceedings of the National Computer Conference. Montvale, N.J., AFIPS Press, 1976, p. 53, 134 refs.
12. Bushkin, A. A.: A Framework for Computer Security. McLean, VA., System Development Corporation, AD-A025 356, June 1975, 158 pp.
13. Campaigne, H., and Hoffman, L. J.: Computer privacy and security. Computers and Automation, *22*(7): 12, 1973.

14. Carroll, J. M., Martin, R., McHardy, L., and Moravec, H.: Multi-dimensional Security Program for a Generalized Information Retrieval System. Proceedings of the Fall Joint Computer Conference, Vol. 39, 1971, p. 571, 5 refs.
15. Carroll, J. M., and McLelland, P. M.: Fast "Infinite-key" Privacy Transformation for Resource-sharing Systems. Proceedings of the Fall Joint Computer Conference, AFIPS Press, 1970, p. 223, 12 refs.
16. Carroll, J. M., and McLelland, P. M.: The Data Security Environment of Canadian Resource-sharing Systems. INFOR, Canadian Journal of Operational Research and Information Processing 9(1): 58, 1971.
17. Carroll, J. M., and Reeves, P.: Security of Data Communications: A Realization of Piggyback Infiltration. INFOR, Canadian Journal of Operational Research and Information Processing 11(3): 226, 1973.
18. Cotton, I. W., and Meissner, P.: Approaches to Controlling Personal Access to Computer Terminals. Proceedings of the 1975 Symposium Computer Networks: Trends and Applications, IEEE Computer Society, 1975, p 32, 19 refs.
19. Crane, H. D., Wolf, D. E., and Ostrem, J. S.: The SRI Pen System for Automatic Signature Verification. Proceedings of Trends and Applications 1977: Computer Security and Integrity, IEEE Computer Society, May 1977, p. 32.
20. Denning, D. E.: Secure personal computing in an insecure network. Communications of the ACM 22(8): 476, 1979.
21. Diffie, W., and Hellman, M. E.: Privacy and Authentication: An Introduction to Cryptography. Proceedings of the IEEE, Vol. 67, No. 3, March 1979, pp. 397–427.
22. Downey, P. J.: Multics Security Evaluation: Password and File Encryption Techniques. Electronic Systems Division (AFSC), Hanscom AFB, Mass., ESD-TR-74-193, Vol. III, in preparation.
23. Evans, A., Jr., and Kantrowitz, W.: A User Authentication Scheme Not Requiring Secrecy in the Computer. Communications of the ACM 17(8): 437, 1974.
24. Jacobson, R. V., Brown, W. F., and Browne, P. S.: Guidelines for Automatic Data Processing Physical Security and Risk Management, National Bureau of Standards, FIPS PUB 31, June 1974.
25. *Glossary for Computer Systems Security,* National Bureau of Standards, FIPS PUB 39, February 1976.
26. *Computer Security Guidelines for Implementing the Privacy Act of 1974,* National Bureau of Standards, FIPS PUB 41, May 1975.
27. *Data Encryption Standard,* National Bureau of Standards, FIPS PUB 46, January 1977.
28. *Guidelines on Evaluation of Techniques for Automated Personal Identification,* National Bureau of Standards, FIPS PUB 48, 1977 (in press).
29. *Guideline for Automatic Data Processing Risk Analysis,* National Bureau of Standards, FIPS PUB 65, August 1979.
30. Fletcher, J. G.: Octopus Software Security. Proceedings of COMPCON 73, IEEE Computer Society, p. 61, 1 ref.
31. Fletcher, J. G.: Software Security in Networks. Lawrence Livermore Laboratory, University of California, 1975, 17 pp.
32. Gasser, M.: A Random Word Generator for Pronounceable Passwords. The MITRE Corporation, Bedford, Mass., AD-A017 676, November 1975, 1830, 3 refs.
33. Hammer, C.: Electronic Data Systems Security. ADP Data Security and Privacy: Proceedings of the Conference on Secure Data Sharing, Bethesda, Md., Naval Ship Research and Development Center, Report 4130, August 1973, p. 188.
34. Held, G.: Locking Intruders Out of a Network. Executive Guide to Data Communications. New York, McGraw-Hill Publications Co., 1976.
35. Herbst, N. M., and Liu, C. N.: Automatic Signature Verification Based on Accelerometry. IBM J. Research Development, May 1977, p. 245, 16 refs.

36. Hoffman, L. J.: Computers and privacy: a survey. Computing Surveys *1*(2): 85, 1969.
37. Hoffman, L. J.: The Formulary Model for Flexible Privacy and Access Controls. Proceedings of the Fall Joint Computer Conference, Vol. 39, 1971, p. 578, 33 refs.
38. Hoffman, L. J.: Modern Methods for Computer Security and Privacy. Englewood Cliffs, N.J., Prentice-Hall, 1977.
39. Data Security and Data Processing. Volume 1. Introduction and Overview. International Business Machines Corporation, (G320-1370).
40. Data Security and Data Processing. Volume 2. Study Summary, International Business Machines Corporation, (G320-1371).
41. Data Security and Data Processing. Volume 3. Part 1 State of Illinois: Executive Overview, International Business Machines Corporation, (G320-1372).
42. Data Security and Data Processing. Volume 3. Part 2 Study Results: State of Illinois, International Business Machines Corporation, (G320-1373).
43. Data Security and Data Processing. Volume 4. Study Results: Massachusetts Institute of Technology, International Business Machines Corporation (G320-1394).
44. Data Security and Data Processing. Volume 5. Study Results: TRW Systems, Inc. (G320-1375).
45. Data Security and Data Processing. Volume 6. Evaluations and Installation Experiences: Resource Security System, International Business Machines Corporation, (G320-1376).
46. IBM introduces more complete security for MVs. Electronics News (July 26, 1976), pp. 16, 28.
47. OS/VS2 MVS Resource Access Control Facility (RACF) Command Language Reference, International Business Machines Corporation, (Program No. 5740-XXH9), August 1976, 78 pp.
48. OS/VS2 MVS Resource Access Control Facility (RACF) General Information Manual, International Business Machines Corporation, (Program No. 5740-XXH), August 1976, 48 pp.
49. Automatic Password Generation for TSO. International Business Machines Corporation, 1976.
50. TSO/Codes Update System: Program Description/Operations Manual, International Business Machines Corporation, (Program No. 5796-PFR), 1976, 34 pp.
51. Jarvis, J. E.: Security in the Time-Sharing Bureau. Proceedings of Computer Security 74, National Computing Centre Publications and IFIP Administrative Data Processing Group, 1974, p. 101.
52. Johnson, S. M.: Certain Number Theoretic Questions in Access Control, Rand Corporation, Report R-1494-NSF, January 1974.
53. Karger, P. A., Schell, R. R.: Multics Security Evaluation: Vulnerability Analysis, Electronic Systems Division (AFSC), Hanscom AFB, Mass., ESD-TR-74-193, Vol. II, June 1974, 156 pp., 33 refs.
54. Karger, P.: Non-discretionary Access Control for Decentralized Computing Systems, SM thesis, M.I.T. Department of Electrical Engineering and Computer Science, NTIS ADA040808, May 1977.
55. Kaufman, D., and Auerbach, K.: A Secure National System for Electronic Funds Transfer. Proceedings of the National Computer Conference, AFIPS Press, 1976, p. 129, 6 refs.
56. Kent, S. T.: Encryption-Based Protection Protocols for Interactive User-Computer Communication (Master's Thesis). Cambridge, MA, Massachusetts Institute of Technology, AD-A026 911, May 1976, 122 p., 42 refs. AD-A017 676, November 1975, 183 pp., 3 refs.
57. Kimbleton, S. R., Wood, H. M., and Fitzgerald, M. L.: Network Operating Systems—An Implementation Approach. Proceedings 1978 National Computer Con-

ference, Montvale, NJ, AFIPS Press, Vol. 47, 1978, p. 773.

58. Lientz, B. P., and Weiss, I. R.: On the Evaluation of Reliability and Security Measures in a Computer Network, Office of Naval Research, Arlington, Va., AD-A002 996, December 1974, 28 pp., 19 refs.

59. Lupton, W. L.: A Study of Computer Based Data Security Techniques, Naval Postgraduate School, Monterey, California, AD-765 677, 1973, 77 pp., 141 refs.

60. McCraney, R.: CDC's Current Procedures for Data Security. ADP Data Security and Privacy: Proceedings of the Conference on Secure Data Sharing, Naval Ship Research and Development Center, Bethesda, Md., Report 4130, August 1973, p. 199–200.

61. Meissner, P.: Report of the 1976 Workshop on Estimation of Significant Advances in Computer Technology. National Bureau of Standards, NBS-IR 76-1189 (August 30–31, 1976), 70 pp. [in press].

62. Muerle, J. L., Swonger, C. W., and Tona, C. J.: EDP Security Through Positive Personal Identification. Proceedings of 1974 Carnahan and International Crime Countermeasures Conference, University of Kentucky, 1974, pp. 246–253.

63. National Bureau of Standards: Proposed Standard Encryption Algorithm for Computer Data Protection. Federal Register *40*(52): 12134, 1975.

64. Neumann, A. J.: A Guide to Networking Terminology. National Bureau of Standards, NBS Technical Note 803, March 1974, 29 pp.

65. Twice-scrambled passwords protect customer accounts. Minicomputer News (October 7, 1976), p. 2.

66. Nielsen, N. R., Brandin, D. H., Madden, J. D., Ruder, B., and Wallace, G. F.: Computer System Integrity Safeguards: System Integrity Maintenance. Menlo Park, California, Stanford Research Institute, SRI Project No. 4059, October 1976.

67. Northup, E. H.: Bank cards vs. the underworld. Banking *67*(9): 66, 68, 70, 73, 1975.

68. Parker, D. B.: Threats to Computer Systems. Lawrence Livermore Laboratory, UCRL-13574, March 1973, 118 pp.

69. Parker, D. B., Nycum, S., and Qura, S. S.: Computer Abuse. Stanford Research Institute, PK-231 320, November 1973, 181 pp.

70. Parker, D. B.: Computer Abuse Perpetrators and Vulnerabilities of Computer Systems. Proceedings of the National Computer Conference, Montvale, NJ, AFIPS Press, 1976, p. 65.

71. Parker, D. B.: Crime by Computer. New York, Charles Scribner's Sons, 1976, 308 pp.

72. Peters, B.: Security Considerations in a Multi-programmed Computer System. Proceedings of the Spring Joint Computer Conference. Washington, D.C., Thompson Book Co., 1967, p. 283.

73. Petersen, H. E., and Turn, R.: System Implications of Information Privacy. Proceedings of the Spring Joint Computer Conference. Washington, D.C., Thompson Book Co., 1967, p. 291, 14 refs.

74. Peterson, B.: Convicted Computer Expert Seeks Role as Security Advisor. Washington Post (August 1974), p. 442, 8 refs.

75. Purdy, G. B.: A high security log-in procedure. Communications of the ACM *17*(8): 442, 1974.

76. Reed, S. K., and Branstad, D. K., (Eds.): Controlled Accessibility Workshop Report. National Bureau of Standards, NBS Technical Note 827, May 1974, 86 pp.

77. Richardson, M. H., and Potter, J. V.: Design of a Magnetic Card Modifiable Credential System Demonstration. Electronic Systems Division (AFSC), Hanscom Field, Mass., MCI-73-3, December 1973, 65 pp.

78. Shannon, C. E.: Communication theory of secrecy systems. Bell System Technical Journal *28*(4): 656, 1949.

79. Taylor, A.: Darmstadt system eliminates check-digit loopholes. Computerworld (September 17, 1975), p. 13.
80. Taylor, A.: Deeds check-digit method possibly valuable DP tool. Computerworld (October 22, 1975), p. 11.
81. Taylor, A.: Statistics improving state of art in "check-digitry." Computerworld (February 23, 1976), p. 17.
82. DAS II: Product Announcement. Tesseract Corporation, San Francisco, California, October 1976.
83. Turn, R.: Privacy Protection in Databanks: Principles and Costs. The Rand Corporation, Santa Monica, California, AD-A023 406, September 1974, 21 pp., 19 refs.
84. Turn, R., and Shapiro, N. Z.: Privacy and Security in Databank Systems—Measures of Effectiveness, Costs, and Protector-intruder Interactions. Proceedings of the Fall Joint Computer Conference, Montvale, N.J., AFIPS Press, 1972, p. 435, 26 refs.
85. Weissman, C.: Security Controls in the ADEPT-50 Time-sharing System. Proceedings of the Fall Joint Computer Conference, AFIPS Press, 1969, p. 119, 20 refs.
86. Wilkes, M. V.: Time Sharing Computer Systems. American Elsevier, New York, 1975.
87. Winkler, S., and Danner, L.: Data security in the computer communication environment. Computer (February 1974), p. 23, 7 refs.
88. Wood, H. M.: On-line Password Techniques. Proceedings of Trends and Applications: 1977—Computer Security and Integrity Symposium, IEEE Computer Society, May 1977.
89. Wood, H. M.: The Use of Passwords for Controlling Access to Remote Computer Systems and Services. Proceedings of the National Computer Conference, AFIPS Press, 1977, pp. 27–33.
90. Wood, H. M., and Kimbleton, S. R.: Access Control Mechanisms for a Network Operating System. Proceedings of the National Computer Conference, AFIPS Press, 1979, p. 355.

Chapter 8

APPLICATION OF CRYPTOGRAPHY

Rein Turn

California State University, Northridge, California

Computers are routinely used in business, industry, government and other organizations to automate accounting, purchasing and sales, manufacturing, research, management, record keeping, and other related functions. The information maintained and processed in these systems is necessary in the daily operation of most of these organizations as well as vital to their long-term growth and competitive positions. This information could also be valuable to their competitors, some of whom may attempt to gain clandestine access to the computer systems and data files for the purposes of industrial espionage.[1] Automated processing has also provided new opportunities for white-collar crime by employees—embezzlement, fraud, and falsification of information. Distributed data processing systems, distributed data bases, and computer networks where computers, data bases, and terminals may be at geographically dispersed locations, but are connected through various data communication systems, further increase the system's complexity and accessibility and, thus, provide new vulnerabilities. For example, the emerging electronic funds transfer systems (EFTS) handle millions of dollars daily in the form of electronic impulses in computer-communication systems. These systems will be attractive targets for persons with computer experience who could intercept funds-transfer messages, modify these to suit their intentions, and reinsert them into the network.

Case histories of computer-assisted crime in the United States and other industrialized countries underscore the reality of the threat to computer and data security.[2] Computers have become targets of terrorist attacks, have been held for ransom, and have been used to defraud their owners or, in conspiracy with the latter, to defraud customers or the public at large. Employees who design their own computer applications, write programs, or operate the equipment have many opportunities to perpetrate acts of computer crime. They have little difficulty with procedural or technical means employed to enforce access controls and, to date, legal deterrence has been nonexistent. The latter is now being improved by enactment of computer crime laws in a number of states, and the likely enactment of a federal computer crime law.[3]

In computer-communication systems the legal deterrence is stronger since the

Communications Act of 1934 prohibits illegal interception of any communications. However, legal deterrence is not enough and technical means must be used to control access to data and messages in communications systems. Principal among these techniques are cryptography and the use of codes. These deterrents will be examined in depth in this chapter.

In a different category of computer applications, personal information records are maintained in computer-accessible data bases by organizations in the private sector and in the government. There are now in existence on the federal government level, in a dozen states, and applicable to a few areas of the private sector, laws that provide individuals with privacy rights vis-à-vis personal data about them maintained in record-keeping systems, and place certain requirements on the record-keeping organizations. Among these are requirements to maintain data quality, integrity, and security; and to control access to the data. Thus, implementation of data security techniques and procedures is indicated.

Finally, the management of computer facilities must maintain positive control over the use of computing and communications resources and the data being processed or communicated. Such control is achieved when the management can be confident that only explicitly authorized users and employees are granted access to those programs and data that are explicitly specified; i.e., the system and the data maintained therein are inaccessible to all others, including persons external to the system who may try to gain access through the communications system by intercepting the communications. This type of access is relatively simple for anyone with technical know-how and resources, even in microwave transmission links.[4] The emergence of low-cost, portable, computationally powerful intelligent terminals has made the eavesdropping task much easier as computers may be programmed to scan the intercepted traffic for certain key words of interest; thus sophisticated wiretapping activities can take place where a terminal may be inserted in a communications link for intercepting, modifying, and retransmitting data communications. Experiments have shown that such "piggy-back" penetration of computer systems is quite feasible.[5]

A different aspect of the management control problem is the lack of signatures or other authenticating material in digital messages, and the ease of forging such messages. Clearly, when two parties enter into a legally binding relationship on the basis of exchanging digital messages, each would require assurances that these messages are authentic and that they could not be altered afterwards. At present such assurances cannot be provided, but techniques for implementation of digital signatures are becoming available, as discussed later in this chapter.

Whether or not a particular computer-communication system is likely to be a target for computer crime from internal or external sources depends on a number of factors, such as the nature of the organization and its operations, the types of applications supported and data bases maintained, the opportunities for economic gain for the would-be perpetrators, the size and nature of the system's user population, and the type and architecture of the system itself. For example, a remotely accessible network of computers which permits its users to submit assembly language programs and uses circuit-switched communications offers more opportunities for computer crime and unauthorized access to communications than would a centralized system that limits its users to a small set of predetermined, fixed format transactions.

Determination of the potential threats against a computer-communication system, and evaluation of the associated potential losses, is the purpose of risk assessment.[6-8] Unfortunately, effective risk-assessment methods and techniques are still to be developed for computer-communication systems.[9] Therefore, it is important that security safeguards be designed into the system, rather than added on later. The computer system management must recognize that security has become just as important a design criterion as are functional capabilities provided, performance, and cost.

The increasing trend toward implementation of distributed computer systems with remotely located terminals, processors and data bases, and toward the use of such systems for transmitting sensitive data, accentuates the need for securing the associated data communications links, and developing message and data authentication techniques. The use of cryptographic techniques for this purpose and the attendant implications on managing such systems are the topics of this chapter.

CRYPTOGRAPHY

Cryptography is the practice of transforming messages or text (the "cleartext") into forms (the "ciphertext") that are unintelligible to all except those who know the reverse transformation. *Cryptology* is the science of secret communications. In addition to cryptography, it includes *cryptanalysis,* the methodology and techniques for transforming the intercepted ciphertext into the original cleartext, or the transformation used. Basic to providing security to messages by cryptographic techniques is maintaining secret the transformation used or the parameter (the "key") that selects a specific transformation from a large space of possible transformations.

Cryptographic techniques are used to provide security to data and messages in communication links and networks; that is, they protect against passive wiretapping (eavesdropping) and against active wiretapping (interception, modification, and reinsertion of data or messages). However, communications security must also satisfy other requirements:[10]

- Prevention of traffic analysis—determination of the frequency, volume, length, and origin-destination patterns of the message traffic
- Detection of message stream modifications
- Detection of denial of message service
- Detection of attempts to establish unauthorized connections.

Cryptographic techniques can achieve the first goal through encryption (application of a cryptographic transformation) where the message address and origin indications are also concealed. A standard practice is to transmit continuously, using dummy messages during pauses in actual message or data traffic. Meeting of the other goals depends more on the use of proper communications procedures (protocols) than on the use of cryptography except when cryptographic techniques are used to authenticate identifications of users, messages, and sources/destinations.

In addition to these goals, security systems for computer networks should be designed to incorporate the following principles:[10]

- Economy of the security mechanism—the use of the simplest possible design that can achieve the desired effect. Not only low cost, but also the effort required for testing and verifying correct operation of the mechanism are important considerations.
- Fail-safe property—design approach where access granting is based on permission, not denial. Failure of the process will then lead to denial of all access requests, rather than permitting access.
- Complete mediation—every access request is tested against access authorization tables. No exceptions are made.
- Open design—the configuration and operation of the protection mechanism is not secret. Protection is not dependent on the ignorance of the attackers, but on the intrinsic strength of the mechanism.
- Separation of privilege—a protection mechanism requiring two keys (in possession on separate individuals) is more robust than a mechanism where a single key is used.
- Least privilege—every program or user, and every security mechanism should be granted only the absolute minimum of capabilities needed to perform their functions. The purpose is to limit the damage that may occur should the element be compromised.
- Least common mechanism—limitation on the number of shared security mechanisms. Each represents a potential information path between users who may attempt to employ it for unauthorized communications (e.g., signalling sensitive data into a less protected part of the system).
- Psychological acceptability—the human interface must be designed for ease of use and as much transparency to the user as possible, so that users do not have incentives to avoid complying with security procedures.

Communications security techniques involve not only the hardware and software mechanisms for access control, identification, authentication, and implementation of the preceding principles, but also cryptography. These former mechanisms have been discussed extensively in the literature.[11-13] This chapter focuses on the use of cryptography as a computer-communications security technique.

Principles of Cryptography

Shannon refers to methods for protecting information in messages and data as *secrecy systems.*[14] He identifies two kinds:

- Concealment systems—the existence of the message is hidden, such as when using invisible ink, or mixing a message with other, unrelated text.
- "True" secrecy systems—existence of the message is not hidden, but its meaning is concealed by using a transformation.

Among true secrecy systems are codes and cryptographic transformations. A code is a transformation where an entire message may be represented by a particular word or string of symbols (usually characters of the alphabet). Coding is usually done with the help of a dictionary (a "code book"). The protection provided depends on maintaining control over the code books and periodic changes of the codes. Besides providing protection, coding also provides a considerable amount of message compression; i.e., many characters are represented by a much shorter string of characters. For example, in telegraphy the code word XYZ may be defined to mean "Happy Birthday." The existence of a code book is a serious vulnerability, however.

A cryptographic system (cryptosystem) for secure communications between a sender, S, and a receiver, R, consists of the following elements (Fig. 8-1):

- A plantext message, M, to be transmitted and protected.
- A very large family of reversible (invertible) cryptographic transformations (ciphers), T. Each transformation, t_k, in the family is uniquely determined by a parameter, k, the key of the cryptosystem. All possible keys, the values of k, constitute the key space, K, of the cryptosystem.
- In the encryption process, a key is selected and the corresponding transfor-

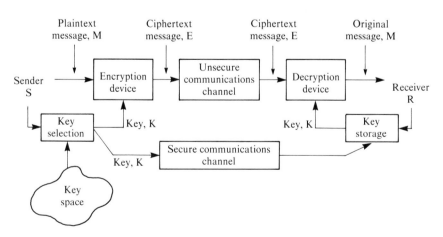

Fig. 8-1.   Application of cryptographic transformations.

mation, t_k, is applied to the message to produce the corresponding ciphertext, E: $E = (M)t_k$. E is transmitted to the destination where the receiver applies the inverse transformation, t_k^{-1}: $(E)t_k^{-1} = M(t_k t_k^{-1}) = M$

Clearly, such a cryptosystem will be effective only if the key, k, is kept secret, and the key space, K, is sufficiently large to make it unlikely that the correct value of k could be determined easily by trial and error methods. It is also necessary that both the sender and receiver use the same value for k—this value must have been exchanged earlier over a secure communication channel.

The ciphertext version of the message, M, is transmitted to the destination over a communication channel that is not secure. Thus, E may be intercepted and subjected to a variety of cryptanalytic attacks. If the cryptosystem is constructed according to the principles stated previously, then its structure is known to the analyst. Security of the message rests entirely on the uncertainty of the analyst regarding which key was used in producing E. However, as discussed later, an extremely large key space and the associated uncertainty in the key are a necessary but not sufficient condition for achieving a high level of security.

Design Criteria

Over 70 years ago, Kerkhoffs formulated a set of effectiveness criteria for cryptosystems (as stated by Shannon[14]):

- The cryptographic transformation used should be unbreakable, if not theoretically then at least in practice.
- Knowledge by the interceptor of the family of transformations used and of the equipment in the cryptosystem should not compromise the protection provided.
- The key should be capable of providing all the protection; it should be easy to generate, apply, store, transmit, and change.
- The transformation should be simple, requiring neither complicated rules nor mental strain.

Kerkhoffs' criteria were derived for manually operated communications systems, but with some modification they are still applicable in computer-communication systems. Since transformations are applied automatically by computers or special-purpose equipment, simplicity is no longer a necessary requirement (even though it is desirable from a performance point of view), and keys can be changed much more readily. On the other hand, computers are now also important tools for cryptanalysis. Their use has greatly reduced the effectiveness of classic cryptographic transformations.[15,16]

Other important characteristics of cryptosystems influence their design and suitability in computer-communication systems:[17]

- Size of the key space. It must be very large in order to make impractical any trial-and-error attempts at finding the key.

- Effect of the transformation on language statistics. Ideally, all language characteristics, such as relative frequencies of single letters, pairs of letters (digraphs), and word structure, should be totally masked and altered.
- Complexity. The transformation should be complex enough to prevent mathematical analysis, as well as contribute to the time required for brute-force search. On the other hand, complexity affects the cost of its application, in terms of both time and the equipment used.
- Effect on message length. Certain transformations expand the message length and, thus, affect the storage and transmission time requirements.
- Error susceptibility. Some transformations propagate a single error throughout the ciphertext requiring retransmission of the message; others permit the use of simple error-correcting codes to handle errors at the destination.
- Key length. Keys that are shorter than the message must be applied several times cyclically in certain transformations. This practice can assist cryptanalysis. Long keys generated by processes that themselves are specified by a few parameters may also be weak since the parameters, not the sequence, must be regarded as the real key. Systems that use randomly selected keys that are longer than the messages sent using a key, and that are used only once, are theoretically as well as practically unbreakable.[14] However, large amounts of key must be available in active systems, and key generation, storage, distribution, and security are severe problems.

Application characteristics that affect the choice of encryption transformations include:

1. Value of the information to be protected. While value is difficult to assess for certain types of information, such as personal data, risk analysis methods can provide assistance.[6-8] Important is time-dependency of the value; if the encryption transformation used can resist cryptanalytic attacks for T hours, but the value of the information decreases below a critical threshold within this time, the selected transformation may provide adequate protection.
2. Language used. Information in a message (or computer record) is expressed in a language characterized by a vocabulary, grammar, syntax, and certain statistical characteristics (e.g., the relative frequency of occurrence of different characters of the language alphabet). If a natural language is used, it has evolved over long periods of time without regard to application of encryption techniques; thus, its characteristics tend to be useful for cryptanalysis.[18,19] However, in the design of artificial languages (e.g., programming languages), the need for providing cryptographic protection can be taken into account in the design phase and the language characteristics designed so as to minimize their usefulness for statistical analyses.
3. Dimensions and dynamics of the application. The volume of messages or records that must be transmitted or stored, the required rates and response

times, the nature of processing to be performed, and tolerance to errors establish criteria for the cryptosystem.

Technical considerations in the application of cryptographic techniques include:

1. Processing capability. The availability of sufficiently high speed processors to perform the encryption/decryption operations within the time constraints of the application, and without unduly degrading the channel transmission capability.
2. Error environment. The error characteristics of the communication channel are important in choosing the encryption system. For example, in a highly error-prone channel the use of transformations that propagate errors, or that require continuous synchronization can lead to much wasted transmission due to the need to retransmit messages that couldn't be decrypted or due to the need to resynchronize the system.
3. Operational environment. The nature of the system and its control (e.g., it is a dedicated communications link, a multi-user system, a public network of computers); the training of operators and users of the system.
4. Key distribution and management. The techniques used for key generation, distribution and control. This aspect of a cryptosystem is most crucial for successful use, but is often overlooked in the beginning. More about it appears in the next section.

The DP system management must consider all of the foregoing aspects when exploring the use of encryption. Training and education of users prior to start-up are equally important. Experience has shown[20] that much of the success of cryptanalysts in breaking complex military and diplomatic cryptosystems has depended on poor practices by the users of these systems.

1. Using the same key many times to transmit different messages when this practice has been contrary to the requirements of the system in use in that the cryptanalyst can simultaneously hypothesize solutions and test them on several ciphertexts.
2. Sending plaintext after several unsuccessful attempts to get the ciphertext transmitted without error.
3. Use of highly formatted, repetitive text in encrypted messages that can be easily guessed through the context of the system, language used, or application and, thus, can provide a source of plaintext for the cryptanalyst.
4. Verbatim publication of a message that was earlier transmitted in encrypted form.
5. Use of the same key for periods longer than specified for the given cryptosystem. This negligence will provide additional material for cryptanalysis beyond what is considered acceptable by the system's designers.
6. Sending a new key using the old one. Clearly, if the old key had been broken, the new one will also be compromised.

In general, despite rigid following of operational restrictions, a great deal of ciphertext and corresponding plaintext fragments can be expected to become available to interceptors/cryptanalysts. Thus it is important to use a cryptosystem that is as effective as possible in view of other considerations in the application, system, performance, and cost.

CLASSIC CRYPTOGRAPHIC SYSTEMS

Historically, there has always existed a requirement to prevent access to information in messages when they are outside the control of either the originator or the intended receiver; that is, when the message is in some communication channel where it is subject to interception. Correspondingly, various cryptographic schemes have been invented through the ages.[20] However, when applied to written messages composed in natural languages, these schemes tend to fall into two general classes: *substitution* of characters or groups of characters of the message alphabet with characters or groups of characters of the cipher alphabet (where both may use the same set of symbols, e.g., those of the English alphabet), and *transposition* of the characters in the message (rearranging their order according to some rules—the key). Transformations of these two types can be combined to obtain *product* transformations.[14] As will be discussed later, product transformations are especially suitable in the age of computer communications.

Substitution Transformations

Substitution transformations are categorized as monoalphabetic and polyalphabetic. Each of these could be either monographic or polygraphic. The latter classification refers to the number of characters being substituted as a group. In monographic substitutions, *single* characters are substituted (independently of each other and the context of the message) by single characters from the cipher alphabet(s) or by groups of characters. In *polygraphic* substitutions, groups of two or more characters of the message are substituted by similar size groups, or larger groups, of characters from the cipher alphabet(s). In the following material, monographic substitutions are made by single characters only.

In monoalphabetic substitutions a cipher alphabet B is chosen or constructed to correspond with the message alphabet, A, such that each character in A corresponds to a unique character in B. It is common to derive B from A by making a permutation of the characters of A. The simplest such permutation is a rotation of the message alphabet, A, by a fixed number of character positions. This number is the key. This cryptographic transformation is called the Caesar cipher, after its originator. An illustration is given in Figure 8-2.

A Caesar cipher is extremely easy to break (i.e., to discover what the key is by cryptanalysis of the available ciphertext) by trial and error, since at most 25 trials need to be made. In general, monoalphabetic substitutions change the individual

Plaintext
alphabet, A: a b c d e f g h i j k l m n o p q r s t u v w x y z

Cipher
alphabet, B: d e f g h i j k l m n o p q r s t u v w x y z a b c

Plaintext message: sell all shares
Ciphertext: vhoo doo vkduhv

Fig. 8-2. Caesar cipher, K = 3.

characters of the message alphabet, but leave the message language statistics unchanged.

Language statistics are the primary "hook" that permits cryptanalysts to "break" classic substitution-type cryptographic systems. Investigations of the structures of natural languages[21,22] have shown that that a number of structural and statistical characteristics of their vocabularies, in normal use, are relatively insensitive of the context and can be used to identify a particular natural language:

- Single character (monograph) frequency distribution. There is a large difference in the usage of letters of the alphabet in the vocabularies of natural languages. For example, on the average, the letter "e" appears 100 times more often than the letter "q" in the English language, but in French the letter "q" occurs 11 times more often than in English.
- Polygram frequency distribution. Relative frequencies of occurrence of pairs of letters (digrams), triplets of letters (trigrams), and so forth. In English the most frequent digrams are "th" and "he," and the most frequent trigrams are "the" and "ing." In French, these are "es" and "en," and "ent" and "que," respectively.
- Word starting and terminal letter frequencies. These differ sharply from the general letter frequency distribution. For example, in English the letter "e" (most frequent in general distribution) ranks fourteenth as a starting letter, and first as a terminal letter. The letters "v," "q," and "j" are almost never found as terminal letters.
- Word usage frequencies. These are much more dependent on the particular application area or topic than letter frequency distributions. The first-ranking words, however, tend to be prepositions, connectives, and pronouns which are used in the same manner in nearly all application areas. For example, the first nine are: the, of, and, to, a, in, that, is, was. The word frequency distributions are the basis of the so-called "probable word" method of cryptanalysis.
- Word structure patterns (isomorphisms). Groups of words which have similar patterns of letter occurrences in a word (e.g., caNNoN, miRRoR, teRRoR have the same pattern – –XX-X). This structural characteristic can be used to place words into congruency classes for use in cryptanalysis.

- Word length frequencies. This also characterizes different languages and, on occasion, application areas. For example, the average word length in English is 4.5, but 5.9 in German.

Various other statistics about word structure, word-to-word transition, and other features have been derived. The statistical structure of a natural language provides a certain predictability in constructing words in that language. This quality can be measured in terms of *redundancy* in the language, i.e., the inefficiency in the use of all possible character sequences as words in the language. For example, analyses of English indicate that 75% of the possible character sequences (up to some maximum length) are not used as words in the language. In general, redundancy of words of length n increases as n increases (there are many more four-letter words in English, for example, than there are seven-letter words). Redundancy provides another tool for the cryptanalyst.

Returning to monoalphabetic substitutions, the Caesar cipher is the simplest such substitution; the most complex one would be to construct the cipher alphabet by randomly rearranging the message alphabet. Since 26! ways are available, the key space is now very large, and trial and error solution in the manner of the Caesar cipher is out of the question (n! denotes "factorial of n," which is the product of all positive integers from 1 through n; 26! is approximately 4×10^{26}, an extremely large number). However, since monoalphabetic substitutions totally fail to conceal any of the language statistics listed previously, they are easily broken.

Language statistics can be hidden more effectively by using *polyalphabetic* substitutions. Here the cipher alphabet, B, is actually a set of M alphabets, $B_1, B_2, \ldots, B_M$ which are used cyclically with period M. For example, the first character of the message is replaced by the corresponding character from B_1, the second with corresponding character from B_2, and so forth, until the M-th character has been replaced with the corresponding character from B_M. Then the cycle begins again with the use of alphabet B_1. The result is that a particular character, say "e," is now substituted by several different characters so its frequency of occurrence has been concealed. The other language statistics are also concealed.

A particular type of polyalphabetic substitution, the Vigenere cipher, uses M

```
Plaintext
alphabet, A:     a b c d e f g h i j k l m n o p q r s t u v w x y z

Ciphertext
alphabets, B₁:   l m n o p q r s t u v w x y z a b c d e f g h i j k
           B₂:   o p q r s t u v w x y z a b c d e f g h i j k l m n
           B₃:   v w x y z a b c d e f g h i j k l m n o p q r s t u
           B₄:   e f g h i j k l m n o p q r s t u v w x y z a b c d
           B₅:   r s t u v w x y z a b c d e f g h i j k l m n o p q
                                    key
              Plaintext message:    sell all shares
                            key:    love rlo verlov
                      Ciphertext:   dsgp rwz nlrcon
```

Fig. 8-3. Vigenere cipher with key "lover".

Caesar ciphers as the alphabets $B_1, \ldots, B_M$. The key is the corresponding letters in these alphabets to the message alphabet letter "a." Figure 8-3 illustrates the Vigenere cipher with key "lover." A special case of the Vigenere cipher is when the number of alphabets (i.e., the key length), M, is equal to or greater than the message length. This transformation is called the Vernam cipher and it can provide a very high level of protection.[14]

The Vigenere transformation has complicated the cryptanalytic attack, but not provided an unbreakable cipher (except when the Vernam cipher is used or, in general, the messages are so short that insufficient ciphertext is available for determining the message statistics). With the help of computers all substitution ciphers, with the preceding exception, are broken easily.[23,24] On the other hand, computers make it feasible to use other types of substitutions where the substitution characters are computed by algebraic techniques.[25] Here the characters of the alphabet are regarded as integer numbers (0 through 25) that are operated upon by techniques of modular arithmetic modulo 26 (divided by 26, only the remainders are used). The simpler substitutions can be implemented in computers in the same way: the message character and the key character are added modulo 26. For example, in Figure 8-3, determination of the ciphertext character corresponding to the first message character "s" can be implemented by noting that "s" is represented by 18, "l" by 11, and, performing arithmetic modulo 26, one gets (18 + 11) mod 26 = 3 mod 26, which corresponds to the letter "d" of the ciphertext.

A note should be made regarding language statistics when computer programs or data are being encrypted. Computer programs are "artificial" languages in the sense that their vocabularies, grammar, and syntax are generated for specific computers or applications. While one tends to make these languages resemble natural languages, significant differences result in their statistics being quite different. For example, while programming languages use English words such as (in FORTRAN) "equivalence, dimension, do, read, write, if, format" and a variety of punctuation marks, the variable names are arbitrary character strings (up to and including six characters). They make up a variable vocabulary that can be chosen so as to produce arbitrary character occurrence frequencies and polygraph frequencies. The data, likewise, are expected to have highly varying distributions of numerals depending on the computations that are performed. On the other hand, artificial languages are based on rigid syntactical rules which can assist cryptanalysts.

Transposition Transformations

Transposition transformations operate on groups (blocks) of message characters by rearranging their positions in the block. The message alphabet, A, is not changed. Thus, the single letter frequencies are unchanged, but digram and higher order polygram statistics are changed. The cryptanalyst's challenge is to reconstruct from the given set of M characters (for transposition block length of M) the original message fragment. Clearly, the difficulty of this task is a function of M.

A classic implementation of the transposition cipher is to write the message into a matrix of M columns, row by row, and then rewrite it by taking the columns in some specified order.

For example, in a block of six characters, with the key specified as (136542), the word "profit" is changed into string "optrfi," where character 3 has replaced the message character 1, character 6 replaces character 3, and so forth, as specified by the key, until character 2 replaces character 1.

A widely used cryptanalytic technique against transposition ciphers is "multiple anagramming," attempting to recover meaningful text from one block and checking the hypothesized key against other blocks to see whether meaningful text also emerges in these blocks as when several blocks transformed by the same transposition key have been intercepted.

Product Transformations

In the age of computers, neither the pure classic substitutions nor transposition alone provide suitable security in computer-communication systems. Rather, transformations which are combinations of these have been developed and are being implemented. Shannon suggests that the language characteristics are most effectively hidden by sequences of interspersed substitutions and transpositions, as well as the use of certain nonlinear transformations. He called these transformations "mixing transformations," or product transformations.[14]

The best-known product transformation is the Data Encryption Standard (DES) approved by the U.S. government for use by the civilian departments of the government. DES will be discussed in detail in the following section. Other transformations based on complex mathematical formulas are also being developed for application in computer-communication systems; these, too, will be discussed in later sections.

THE DATA ENCRYPTION STANDARD

Responding to the growth in computer-communication systems and distributed data processing networks, the National Bureau of Standards in 1977 approved as a federal standard a specific cryptographic transformation, the so-called Data Encryption Standard (DES), and made its use mandatory for any civilian agency of the federal government that had a need for encryption.[26] The design of the DES takes cognizance of Kerkhoffs' rules and, thus, the DES algorithm has been published in full detail. The security it provides rests on the complexity of the algorithm, the thorough mixing it applies to a data block, and the size of the key space (approximately 7.2×10^{16}). Naturally, the keys used must be kept secret.

The DES is a product transformation of substitutions, transpositions (permutations), and nonlinear operations which are applied iteratively (16 iterations) to 64-bit message blocks to produce 64-bit ciphertext blocks. The key is 56 bits long

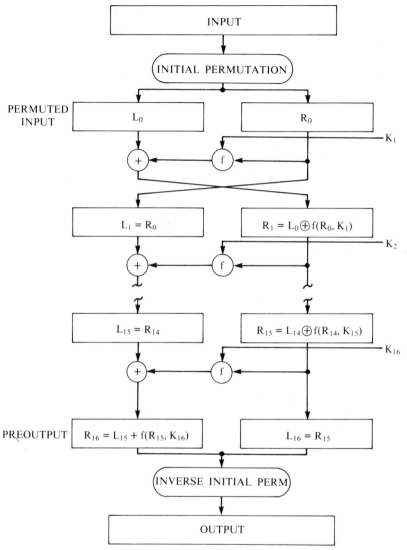

Fig. 8-4.   Enciphering computation with DES.

(actually a 64-bit key word is used in order to include 8 parity bits).   The DES
algorithm, when used in reverse, will decrypt the ciphertext block to yield the
original message block (the same key must be used, of course).   The DES transformation is applied as follows (see Figs. 8-4, 8-5, and 8-6):

1. Given the 64-bit data block, M, it is first divided into left and right parts of
    32 bits each, L_0 and R_0, respectively.   The 56-bit key, K, is similarly de-
    composed into two 28-bit parts, C_0 and D_0.

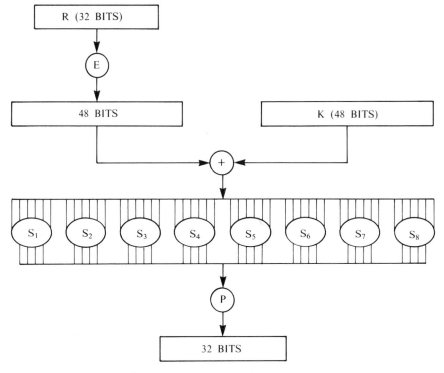

Fig. 8-5.   Generation of $f(R,K)$ in DES.

2. The following operations are now repeated 16 times. The following is a description of the first pass:
   a. The key to be used, K_1, is produced by generating C_1 and D_1 from C_0 and D_0 by left-shifting these a specified number of places. Then, the 48-bit K_1 is composed by selecting 24 specified bits from D_1 and C_1, as shown in Figure 8-6.
   b. L_1 is produced by making it equal to R_0.
   c. R_1 is produced by computing a function, $f(R_0,K_1)$, and then summing it on a bit-by-bit basis with L_0. In computing $f(R_0,K_1)$, as shown in Figure 8-5, R_0 is first expanded to a 48-bit word, then summed with K_1, 32 bits are chosen from the sum, and then a transposition (permutation) is applied. Thus, $R_1 = L_0 \oplus f(R_0,K_1)$. The strength of the entire DES transformation rests mainly on the nonlinear operations in computing $f(R_0,K_1)$— expansion of R_0 to 48-bit size, and selection of the 32-bit word from the sum with K_1.
3. The last operation is combining L_{16} and R_{16} and applying a permutation that is inverse to the initial permutation performed on M before it was split into R_0 and L_0. The result is the 64-bit ciphertext, E, of M.

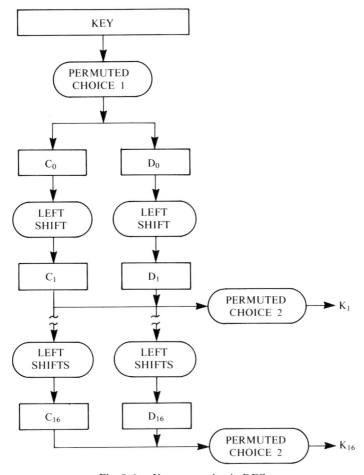

Fig. 8-6.   Key generation in DES.

There are three basic methods for using the DES in a communication system.[27]   The first is an *electronic code-book* form where, as described previously, the 64-bit data block M is transformed to produce E.   When the same key is used each time M is encrypted, the same E is obtained, very much like checking in a code-book.   The second mode is *cipher feedback* mode where E_0 is produced from an initializing block, I_0, and then G_1 is produced by applying the transformation to E_0. E_1 corresponding to M_1, the first data block to be encrypted, is produced by summing G_1 and M_1.   Thus, the data blocks themselves will not go through the DES transformation.   The third mode is *block chaining* where the data block M_2 is first summed with the ciphertext, E_1, from transforming data block M_1, and then the sum is transformed in the DES device.   This mode is viewed as providing stronger protection than the first two modes.   The last two modes are useful when

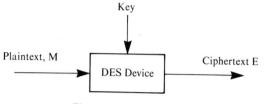

a. Electronic code-book mode

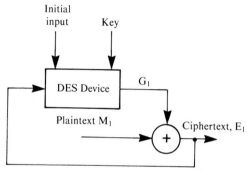

b. Cipher feedback mode

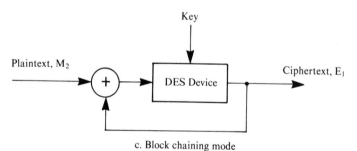

c. Block chaining mode

Fig. 8-7.   Principal modes for the DES use.

encrypting serial data for storage, or stream-mode communication of character-oriented data.   They are not useful for encrypting data that are to be randomly accessed in storage, or encrypting across packets in a packet communication system where the packets may arrive out of sequence.   The electronic code-book mode is suitable for these applications.   Figure 8-7 illustrates the three modes of using DES.

Since all details of the DES application have been published, i.e., the permutations used, the way key bits are selected, the way the 32-bit R is expanded to 48-bit length and combined with a 48-bit segment of the key and then reduced to 32-bit length again, and so forth, the entire protection burden falls on the key and the computational difficulty in breaking it. DES is very complex and the key space is very large. Thus, it is not likely that the cryptanalytic attacks used on classic cryptographic transformations will work (i.e., when only ciphertext is available, and some knowledge of the language used or of the application area to which the messages pertain). A question has been raised,[28] however, over the adequacy, or future adequacy, of DES in the case of "known plaintext" attack, i.e., when the cryptanalyst has several messages of plaintext and the corresponding ciphertext blocks, but does not know the key that was used. The question is, is it possible to discover the DES key used?

The known plaintext situation can arise in various ways: a previously encrypted message may be released later verbatim, or certain text is known to occur in the message (such as the address, salutation, reference to an organization), or the analyst may be able to insert a message of his own choosing in the system. Given a plaintext-ciphertext pair, the analyst would have to try different keys on the plaintext to see which one produces the corresponding ciphertext. Two assessments of the success of a known plaintext attack of DES have been made.[28,29] One maintains that it is technically and economically feasible to construct a microcircuit computer which can make a million trials per second, and to assemble one million such computers in a facility which, then, has the capability of testing all of the 7.2×10^{16} possible keys in 7.2×10^4 seconds (approximately 20 hours).[28] The cost of such a machine was estimated at $20 million. The conclusion was that the 56-bit key is too short to provide a high level of protection with high confidence that would last for some time into the future as a standard should, especially in view of the rapid technology advances.

The other assessment took a different viewpoint, namely that the development of a 10^6 processor array for known plaintext attack on the DES key is not feasible technically and economically for some time to come since the system would require millions of watts of power, be over 256 feet long, and cost over $70 million.[29]

At present a number of microcircuit implementations of the DES algorithm are underway, with some already on the market.[30] In general, the DES is finding acceptance in the private sector, too. No one doubts its usefulness for at least 5 years. Additional security could be obtained easily by running two DES units in tandem. Data rates up to 1.6 million bits per seconds can now be supported by DES processors chips. The costs range from $1000 to $5000 when implemented as stand-alone units. The DES chip itself is in the $200 to $500 range.

One reason for the controversy surrounding the DES and its resistance to cryptanalysis is the lack of information about its design theory and principles, and about any testing that was performed by IBM (the originator of the DES concept in an earlier system, the Lucifer[31]) or the government agencies responsible for security in general (e.g., NSA performed considerable testing on the DES). Thus, no guidelines exist for modifying the DES, such as, for example, to permit increase or decrease of the key length, change the block size, or change the number of iterations and still have an effective transformation. Some research on the design of DES-like transformation is being conducted, however, and results are becoming available.[32]

NETWORK APPLICATIONS OF CRYPTOGRAPHY

The principal application area for cryptographic transformations is in providing security for computer-communication networks. Typically, these networks consist of a number of *nodes* where computers are located, and a communication network that interconnects the nodes. The communication network consists of communication links that connect computer nodes to switching centers and the latter to each other. Several types of communication networks exist:

1. *Circuit switched networks* where a physical circuit is established between the sender and the receiver before communication begins, and is held throughout the communication.
2. *Message switched networks* where messages are routed from switching center to switching center, but the full circuit from sender to receiver is not established.
3. *Packet switching networks,* where messages are partitioned into fixed-length packets and each packet is routed independently.

Design Choices

Cryptographic techniques may be implemented in a communication network in three basic ways:

• Link-by-link encryption. Each communication link from a switching center to the neighboring switching center has its own encryption key. Within switching centers, incoming messages are decrypted, and then encrypted again using the key for the next link that is to be used to forward the message. Thus, security is required within the switching center. Further, the message is entirely in plaintext form (i.e., "in the clear") in any node's computer. An advantage is that any user of the network needs no other keys but the key to his nearest switching center. Figure 8-8 illustrates link-by-link implementation.

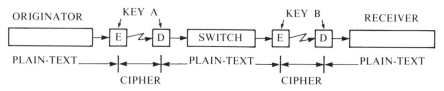

Fig. 8-8.   Link-by-link encryption.

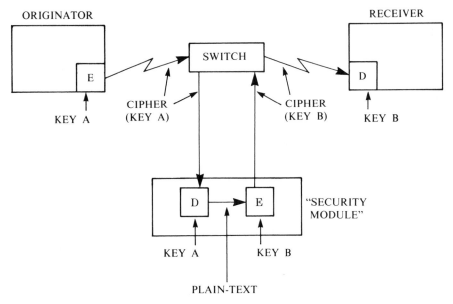

Fig. 8-9. Node-by-node encryption.

- Node-by-node encryption. A variation of link-by-link encryption where each link uses a unique key, as before, but the "translation" from one key to another occurs in a special security module in the switching center or the computer node. This reduces the potential exposure of the message when it is in plaintext form. Of course, any addressing and routing information in the message must be in the clear to permit forwarding of the message. Figure 8-9 illustrates node-to-node encryption.
- End-to-end encryption. The sender encrypts the message and it remains encrypted while it is transmitted through the network until it is received and decrypted by the receiver. This approach offers the best security, but requires each sender-receiver pair to have the same key. This requirement can be handled by prearrangement, or a network function must be established to set up secure communication sessions. Figure 8-10 illustrates end-to-end encryption.
- Super-encryption. Both link-by-link (or node-by-node) encryption implementation and end-to-end encryption are used for increased security; that is, the message submitted for transmission in a link-encrypted network has been encrypted itself and the receiver has the key.

The application of the encryption algorithm may be in the form of *stream* ciphering where each character of the message is encrypted independently of the others and can be transmitted as soon as it has been transformed. The pure substitution cryptosystems can be implemented readily as stream ciphering systems.

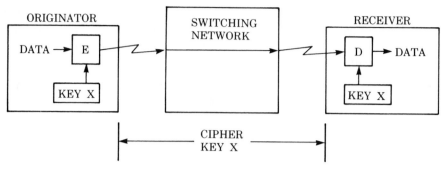

Fig. 8-10.   End-to-end encryption.

Transpositions and mixing transformations such as the DES are examples of *block* ciphers, since an entire block of characters must be encrypted before any of them may be transmitted. Block ciphers, thus, incur a transmission delay equal to the time required to complete the block encryption operation.

Stream ciphers work correctly only when the encryption and decryption devices, and especially the key generators, are synchronized in time; that is, both devices are in correct initial states when transmission begins and remain in synchronism throughout the communications session. In these systems the key generators are often some type of pseudo-random sequence generators,[32] or block ciphers that run in cipher-feedback mode. Block ciphers that operate in other modes usually do not require time synchronization, but the first block of a message must be clearly identified and the other blocks must have sequence numbers. The DES transformation is self-synchronizing. In general, the need for synchronization exposes the system to jamming attacks through deliberate insertion of noise in a communication link to break synchronization.

Other practical considerations exist when introducing encryption into an existing system in the commercial environment:

1. Security in the system should depend on a minimum amount of manual operations, and on minimum personnel, thus limiting the number of people who must be cleared to handle encryption keys.
2. The daily, routine users of the data terminals, and the system operators, should not need to handle keys or require special training to transmit encrypted messages.
3. Data link control procedures and protocols, and network control programs should not require major modifications when encryption is introduced.
4. Data link throughput should not be reduced noticeably in the encrypted transmission mode, particularly not because of artificially added redundancy (such as padding of plaintext messages with random characters, or the use of polygraphic substitutions).
5. The encryption transformations should not produce and transmit character groups that are also used by the communication system to control data links,

switches, etc. Means must be implemented to filter out such forbidden character groups or, at least, to identify clearly the ciphertext portions of a transmission such that these character groups would be ignored by the network control programs.

Other considerations and requirements in the operation of computer-communication systems may be affected in varying degrees by the introduction of security requirements, encryption in particular, or may themselves affect the choice of encryption transformations. Some 35 such requirements are examined in a recent publication,[33] which covered network reliability, availability, recovery from failures, protocols for formatting, routing, error control, and so forth.

Key Management

It is clear from the previous discussion that the security provided by a cryptosystem hinges on the security of the keys that are used, especially in cryptosystems where all details of the transformations used are public knowledge, such as the DES. The problem, then, is to generate, distribute, store, and apply keys in a secure manner. Furthermore, this is not a one-time effort, but a continuous activity, since keys must be changed as time passes, when there are changes in the users' population, or when it is feared that the keys have been compromised. The associated procedures and considerations are called key management.

The importance of keys suggests that they should be given greater protection than the data that are to be protected. Therefore, it is prudent to keep secret the key management procedures in an organization, only the minimum necessary number of employees should be involved, and tight discipline should be enforced.[34] The keys themselves should be unpredictable, preferably random numbers. The danger of using keys that are easy to remember has been demonstrated in the case of passwords where nearly 86% of the passwords used were found by an exhaustive search using the dictionary, lists of names, and other material that is likely to be used to find easy-to-remember code words.[35] While, in principle, 26^n possible n-character words can be composed using the English alphabet, many fewer such words are in use. Other precautions must be taken with key storage; they should be encrypted themselves with some master key, and with key distribution.

There are essentially three methods for key distribution: by registered mail, by courier, or over the computer-communication network itself. The last requires development of special protocols and facilities, and certain commonsense precautions. For example, the key currently in use should not be used to encrypt the new keys being distributed. Instead, a hierarchy of keys is defined:[36]

- Communication session key—established for one end-to-end interaction between sender and receiver. This key would be temporary and would be discarded after the communication session ends.
- Submaster key—used for encryption of the session keys as they are stored in key files or transmitted over the network to establish a session.

- Master key—used to protect submaster keys stored in files. This key must be kept physically secure by a trusted employee of the network, since it has no encryption protection.

The type of encryption system employed determines the details of the key management function and its implementation. In systems where keys are handled automatically, increased emphasis must be placed on reliable identification and authentication of the users as well as systems and subsystems (computers, terminals) involved in the communication process. Networks of computers are an especially demanding environment for key management when they service many users who may wish to engage in encrypted end-to-end communication with each other, or who may require secure communications when interacting with a variety of systems in the network.

In link-to-link encryption systems (see Fig. 8-8), each link has a separate key which may be changed automatically each time a message is transmitted, or less frequently. The keys can be stored in the (tamperproof) encryption device in a read-only memory which could be physically distributed to switching centers at required intervals. Thus, key management in this system is relatively simple and secure. If headers of messages are not encrypted, then there is no need for the switch to have access to the decrypted message, and decryption and encryption for the next link could all be done within the device. At the receiving terminal, au-. thentication of the receiver's identity must be required before he is allowed access to the received message. This process could be handled by standard identification/authentication techniques, such as the use of passwords, or some individual characteristics (signature or fingerprint). Key sets to be used in the two ends of a communication link can be delivered by conventional means (e.g., by courier), and kept encrypted until used.

In end-to-end encryption it is impractical for every subscriber to possess a separate key for every possible subscriber or system with which he may wish to communicate at some time. Instead, using the key hierarchy approach previously mentioned, the network itself can distribute a session key to the communicators. For this function, a network security center (NSC) is established.[36-38] The NSC can communicate with each subscriber's encryption device using a submaster key that is unique to that device; the device uses the same key. The following is an example of a protocol that may be used to set up secure communications between users X and Y, at terminals T_x and T_y, respectively:

1. A user, X, who wants to communicate over an encrypted channel with another user, Y, using end-to-end encryption, identifies and authenticates his terminal, and then himself, to the Network Security Center (NCS), and then requests a key for communication with Y.
2. NCS verifies from its data base the authority of X to communicate with Y, then contacts Y, and identifies/authenticates Y's terminal and Y.
3. NCS now uses its submaster key (which is not available to X or Y) to com-

municate with the two terminals to deliver a key for the communication session between X and Y.
4. At the end of the session the session key is discarded.

The described approach is quite promising for implementation in networks with a large user community. In smaller networks, more conventional key distribution approaches are appropriate, such as physical delivery of the keys to communicators who require end-to-end encryption. The selection of the key could then be made by referring to some identification number or code associated with each key. Such a selection could use a non-secure channel if confidence is high that neither the list of keys nor their identification system has been compromised.

PUBLIC KEY CRYPTOSYSTEMS

The previous sections have identified key distribution as one of the weak links in the use of cryptographic techniques; i.e., either physical transportation of the keys must be used, or special network facilities must be set up. This need arises because the same key, K, is used to encrypt a message, and to decrypt it again. Recently it was realized that if there were two different keys, K_E for encryption, and K_D for decryption, both generated together but with the property that given K_E it is computationally infeasible to derive from it the decryption key, K_D, then K_E could be made public without compromising the security of the system.[24,39-41] Such a system is called a public key cryptosystem. No key distribution is required in this system since each user of the system generates his own key pair, T_E and T_D, makes T_E publicly available, but keeps K_D secret. He is the only one who needs to know K_D.

As in the non-public key cryptosystems (the classic cryptographic transformations and the DES), the following properties should hold for the public key cryptosystem. Letting M and E correspond to the message (plaintext) and ciphertext, respectively, and K_E and K_D correspond to the encryption transformation with key K_E and decryption transformation with key K_D, respectively:[40]

1. Decryption reverses encryption

$$T_D(T_E M) = M$$

2. Decryption cannot be achieved without K_D:

$$T_E(T_E M) \neq M$$

3. It is practical (easy with a computer) to generate the encryption and decryption key pair (K_E, K_D).
4. It is computationally impractical to obtain K_D from K_E.
5. Encryption reverses decryption

$$T_E(T_D M) = M$$

Given the desirable principles for public key cryptosystems, transformations that satisfy these principles have yet to be found. Several have been proposed, based on mathematical operations that are difficult to perform.[42,43] The best known of these is based on the difficulty of factoring large integers into their prime factors.[42] The system works as follows:

1. The message, M, is represented as a positive integer (as are the resulting ciphertext and various components of the keys and transformations used).
2. The encryption and decryption keys are designed as follows:
   a. Two large prime numbers, p and q, are chosen (each with at least 100 decimal digits). Two quantities are formed:

   $$n = pq \text{ and } r = (p - 1)(q - 1).$$

   b. An integer, F, is selected randomly such that $3 < F < r$, and that F has no common factors with r (they are relatively prime). Then another integer, D, is found which is the "inverse of F modulo r;" that is, the product FD = 1 mod r, differs from 1 by a multiple of r.
   c. Then the encryption key, K_E, consists of the pair (F,n), and the decryption key, K_D, is the pair (D,n).
3. Given a plaintext message, M, which is an integer between 1 and $n - 1$, the encryption is performed to produce ciphertext, E, as follows: $E = M^F$ mod n; that is, M is raised to the power F, then divided by n; E is the remainder of that division.
4. Decryption is done by raising the ciphertext E to the power D, then dividing by n. The remainder is the original message, M; that is, $M = E^D$ mod n.

The strength of this system lies in the difficulty in finding D given F, since it is necessary to factor n (available along with F) into its prime factors. When n is approximately 200 digits long, this task would take a billion years using a computer with a 1-microsecond instruction time.[39] On the other hand, computation of the key parameters F and D is quite straightforward since one need only verify whether two numbers selected, p and q, are prime.

Operational use of the public key cryptosystem just described requires modular exponentiation—raising messages (integers) up to 200 digits long to integer powers with exponents up to 200 digits long. This operation requires considerable multiple-precision computation but is not infeasible since the exponentiation can by itself be factored (i.e., $X^{10} = X^{5+5} = X^5X^5$). Nevertheless, it will be difficult to perform these operations sufficiently fast to permit data transmission speeds of hundreds or thousands of characters per second. Current research in the public cryptosystem area is focused on finding functions that provide high levels of security but are simpler to apply computationally.

The following simple example illustrates the application of the preceding public key cryptosystem.[24] Let p = 17 and q = 31. Then n = pq = 527, and r = (p − 1)(q − 1) = 480. If F is chosen to be 7, then its inverse modulo 480 is 343 (i.e., $7 \times 343 = 5 \cdot \times 480 + 1$). Now, let the message M = 2. Then $E = M^F$ mod n =

$2^7 \bmod 527 = 128$, and E is transmitted in the system. Upon receipt, decryption is performed: $M = E^D \bmod n = 128^{343} \bmod 527 = 128^{256}\, 128^{64}\, 128^{16}\, 128^4\, 128^2$ $128^1 \bmod 257 = 2 \bmod 527 = 2$, which is the original message. Here the exponent 343 was factored into its power of 2 components.

DIGITAL SIGNATURES

Authentication of digitally transmitted and stored messages as to their source and veracity is an important problem in computer data bases, and in cases where these messages are used for making legally binding arrangements or for disbursing resources. Electronic funds transfer systems and various interbank clearinghouses are examples, as are computer-generated purchase orders, contracts, and other such instruments. In the manual world, signatures and seals serve the purpose of authenticating a document, and it is easy to detect any attempts to alter the document: erasures will leave traces. But this is not the case in computer storage; it is easy to change data values and leave no trace. Hence, what is required is a digital equivalent of the analog signature, with the following properties:[44]

1. Unforgeability. No one but the actual sender or author of the message should be able to produce the signature.
2. Authenticity. There should be a simple and indisputable way to demonstrate that the signature is authentic and could have been produced only by the sender.
3. No repudiation. It should not be possible for the signer later on to disclaim the authorship or charge that the message he signed has been altered.
4. Low cost and high convenience. Clearly, the more these properties are achieved, the more the system will find acceptance.

An attractive way to implement digital signatures with all the preceding properties is to make use of the public cryptosystem idea for those systems where the property holds that encryption reverses decryption: $T_E(T_D M) = M$, as is the case for the system discussed in the previous section.[42] The system works as follows:

1. The sender of a signed message, M, first operates on M with his *decryption* transformation using his decryption key K_D. This produces $E = T_D(M)$, which is then sent to the other party or parties.
2. Anyone can now apply the sender's public *encryption* key, K_E, to recover the message: $M = T_E(T_D M)$. This verifies that it was the sender who originated the message because only he could have decrypted it with K_D (no one else should have that key). The receiver(s) save E as the proof.
3. Since no one else has the sender's K_D, messages cannot be forged with the sender's signature. If secrecy is also required, the sender can apply the receiver's encryption key, K_{Er}, after using his own decryption key, K_{Ds}, to sign the message:

$$E = T_{Er}(T_{Ds}M) \text{ and the receiver reverses it } M = T_{Dr}(T_{Es}E)$$

Digital signatures have an important advantage over the usual signatures in that digital signatures are context-dependent, whereas the usual signatures are not. The digital signature will be different when a single character is changed in the message. Thus, once the specifics of a transaction and the date and time are included in the message, they will affect the signature and cannot be surreptitiously changed later.

The described signature implementation certainly authenticates the content of the message involved, but a dispute may still arise over the keys themselves. Namely, did the key pair K_{Es}, K_{Ds} actually belong to the sender? Did someone else have a copy of K_{Ds}? To handle the first question, a registry of keys and authentication of owners is needed. The second problem is more difficult: if K_{Ds} is compromised (even leaked deliberately by the owner), all messages signed by it are in doubt as they could have been produced later by others in possession of K_{Ds}. These problems suggest that a third party must enter the signing process, a "notary public equivalent" that is certified and trusted. Without such intercession by a third authority there would be two fatal flaws:[44] the validity of a signature would rest on its *future* as its compromise in the future invalidates all past uses, and the signer himself can compromise the key and thus invalidate all his past signatures. The latter is directly in opposition with the concept that signatures cannot be repudiated by the signers.

In a computer-communication network where digitally signed messages are likely to be used, the notary public concept can be implemented by a central Network Registry (NR) or a system of distributed NRs. An NR would receive the sender's signed message, $E_s = T_{Ds}(M)$, verify the sender's authenticity, include a registration block to E_s to produce $M_{nr(s)}$, which it will then sign with one of its many signatures, $K_{Dnr(i)}$, and send $E_{nr(s,i)}$ to the receiver along with $K_{Enr(i)}$ either in the clear, or encrypted by the receiver's K_{Er}. Now the sender cannot invalidate his past signatures by making K_{Ds} public since the registration block in the message fixes the signing time and other particulars. Compromise of the NR is also required for full invalidation of the signatures. Thus, the NR security must be very high and the signature registry must be highly protected by hierarchical encryption to the level that even the master key is not in the possession of a single trusted individual or facility. One approach to key partitioning between a group was recently proposed:[45] any n members of the group of N trusted individuals could generate the full master key.

MANAGEMENT CONSIDERATIONS

The preceding sections of this chapter have described a variety of techniques for achieving security in communications links through the use of encryption. Implicit has been an assumption that the cryptographic transformations used are applied correctly, and that keys are secure. However, since the transformations and key management are expected to be applied automatically by the network components, the security of the system has now been predicated on the security of the computers being used and the procedures being applied; that is, the adequacy of the security features in the computer hardware, software, communications protocols, and personnel procedures must be assessed. For example, in the case of DES application (as well as in the use of other encryption transformations that themselves may have been found to provide adequate cryptographic security), the following measures must be taken:

- Prevent inadvertent transmission of plain text.
- Prevent theft or unauthorized use of the cryptographic equipment when it contains a key.
- Prevent unauthorized acquisition or modification of the key while it is in the cryptographic equipment.
- Provide for erasure of the key in the cryptographic equipment upon instruction by the operator or upon attempted entry into the equipment.
- Prevent inadvertent transmission of the key or any part of it.
- Prevent transmission of messages, and provide alarms when critical failures take place (i.e., those that weaken cryptographic protection provided by the system).

These measures can be implemented by built-in functions in the cryptographic equipment, software in the network protocols, and personnel procedures. For example, any controls in the equipment should be protected by physical, key-operated pickproof locks, and the equipment itself should be mounted in a theft-resistant manner with an interlock that would erase the cryptographic key if the device is forcibly removed from its mounting. The key itself could be entered manually using a keyboard, or automatically from another electronic device. In both cases, there must be means for checking for errors in key transfer. A number of other requirements for secure operation of the cryptosystem are needed, especially for testing its correct operation.

Cryptographic protection is but one element in the general system of providing data security in a computer-communications network. Even more broadly, security itself is one facet of maintaining management control over the operations and resources of the system, so it is necessary to implement techniques and features that:

- Provide for control over the system and its resources, and the processing activities; provide for accountings of the resources used.
- Prevent accidental physical harm to the system, interference of users with one another, modification of data or programs, and preemption of resources by some small subset of the users.
- Provide safeguards against deliberate, unaccounted use of the system or its resources, disruption of the services, physical attack against the system, modification of data or programs, and illegal uses of the system.

- Comply with legal and regulatory requirements such as privacy protection laws, auditing requirements, and other requirements that may apply to the organization and its business.
- Assure that these security measures continue to be in effect not only when the system operates normally, but also when it is in a degraded mode of operation, is being maintained or repaired, or is using backup features or systems.

It is now reasonably well understood how to implement management control and provide security against most of the threats, accidental and deliberate, that can be identified,[46] and what needs to be done to audit the system.[47]

- Physical safeguards, such as locks, fire protection, water protection, and other techniques against disasters can reduce physical damage to the equipment and data.
- Computer hardware techniques, such as memory protection, virtual memory feature, and hardware-implemented identification systems are necessary for establishing effective access control mechanisms between users and data files, and for isolating users from each other.
- Software safeguards, such as file access control schemes, must provide (in conjunction with the hardware) barriers between users and those data files that they are not authorized to access, but permit easy access to those files that users are authorized to access.
- Communications safeguards, such as discussed in this chapter, are needed to protect information in transit in channels not controlled by the system.
- Personnel safeguards, such as background checks, bonding, training, and disciplinary actions, are needed to deter potential leakage of information due to some employee's deliberate actions.
- An administrative and management system must be created to oversee all aspects of the security safeguards; to inspect, test and audit their performance; and to control employees and users and their actions in the system.

Detailed discussion of the security safeguards that are required to support management control is beyond the scope of this chapter. However, a general overview can be presented along with certain caveats on the safeguards and their use.

In general, the techniques for protecting computer systems against accidental damage and natural disasters using physical security mechanisms are well in hand.[48] A variety of equipment and techniques exist for extinguishing fires in the computer room, preventing physical access to the facility, providing safe storage, and the like. Nevertheless, the application of these techniques requires careful analysis and engineering. For example, a ceiling sprinkler system may not be appropriate in a computer room and although a tear-gas dispensing system may keep out a rioting mob, tear gas also corrodes computer circuitry.

Problems still exist in generating secure operating systems and applications software.[49] The problem is mainly in the complexity of such software and the difficulty in assuring that the software system not only performs all specified tasks correctly, but also performs no other tasks.[50] Approaches to production of secure software now include the identification of a "kernel" of operating system functions that are essential for access control and security, and carefully verifying the correctness of the kernel. It is then expected that, since all accesses must be processed by the kernel, full control can be achieved and penetrations of the system can be prevented.[51] Other techniques are being developed for designing operating system software in which the correctness can be assured by formal proofs in each design step.[52]

Finally, some caveats can be stated regarding security in large computer systems and computer-communication networks:

1. Absolute security is unachievable in an automated, multi-user, resource sharing computer system; that is, it is not yet feasible to prove the correctness of the design and implementation of the operating system, and the application programs and data management systems that are needed. Some design flaws and implementation errors are certain to remain; hardware and personnel reliability cannot be assured.
2. Personnel trustworthiness cannot be reliably predicted, assured, or maintained.
3. Physical security cannot be assured against massive attacks or disasters, or against sophisticated sabotage.
4. Available data encryption techniques, such as DES, can offer very high levels of protection, but they have not been proven secure against massive attacks based on advanced computer technology.

To date, no system has been required to implement absolute security, but even reasonable security may be unachievable in some provable manner in large systems. Several factors support this contention:

1. Risk analysis techniques and methodology are not yet adequately developed to be used as guidelines on how to satisfy requirements for some specified level of security. Lacking are quantitative metrics for value of information and effectiveness of security measures.
2. Complexity of large software systems defies analysis for design weaknesses or implementation errors; exhaustive identification of vulnerabilities and associated security threats is very difficult.
3. Threat detection and monitoring techniques in computer systems are not adequate for detection of covert penetration attacks within the system.

Risk analysis is an important tool in the design of computer security systems and in associated trade-off analyses. It is important to avoid excessively costly and constraining security practices while still providing adequate security in view of the value of the data that are protected, the perceived threats, and the cost of safeguards. While achieving a general answer to the risk assessment problem is difficult,[9] progress has been made in specialized areas such as physical security risk assessment,[48] and data processing security in the financial and business sectors.[6,7] For example, a particular risk assessment approach is based on obtaining estimates of expected losses and their probabilities with order-of-magnitude accuracy rather than striving for greater precision. This approach permits comparing relative magnitudes of risks and identifies critical deficiencies in security safeguards. However, still open to criticism are claims that this method also produces credible recommendations on expenditures that should be made to improve security safeguards of the system. At present it is clear that much more research is required in risk assessment before it can be used with confidence in the design of security systems.

Software shortcomings are a general problem in producing reliable systems, but security requirements add a new dimension. Not only should programs correctly perform all tasks they are designed to do, but they should also not do anything they are not intended to do (the latter is often used for penetration of operating systems—these were designed to be used according to design specifications, and not to be experimented with). Verifying that a program satisfies such stringent requirements is difficult. Very little progress has been made in developing practical program correctness proving techniques.

In the absence of totally effective security safeguards in contemporary computer systems, various auditing procedures are used to discourage the curious or slightly larcenous users (the expert penetrators will not be thwarted) and to maintain control over the system. Typically, records are made of all jobs processed and resources used in the system, of all log-ons at on-line terminals, accesses to files, exception conditions detected by the operating system, and the like. If an audit log is properly designed, it can permit tracing anomalous user actions in the system and, thus, establish accountability through ex post facto analysis; moreover, active and dynamic audits can also intercept some penetration efforts in progress. Ideally, the equipment used to maintain audit logs should be constructed along the lines of aircraft flight recorders; they should be highly protected and should not permit erasures.

Advances in computer technology have made possible the incorporation of microprocessors into computer systems to perform a variety of control and housekeeping functions. Such processors could be incorporated also for security purposes (as they already are for implementing cryptographic functions). For example, they could monitor message traffic within the computer and compare the traffic with expected patterns. In this role they may detect that actions requested from some terminals are not normal, or that certain data are flowing to terminals or other computers in the system that are not expected to receive these data. In summary, advances in technology will permit implementation of "intelligent security" and distributed security functions throughout the system or the network. The outcome, hopefully, will be increased protection and lessened probability that security penetrations will be attempted.

REFERENCES

1. Greene, R. M., Jr. (Ed.): Business Intelligence and Espionage. Homewood, Ill., Dow Jones-Irvin, Inc., 1966.
2. Parker, D. B.: Crime by Computer. New York, Charles Scribner's Sons, 1976.
3. Taber, J. K.: On computer crime. Computer/Law Journal, Winter 1979, pp. 517–543.
4. Taps to steal data. Security World, December 1972, pp. 45–46.
5. Carroll, J. M., and Reeves, P.: Security and Data Communications: A Realization of Piggy-Back Infiltration, INFOR (Canada), October 1973, pp. 226–231.
6. Courtney, R. H., Jr.: Security Risk Assessment in Electronic Data Processing Systems. AFIPS Conference Proceedings, Vol. 46, 1977 National Computer Conference. Montvale, New Jersey, AFIPS Press, June 1977, pp. 97–104.
7. Reed, S. K.: Automatic Data Processing Risk Assessment. NBS/IR 77-1228, Washington, DC, National Bureau of Standards, March 1977.
8. Campbell, R. P., and Sands, G. A.: A Modular Approach to Computer Security Risk Management. AFIPS Conference Proceedings, Vol. 48, 1979 National Computer Conference. Montvale, New Jersey, AFIPS Press, June 1979, pp. 293–303.
9. Glaseman, S., Turn, R., and Gaines, R. S.: Problem Areas in Computer Security Assessment. AFIPS Conference Proceedings, Vol. 46, 1977 National Computer Conference. Montvale, New Jersey, AFIPS Press, June 1977, pp. 105–112.
10. Kent, S. T.: Network security: a top-down view shows problem. Data Communications, June 1978, pp. 57–75.
11. Denning, D. E., and Denning, P. J.: Data security. ACM Computing Surveys, September 1979, pp. 227–250.
12. Linden, T. A.: Operating system structures to support security and reliable software. ACM Computing Surveys, December 1976, pp. 406–445.
13. Saltzer, J. H., and Schroeder, M. D.: The protection of information in computer systems. Proceedings of the IEEE, September 1975, pp. 1278–1308.
14. Shannon, C.: Communication theory of secrecy systems. Bell System Technical Journal, October 1949, pp. 654–715.
15. Tuckerman, B.: RC 2879, A Study of the Vigenere-Vernam Single and Multiple Loop Enciphering Systems. Yorktown Heights, New York, IBM T. J. Watson Research Center, May 14, 1970.
16. Tuckerman, B.: RC 4537, Solution of a Substitution-Fractionation-Transposition Cipher. Yorktown Heights, New York, IBM Thomas J. Watson Research Center, Sept. 21, 1973.
17. Turn, R.: Privacy Transformations for Databank Systems. AFIPS Conference Proceedings, Vol. 43, 1973 National Computer Conference. Montvale, New Jersey, AFIPS Press, 1973.
18. Gaines, H. F.: Cryptanalysis. New York, Dover Publications, 1956.
19. Sinkov, A.: Elementary Cryptanalysis—A Mathematical Approach. New York, Random House, 1968.
20. Kahn, D.: The Codebreakers. New York, Macmillan, 1967.
21. Miller, G. A., and Friedman, A. E.: The reconstruction of mutilated English texts. Information and Control, 1975, pp. 38–55.
22. Shannon, C. E.: Prediction and entropy of printed English. Bell System Technical Journal, 1951, pp. 50–64.
23. Fiellman, R. W.: SRC-82-A-65-32, Computer Solution of Cryptograms and Ciphers. Cleveland, Ohio, Case Institute of Technology, 1965.
24. Diffie, W., and Hellman, M. W.: Privacy and authentication: an introduction to cryptography. Proceedings of the IEEE, March 1979, pp. 397–427.

25. Levine, J.: Variable matrix substitution in algebraic cryptography. American Mathematical Monthly, March 1958, pp. 170–178.
26. Data Encryption Standard, FIPS PUB 46, Washington, DC, National Bureau of Standards, January 15, 1977.
27. Branstad, D. (Ed.): Computer Security and the Data Encryption Standard, SP 500-27, Washington, DC, National Bureau of Standards, February 1978.
28. Diffie, W., and Hellman, M. E.: Exhaustive cryptanalysis of the NBS data encryption standard. Computer, June 1977, pp. 74–84.
29. Report on the Workshop on Estimation of Significant Advances in Computer Technology. National Bureau of Standards, Aug. 1977.
30. Hindin, H. J.: LSI-based data encryption discourages the data thief. Electronics, June 21, 1979, pp. 107–120.
31. Feistel, H.: Cryptography and computer privacy. Scientific American, May 1973, pp. 15–23.
32. Kam, J. B., and Davida, G. I.: Structured design of substitution-permutation encryption networks. IEEE Transactions on Computers, October 1979, pp. 747–753.
33. Shankar, K. S., and Chandersekaran, C. S.: The Impact of Security on Network Requirements. Symposium Proceedings, Trends and Applications 1977: Computer Security and Integrity. Long Beach, California, IEEE Computer Society, May 1977, pp. 96–99.
34. Sykes, D. J.: NBS SP 500-27, The management of encryption keys. Computer Security and the Data Encryption Standard. Washington, DC, National Bureau of Standards, February 1978, pp. 46–53.
35. Morris, R., and Thompson, K.: Password security: a case history. Communications of the ACM, November 1979, pp. 594–597.
36. Everton, J. K.: A Hierarchical Basis for Encryption Key Management in a Computer Communication Network. Proceedings, 1978 International Communications Conference, Toronto, June 1978, pp. 46.1.1–7.
37. Ehrsam, W. F., et al.: A cryptographic key management scheme for implementing the Data Encryption Standard. IBM Systems Journal, No. 2, 1978, pp. 106–125.
38. Branstad, D.: Encryption Protection in Computer Data Communications. Proceedings, Fourth Data Communications Symposium, Quebec, October 1975.
39. Hellman, M. E.: An overview of public key cryptography. IEEE Communications Society Magazine, November 1978, pp. 24–32.
40. Adleman, L. M., and Rivest, R. L.: The use of public key cryptography in communication system design. IEEE Communications Society Magazine, November 1978, pp. 20–23.
41. Hellman, M. E.: The mathematics of public-key cryptography. Scientific American, August 1979, pp. 146–157.
42. Rivest, R. L., Shamir, A., and Adleman, L.: On digital signatures and public key cryptosystems. Communications of the ACM, February 1978, pp. 120–126.
43. Merkle, R. C., and Hellman, M. E.: Hiding Information and Signatures in Trap Door Knapsacks. IEEE Transactions on Information Theory, September 1978, pp. 525–530.
44. Kline, C. S., and Popek, G. J.: Public Key Vs. Conventional Key Encryption. AFIPS Conference Proceedings, Vol. 48, 1979 National Computer Conference. Montvale, New Jersey, AFIPS Press, June 1979, pp. 831–838.
45. Shamir, A.: How to share a secret. Communications of the ACM, November 1979, pp. 612–613.
46. Ruder, B., and Madden, J. D.: An Analysis of Computer Security Safeguards for Detecting and Preventing Intentional Computer Misuse, NBS SP 500-25. Washington, DC, National Bureau of Standards, January 1978.

47. Ruthberg, Z. G. (Ed.): Audit and Evaluation of Computer Security, NBS SP 500-19. Washington, DC, National Bureau of Standards, October 1977.
48. Guidelines for Automatic Data Processing Physical Security and Risk Management, FIPS PUB 31. Washington, DC, National Bureau of Standards, 1974.
49. Linden, T. (Ed.): Security Analysis and Enhancement of Computer Operating Systems, NBS IR 76-1041. Washington, DC, National Bureau of Standards, April 1976.
50. Linde, R. R.: Operating System Penetration. AFIPS Conference Proceedings, Vol. 43, 1975 National Computer Conference. Montvale, New Jersey, AFIPS Press, June 1975, pp. 361–368.
51. McCauley, E. J., and Drongovski, P. J.: KSOS—The Design of a Secure Operating System. AFIPS Conference Proceedings, Vol. 48, 1979 National Computer Conference. Montvale, New Jersey, AFIPS Press, June 1979, pp. 345–353.
52. Feiertag, R., and Neumann, P. G.: The Foundations of a Provably Secure Operating System (PSOS). AFIPS Conference Proceedings, Vol. 48, 1979 National Computer Conference. Montvale, New Jersey, AFIPS Press, June 1979, pp. 329–334.

Chapter 9

DEPARTMENT OF DEFENSE NETWORK SECURITY CONSIDERATIONS

James D. Scharf

Defense Communications Agency, Command & Control Technical Center, Washington, D.C.

Virgil Wallentine and Paul S. Fisher

Department of Computer Science, Kansas State University, Manhattan, Kansas

OVERVIEW

This chapter provides a managerial and user survey of those secure Department of Defense (DOD) computer networks currently in existence and others which are still in the research stage. It also assesses current developments in computer network security. The information is based upon current literature, especially DOD computer network security implementation guides, planned implementations, and DOD areas of research in computer network security. The emphasis is on DOD networks because the majority of research in network security and computer security in general was started by and continues to be heavily supported by DOD.

The need for computer network security is particularly pressing within the DOD, since some of the DOD computer networks deal with classified information handling and many others carry information regulated by the Privacy Act of 1974. Some of the initial impetus in the computer security field and particularly in computer network security came from the DOD, and research is constantly underway to find a "trusted" computer network. This chapter provides computer network security sources and techniques that have been implemented as well as information on areas currently under research.

The technical scope of this chapter cannot encompass the implementation of a secure computer network, but the references provide a basic framework plus a guide to other sources which will permit implementation, and these sources will be identified.

DOD SECURITY POLICY

The DOD has set forth its security standards for resource-sharing computer systems, to include computer networks, in DOD Publication 5200.28, and has provided draft procedures for implementation in DOD Publication 5200.28-M, entitled "Techniques and Procedures for Implementing, Deactivating, Testing and Evaluating Secure Resource-Sharing Computer Systems." These documents, augmented and refined by each of the departments and agencies within the DOD, provide the framework for the present security levels for computer networks operated by and between elements of the DOD.

The DOD approach to computer security is flexible, as much driven by current technology as by well-established requirements. DOD 5200.28-M contains the caveat that "rigid adherence to all techniques, methodologies, and requirements . . . could adversely impact upon the present and future use of the system under today's rapidly changing ADP technology."

CLASSIFIED VERSUS UNCLASSIFIED SYSTEMS

Paragraph 1-101b of DOD 5200.28-M states that the ". . . manual is applicable to . . . all (DOD agencies) . . . which process, use or store classified data or produce classified information in resource sharing ADP systems." The military services have largely interpreted this statement to exclude applying those provisions to systems that do not process classified information, with the result that a large number of DOD EDP systems and networks which handle unclassified data have only that security which the local site supervisor or his commander feels is necessary. This security ranges from none to some portion of that required by DOD 5200.28-M, with the result that some systems which process large amounts of cash or high dollar-value material are open to easy penetration.

The implementation of DOD 5200.28-M for classified systems requires the preparation of security checklists, as covered in the next section. Although not required for sites processing unclassified information, a publication which provides comprehensive guidelines for computer facility physical security and risk management is Federal Information Processing Standards Publication 31.[16] Another excellent publication on total EDP system security, covering all phases of operation, is the American Federation of Information Processing Societies (AFIPS) System Reference Manual on Security.[43] This manual covers topics such as personnel, physical, communications, organization, administrative, and some EDP security, and provides extensive checklists in each area covered. This document would be a valuable aid to computer installation managers as it provides a ready means to check on security.

The next section describes techniques used within the DOD to implement computer network security. The next major section, Computer Network Security Research, contains a discussion of some of the research which the DOD is undertaking to improve computer security and provides sources of information on those research areas. The last section contains the author's assessment of both the effectiveness of current computer and network security as well as the direction of DOD research with relation to the state of the art in computer network security.

PRESENT DOD IMPLEMENTATION OF NETWORK SECURITY

This section presents DOD computer security implementation philosophy, provides a background for DOD computer network implementation, and describes current DOD computer network security procedures.

As an overview, the following "security algorithm" may be used to relate the various areas involved in network security. Although not quantifiable, the algorithm represents a method of viewing the required interaction between the various aspects of computer network security. The algorithm expresses security as a multiplicative function of the six components which are described in various security checklists.[16,25,43,59] The function, f, is expressed as:

$$S = f(P1 * O * P2 * A * C * E),$$

where:

> S is total system security,
> P1 is personnel security,
> O is organizational security,
> P2 is physical security,
> A is administrative security,
> C is communications security,
> E is EDP security.

Each element of the algorithm may be thought of as varying between 0 and some weighted value determined by the approving authority for site security, with 0 providing no security and the upper bound providing the maximum amount of security possible for the site. It is easily seen from the multiplicative nature of the algorithm that if any one area is totally deficient, there is no system security, and the less security that is provided in each area, the larger effect this deficit will have on the total system.

Current DOD Secure Computer Network Implementation Philosophy

DOD implementation of computer networks came about more as the result of necessity than of design. Although much design work went into the formation of the existing DOD computer networks, many of the networks were formed from hardware which was already installed and software which was in use for production work. Thanks to the constant DOD emphasis on standardization, most of the systems which were implemented had homogeneous hardware and at least a partially common set of systems and applications software. Unfortunately, this standardization did not extend outside the design of individual systems, so little standardization exists in the design and implementation of even systems which perform similar functions within the same branch of service of the DOD.

Examples of computer systems which were first implemented as individual sites with standard hardware and some standard software are the worldwide Military Command and Control System (WWMCCS), which uses Honeywell 6000-series computers and DEC PDP-11 series minicomputers; the Community On-line Intelligence Networking System (COINS), which is implemented on the DEC PDP-11 series; and the US Army Forces Command operations network and WWMCCS Entry System, which is a nationwide network of terminals and concentrators connected to the Honeywell 6000 computer at the US Army Forces Command headquarters in Atlanta, Georgia. This network may be selectively connected through a communications facility to the WWMCCS network.

Even these systems, however, were allowed the development of site-specific applications for their systems, both in operating system software and in applications software. Some systems, such as the US Army Tactical Fire Direction System (TACFIRE) and the prototype Division Level Data Entry System (DLDES) in use at Ft. Stewart, Georgia, were developed with network design as one of the design criteria, and software changes are limited to those promulgated at the system level; the users are allowed no site-specific modifications.

The prevailing network security philosophy in the DOD and the only one which can be certified for implementation involves the establishment of a benign environment system envelope which encompasses every portion of the network to be secured. All computer centers, every remote device connected to the network, all users, and all software must be protected at the level of classification established for the most highly classified portion of the network. All communications links in the network must be protected with approved communications encryption devices which meet the required level of classification. Some links in the system are super-encrypted for the protection of compartmented information. This super-encryption is strictly in the communications processes at present, although research is also being conducted in the use of data encryption techniques for this purpose.

Background for DOD Network Implementation

The DOD has several secure computer networks, but the configuration and methods of operation of most of them are classified, as they support the national intelligence missions of the various departments of the DOD. The Worldwide Military Command and Control Systems (WWMCCS), however, uses a computer network in support of the operational role of the DOD, and the configuration and much of the methods of operation of this network are unclassified and will be used in this report as an example of current DOD computer network security implementation.

As background, WWMCCS facilities around the world provide a means for the Joint Chiefs of Staff (JCS) to exercise daily control over deployed US military forces in both crisis and non-crisis situations. WWMCCS consists of over 35 Honeywell 6000-series computers located at sites throughout the world wherever a significant number of US forces are stationed. Most of these computers operate in a standalone mode, with information fed into them by manual means or by removable magnetic media which can be transported between sites. WWMCCS also includes an extensive communications network which is the prime means of control for the JCS. This communications network provides the redundant circuitry necessary to ensure constant control, and it is tested continuously to maintain its configuration.

In September 1971, the JCS[27] identified the need for ". . . faster and more accurate information flow in support of crisis management actions and for continuity of operations of the National Command Authorities . . ." The solution which was proposed for this need was a network of the computers which comprised the heart of the WWMCCS operation. A development plan[28] for this network was written in 1975, and a prototype network was designed which included three of the WWMCCs computers in the Washington, DC, area. This network was later extended to the locations shown in Figure 9-1, and two operational experiments were conducted in 1976. In July 1977 the JCS approved and validated the operational requirement for WWMCCS computer internetting, and the WWMCCS Intercomputer Network (WIN) was established. The WIN is a set of independent computer systems interconnected as shown in Figure 9-2. The network uses the ARPANET packet switching technology for handling intercomputer transactions. Each host computer in the system uses a communications front-end minicomputer to handle transactions with both local users and the interface message processor (IMP). The IMP provides the packet switching capability for the network, and a special configuration of the IMP in the Pentagon allows it to monitor and collect statistics on the entire network. The main trunks in the network, indicated by the numbered lines in Figure 9-2, are 50,000 bit-per-second commercially leased communications lines which are especially conditioned for data transmission. There is an ongoing effort to expand this network to include as many of the WWMCCS sites as possible, both in the continental United States and in the European and Pacific theaters of operation.

Network Security Procedures

The WWMCCS EDP System Security Officer Manual[59] describes all of the security measures to be taken in establishing the benign system envelope for the WIN. This section will use those measures to establish a reference framework for computer network security as it is currently implemented within the DOD.

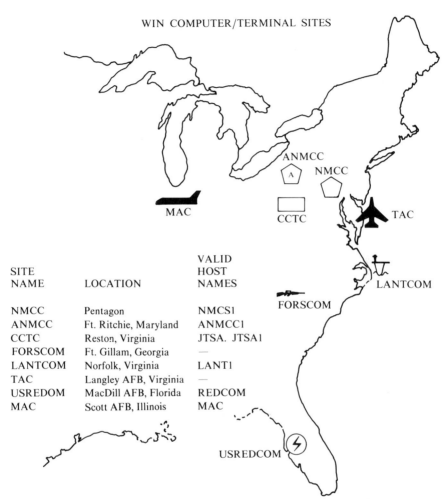

WIN COMPUTER/TERMINAL SITES

SITE NAME	LOCATION	VALID HOST NAMES
NMCC	Pentagon	NMCS1
ANMCC	Ft. Ritchie, Maryland	ANMCC1
CCTC	Reston, Virginia	JTSA. JTSA1
FORSCOM	Ft. Gillam, Georgia	—
LANTCOM	Norfolk, Virginia	LANT1
TAC	Langley AFB, Virginia	—
USREDOM	MacDill AFB, Florida	REDCOM
MAC	Scott AFB, Illinois	MAC

Fig. 9-1. WWMCCS computer node locations. (From WWMCCS İntercomputer Network User Handbook.[9])

Organizational and Administrative Security

Each computer site in the WWMCCS is required to have its own full-time WWMCCS EDP System Security Officer (WASSO), whose responsibility is to ensure that the WWMCCS security provisions are carried out at that site. The WASSO is not only the security manager for the site, but also the lead technician in establishing site security. The qualifications for appointment as a WASSO include security training, experience as a systems software programmer, experience in computer facility operations, and completion of the Honeywell GCOS (systems software) analysis course for the H6000 series computers. Each site which is remote from the central computer facility of a WWMCCS site is required to have

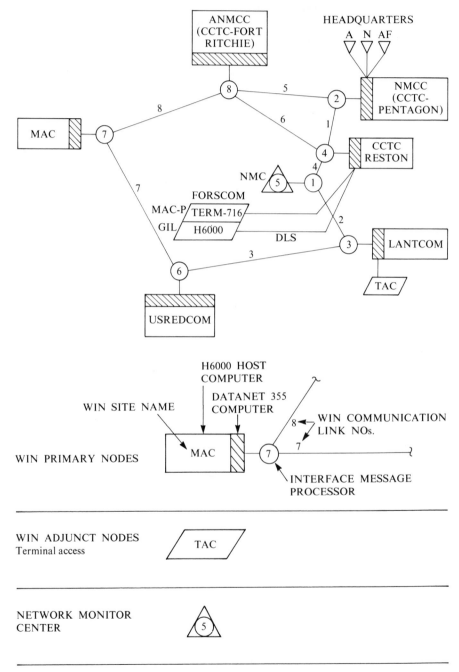

Fig. 9-2.   DOD computer network interconnection scheme.

an individual appointed who is responsible for the security of that site. Although this individual does not work directly for the site WASSO, he obtains all needed security guidance from the WASSO and deals directly with the WASSO on any security problems that might arise.

The creation, dissemination, control, and destruction of classified information within the DOD is regulated by a DOD-level directive[13] along with supplementary regulations published by each of the departments and agencies of DOD. The hierarchy of classification is promulgated in reference 13, and the department and agency regulations refine this directive and provide for compartmentation of information as needed. Special instructions for handling computer-generated classified material within the WWMCCS are contained in reference 59 and in similar documents for each of the DOD departments and agencies. Much of the guidance and part of the checklists provided in reference 59 have been incorporated into the other military services computer security documents.

Personnel Security

The DOD personnel security program is a long-established program which requires extensive background investigation before a security clearance can be granted. The WWMCCS benign environment is protected in this area by the requirement that individuals have a Top Secret security clearance before they can initiate a user account on any part of the WWMCCS. Physical access to any part of a WWMCCS computer facility, including remote terminal areas, requires a properly cleared escort if the individual requesting access does not have an adequately verified Top Secret clearance.

Physical Security

Physical security provisions for the WWMCCS provide a large portion of the benign environment which has been established. DOD-level security guidance[13] and WWMCCS regulation[59] specify physical security requirements, which include vault-type operations facilities, guards, access control lists, and alarms. Almost all of the physical security requirements discussed in references 16, 36, and 43 are implemented for the WWMCCS.

Communications Security

Communications security is established for the WWMCCS by communications encryption measures and regulation of compromising emanations. DOD approved communications security encryption devices are used on every link in the WIN which extends outside a physically secured area. Protected wireline distribution systems are used within the security control zone, and all communications facilities comply with established RED/BLACK separation requirements.[40] Encrypted and plain-text signals are electrically separated, and isolation devices in the facilities provide electrical isolation of even the encrypted signals until they have left the interface. Control and switching of all WIN computer assets and peripherals is accomplished by a small technical control facility established within the Top Secret control zone of the computer facility.

EDP Security

The GCOS III operating system used throughout the WWMCCS has been proven to be insecure from a penetration viewpoint,[8,34] but the benign environment which has been described previously protects the security of the system as a whole to the point that it may be certified for operation at the Top Secret level. Various security precautions taken from an operating system viewpoint also enhance the security of the system, but none of them are foolproof.

Some of these precautions[59] include assignment of unique system user identifications (USERID) and passwords; passwords of eight characters which are randomly generated; frequent changes of passwords; and an audit trail system which provides the system security personnel a valuable means to track user activity through the system. Unfortunately, this audit trail system is not real-time, but a system of checks and alarms to the security console of the system gives a real-time indication of arrests, such as system log-on violations, file access violations, and attempts to perform privileged functions.

Data encryption is not used at this time in the WWMCCS system. The operating system protection of files and programs provides sufficient isolation for normal users; and since all users are required to possess a Top Secret clearance, any inadvertent release of information would not result in a security compromise. The other reason that data encryption is not used within WWMCCS is that no DOD-certified method of encrypting data may yet be implemented at the Top Secret level.

COMPUTER NETWORK SECURITY RESEARCH

Current Secure Software Requirements

A large area of ongoing research concerns certifiably secure software and its uses in developing secure and trusted operating systems. Because of the emphasis on establishing multi-level security and thus being able to dispense with the benign environment or "system-high" concept of operating a secure EDP system, the DOD has expended large amounts of resources in the development of securable, certifiable software. The DOD Computer Security Initiative was established in 1978 by the Assistant Secretary of Defense for Communications, Command, Control and Intelligence (C3I) to achieve the widespread availability of trusted EDP systems for use within the DOD. Mr. Steven T. Walker, Office of the Assistant Secretary of Defense (C3I), described the DOD Computer Security Initiative in an address to the Second US Army Automation Security Workshop in September 1979.[57] He stressed that widespread availability implies the use of commercially developed trusted EDP systems wherever possible. He was careful to delineate between "trusted" and "secure" EDP systems, stating that the DOD already has secure EDP systems because of the benign environment established for them, but that the systems still could not be trusted to know who needs what information. In his address he reviewed the progress of the DOD Computer Security Initiative and described the current interaction with computer manufacturers and their progress in implementing trusted computer systems. He identified the three critical elements of the DOD Computer Security Initiative as:

1. The effective demonstration of the technology for building usable trusted EDP systems.
2. A mechanism for approval of trusted EDP systems instead of the ad hoc, case-by-case, independent system approval means presently used.
3. Vendor involvement in security development to spread the availability of trusted EDP systems.

He pointed out that today's approval methodology provided no technical assistance for the Designated Approving Authority (DAA) other than that available in his organization. Under the DOD Computer Security Initiative, certification techniques for design and implementation will be developed and a single, central, DOD "laboratory" will be designated as the technical approving authority. This laboratory will develop an "evaluated product list" of hardware and software to be furnished to the DAA, who may then apply site-specific threat and risk analyses to select the level of protection required. Walker pointed out that specifications for trusted EDP systems are still being defined as to levels of trust involved and operating environments to be designated. When these specifications are coordinated through the DOD and its departments and agencies, and are approved (tentative estimate is 1982), a single DOD agency will be designated or created to be the trusted EDP system laboratory. This agency would possibly be modeled after the Electromagnetic Communications Analysis Center (ECAC), which is the DOD agency providing coordination of electromagnetic frequency spectrum use for all agencies and departments of the DOD.

Security Kernel Development

The primary area of development for secure software is the security kernel approach. Steven Walker also has written extensively on this approach[56] and provided quite a strong background leading to its development. A chronology of the development of the security kernel and some of the interaction involved is shown in Figure 9-3. Walker's background material indicated that early research efforts (1968–1974) organized "Tiger Teams" to penetrate the access control mechanisms of existing operating systems. These teams succeeded in subverting every commercial operating system that they confronted. Evaluations of some of these penetrations may be found in references 4, 8, 20, 31, 33. One of the methodologies used in the penetrations is explained in reference 34. The research community was so concerned with the ease with which these systems could be broken that a major effort was organized to inform the public of the vulnerability of computer

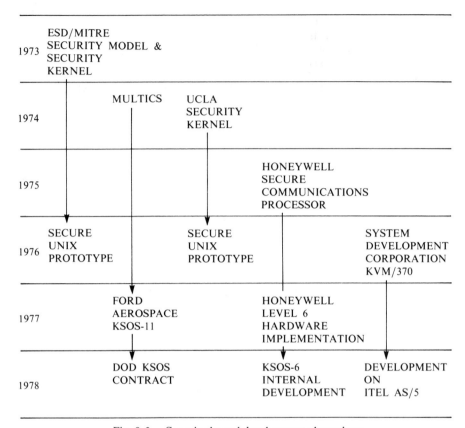

Fig. 9-3.   Security kernel development chronology.

systems. We believe that a large percentage of senior managers, both within the DOD and outside of it, are still unaware of the vulnerability of computer systems. As was stated in the first section of this chapter, computer system security is low except in the cases of computer systems which handle classified information, when they meet the standards of secure computer systems through the establishment of a benign environment.

Walker goes on to say that in the early 1970's the Air Force Electronic Systems Division (ESD) conducted in-depth analyses of the requirements for secure systems.[2] The concepts which emerged from their efforts are the basis for most major secure computer system developments. The basic concept is a Reference Monitor or Security Kernel which mediates the access of all active system elements (people or programs), referred to as subjects, to all system elements containing information (e.g., files and records), referred to as objects. A good technical description of this concept is provided in reference 35, and an example of a protection matrix within the kernel using this concept is in Figure 9-4. In the example, the protection matrix establishes privileges for User B, a systems software analyst, far in excess of those

OBJECTS / SUBJECTS	TIME SHARING SUB-SYSTEM	EDITOR	FILE A1	FILE B1
USER A	ENTER	ENTER	CREATE DELETE READ WRITE EXECUTE	EXECUTE
USER B	ENTER MODIFY	ENTER	READ WRITE EXECUTE	CREATE DELETE READ WRITE EXECUTE
EDITOR COMMAND MODULE	ENTER	READ		

Fig. 9-4. Protection matrix access diagram.

given to User A, an applications programmer. The protection matrix can also establish privileges for programs, such as the Editor Command module in the example, to ensure that they act only within the purview of their established limits. Matrices of this type are established for all subjects and all objects which must interact in the system, and they are contained within the security kernel to preserve their integrity. All of the security relevant decision-making functions within a conventional operating system are collected into a small, primitive but complete operating system known as the security kernel. The three essential characteristics of this kernel are:

1. That it be complete (i.e., that all accesses of all subjects to all objects be checked by the kernel).
2. That it be isolated (i.e., that the code that comprises the kernel be protected from modification or interference by any other software within the system).
3. That it be correct (i.e., that it perform the function for which it was intended and no other function).

The reference monitor system and the formal methodology employed in this development were described in a 1978 Congressional report submitted by the General Accounting Office.[10] Since these Air Force studies were completed, considerable effort has gone into building security kernels for various systems. The reference monitor concept was the basis for work by Massachusetts Institute of Technology, the MITRE Corporation and Honeywell Information Systems in restructuring the MULTICS operating system.[52] MITRE and UCLA have built prototype security kernels for the Digital Equipment PDP-11 minicomputer system.[30,60] System Development Corporation (SDC) is at this time building a security kernel for the IBM VM370 operating system.[22]

Walker further states that a difficult challenge for computer security researchers has been uncovering how to demonstrate secure systems concepts effectively. One way is to build a new operating system from scratch, but development of this type with all the necessary support tools is a complex and expensive operation, and often too difficult for limited computer security research budgets. The alternative approach of patching flaws in an existing system to provide add-on security (the "patch and pray" methodology, as described by DeLashmutt) is known to be unsuccessful, with patches often causing more flaws than they correct.

The ideal solution would be to create a new secure operating system with the external appearance of an existing operating system so that the existing support software and applications programs could be used without modification. The secure operating system would be a completely new system but it would emulate the external characteristics of the existing operating system. Walker maintains that the most difficult aspect of this approach is finding an operating system to emulate in which the user interface will not be severely altered by the process of creating the secure system. Any primitive user functions on a system which cannot be performed in a secure manner must be eliminated or restricted in the secure version of the system, and these changes alter the compatibility of the operating system with its environment. Most operating systems today would be so altered in a secure version that compatibility would not exist, but the emulator approach was still considered to be the most effective if it were possible to find an operating system which would remain compatible after being secured.

After examining a wide range of operating systems, DOD researchers selected the UNIX operating system, which was developed by the Bell Laboratory at Murray Hill, New Jersey, in the early 1970s.[46] UNIX is an interactive system with a simple, unified design. This efficient system has widespread use within the Bell System, and Western Electric also offers licenses for non-Bell System users, so there is a growing community of UNIX users in university and commercial environments. The main reason for selection of the UNIX operating system was its characteristic of maintaining its internal data structures in a manner which was transparent to user programs, thus allowing almost complete restructuring of the system for security while maintaining its external characteristics. In 1976, both UCLA and MITRE adapted their security kernels to support a prototype secure operating system which is compatible with UNIX support software and application programs, and both systems use the reference monitor concept within different architectures.

DOD Kernelized Secure Operating System (DOD KSOS)

Based upon the preceding research background, the DOD initiated an effort in 1977 to design and implement a production quality, certifiably secure operating system which would emulate the UNIX system. This effort is entitled the DOD Kernelized Secure Operating System (DOD KSOS), and a chart of the development to date is contained in Figure 9-5.

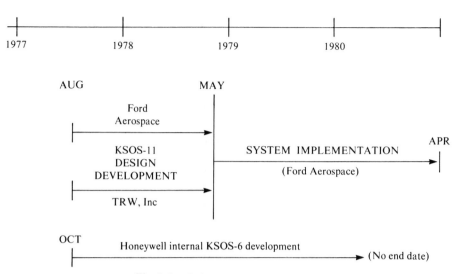

Fig. 9-5. DOD KSOS development.

The decision to emulate the UNIX system in DOD KSOS reflected the facts that UNIX has a widespread installed computer base on the PDP-11 series of computers and that Bell Laboratories as well as other manufacturers are in the process of implementing UNIX on hardware other than the PDP-11, which will make its use even more widespread. The major deliverable product at the end of the Design Phase of the DOD KSOS was a detailed system level specification. This specification contains functional descriptions of each module of the security kernel and the operating system, and could be used to direct the efforts of other manufacturers in the development of the DOD KSOS on other hardware. As shown in Figure 9-5, the implementation phase contract for the DOD KSOS was awarded to the Ford Aerospace and Communications Corporation in May 1978.

It should be pointed out that the actual UNIX software from Bell Laboratories will not be used in the development of the DOD KSOS, but that the operating systems which are developed will interface with all support software and application programs currently in use with UNIX.

Applications Envisioned for the DOD KSOS

The DOD KSOS will fulfill a number of requirements for increased security in DOD ADP systems. Three general classes of applications are presently envisioned by Walker.[56]

The first application will enable the implementation of multi-level security links between EDP systems, something which has not been substantially accomplished to date. The DOD KSOS is used in what is termed a Guard mode, as shown in Figure 9-6. Two commercially available, untrusted data management systems,

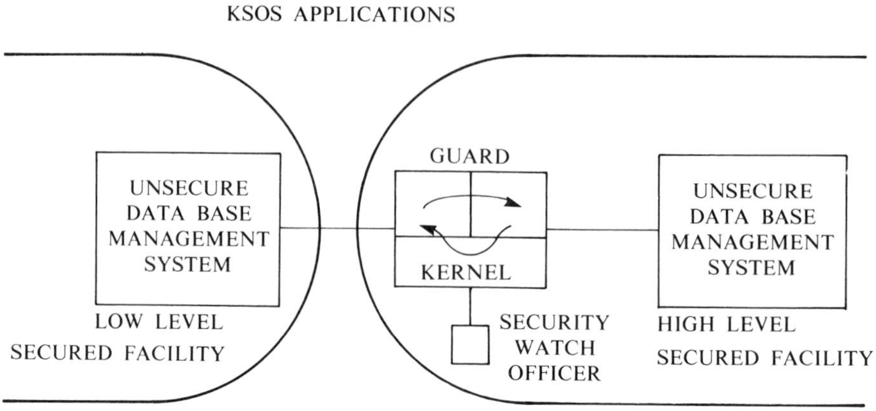

KSOS APPLICATIONS

Fig. 9-6.   DOD KSOS used in Guard mode.   (From Walker.[56])

each operating at a different security level, are connected through a Guard, which is a DOD KSOS based security filter.   Queries from the lower level system which might require answers containing a high security classification have the replies sanitized by either operators or software on the Guard system.   Before any information is passed to the system with the lower security level, it is presented to the Security Watch Officer for a determination of the appropriate classification of the reply.   If the sanitized classification is releasable to the lower-level system, the reply is forwarded; if not, it is returned for further sanitization.

The functions of the Guard mode are now being performed manually, with editing assistance from computer systems, at some of the compartmented intelligence activities of the DOD.   The KSOS will enable more of these sanitization functions to be automated, thus relieving the SWO of some of the time-consuming sanitization duties and allowing more time for proper inspection of the outgoing traffic.   Although this is a relatively simple application of the KSOS, it will fill a very useful function for the DOD and will have widespread application.

The second application of the DOD KSOS is proposed for use as a secure network front-end (NFE),[56] as shown in Figure 9-7.   The DOD is rapidly expanding its use of computer networks, and many of the networks which are being built require the use of untrusted host computers.   In accordance with current network design philosophy, much of the network protocol and terminal access functions are being moved from the host machine to a smaller NFE.   As was described for the WWMCCS EDP system, a benign environment must be established for the entire computer network, and this undertaking can be very expensive as well as possibly precluding the establishment of some needed interconnections in the network. Walker proposes that NFE's be implemented as KSOS's and that the network be established as secure interconnection of subnetworks, each operating at its own security level.[56]   As was stated by Walker, "A set of cooperating secure network frontends could provide a significant improvement to today's system high operating environment with no change required to large systems."

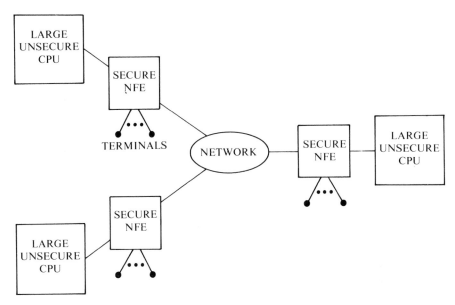

Fig. 9-7.   DOD KSOS used as a network front end.   (From Walker.[56])

The DOD's multitude of message handling systems provides a third very useful application for the DOD KSOS.   A characteristic which is common to all of the DOD message handling systems is the requirement for internal integrity with the systems.   Security constraints in the handling of some highly classified information may preclude the transmission of this information over a message handling system because all of the organizations connected by the system do not have the complete set of security accesses necessary for receipt of the information.   This problem has led to proliferation of special-purpose message handling systems to serve different users and to the denial of ready access to needed information by an organization not connected to the proper message handling system.   If the access isolation mechanisms of the DOD KSOS could be applied to the design of message handling systems, message sources with different security levels could be integrated into a single message handling environment with enough isolation guaranteed to protect the sensitive information involved.

With the identification of the preceding applications, interest in the DOD KSOS increased in the computer manufacturing community.   In addition to Ford Aerospace, which had the DOD development contract, Honeywell Avionics Division initiated an internally funded project called KSOS-6, and Systems Development Corporation entered their Kernelized Virtual Machine/370 (KVM/370) into consideration as a security mechanism for the DOD, thus partially realizing one of Walker's DOD Computer Security Initiative goals, that of manufacturer involvement.   Other efforts which support the DOD Computer Security Initiative are verification and validation standards for software,[55] software specification languages,[3,37,41,42] and software proving mechanisms.[37,41,42] These developments will not be addressed in this chapter.

Ford Aerospace KSOS-11 Development

Dr. E. J. McCauley of Ford Aerospace defines the long-term goal of the Ford Aerospace KSOS-11 effort as the development of a commercially viable operating system for the DEC PDP-11/70, which (1) is compatible with the Bell Laboratories UNIX operating system, (2) is capable of efficiency comparable to that of the standard UNIX, (3) enforces multilevel security and integrity, and (4) is demonstrably secure.

As described in the KSOS Executive Summary,[38] the basic design of KSOS-11 consists of a Kernel that supports multilevel security, the trusted Non-Kernel Security Related Software which, though outside of the Kernel, is trusted to deviate from the multi-level security policy to provide critical system functions, an Emulator that provides UNIX support and User interface, and the untrusted Non-Kernel

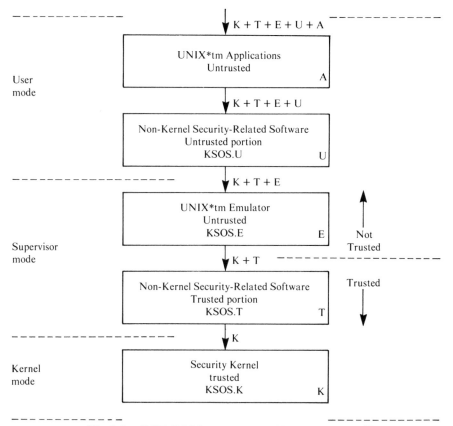

Fig. 9-8.   DOD KSOS components.   (From Neumann.[41])

Security Related Software, which provides user services such as secure mail and output spooling. A block diagram of the KSOS design is shown in Figure 9-8. The diagram is hierarchical in that a given design level is permitted to depend only on lower design levels. , Note that the design has three modes of operation: the User mode, the Supervisor mode, and the Kernel mode; and that the Supervisor mode is split between trusted and non-trusted software. This arrangement allows the UNIX Emulator to be nontrusted but to make calls on the Kernel and the Non-Kernel Security Related software.

Honeywell KSOS-6 Development

Honeywell Information Systems, Inc., is developing what DOD representatives are calling KSOS-6, based on the Honeywell Level 6 series of computers. The Honeywell name for this internally funded development project is "Secure Communications Processor" (SCOMP). The Honeywell Level 6 hardware used for the project has an add-on hardware component called the Security Protection Module (SPM), and the software consists of a security kernel and a UNIX emulator.

Honeywell has not specified dates for completion of the software development, but did state that software development was lagging hardware development "somewhat." [32] The formal specification for the kernel is being written in Stanford Research Institute's SPECIAL, and the detailed design and coding of the program will be done in UCLA PASCAL. The preliminary design of the UNIX emulator is complete and the emulator will be coded in Bell Laboratory's C language, as UNIX itself is, because the Level 6 computer already has a C compiler.

ASSESSMENT

Present DOD Security Environment

The DOD has the capability to establish secure computer systems and to combine those systems into a certifiably secure network at almost any classification level that is required. Any data that are transferred between systems with different levels of protection must be manually sanitized before release, and the volume of data that must be transferred is growing rapidly. The present secure network capability does not satisfy all operational requirements, because the establishment of a benign environment as a total system or network envelope is both expensive to accomplish and limited in its dissemination of needed information.

As was pointed out in the preceding section, "secure" does not connote "trusted" in the sense that the system can infallibly direct the information flow to the required users with no possibility of outside interference with or change to the flow methodology. What is needed is a multi-level security system which can be certified for operation at the highest, most compartmented levels of classification, yet have the facility to allow access by users with low-level security clearances. A multi-level security system has been designed and certified by the US Air Force for use at the USAF Data Services Center in the Pentagon,[11] but none of the DOD intelligence agencies will certify the Air Force approach as acceptable for processing compartmented intelligence data, because the system will not pass the rigorous and exhaustive testing required to the wide range of classifications involved.

DOD Network Communications Environment

DOD communications encryption technology is very good at present. Both link-by-link and total end-to-end circuit encryption can be available in existing communications systems, and the level of protection provided by the encryption systems is adequate to protect even the most sensitive of compartmented information. Data encryption, however, is still an unsolved problem. Although many data encryption algorithms have been proposed and some of them are quite good, certification and approval for use in functions requiring access to compartmented information is still being withheld because of the lack of ability in the DOD to certify any software system, which is what the data encryption algorithms are. Implementation of a data encryption algorithm in hardware with a changeable key similar to that used on the communications circuits is one solution, but a very expensive one in terms of implementation. A separate piece of hardware would have to be provided per user or possibly per file on the computer system, depending on the sensitivity of the information to be protected. If a technique that can prove and therefore can certify software is developed, data encryption will quickly become an everyday part of the implementation of secure DOD computer systems and networks.

DOD Secure Operating System Research

The kernelized subsystem approach to secure operating system development has been widely touted as the solution to operating system software multi-level security problems.[5,22,30,32,39,52,56,60] The basic concept, as explained in the previous section entitled DOD Implementation of Network Security, is sound, but as in the development of data encryption mechanisms, the problem of proving that a program does exactly what it is supposed to do and nothing more has prevented any secure software from being certified for use with highly sensitive information. Ford Aerospace has a delivery date of April 1980 for the KSOS-11 secure operating system to selected test sites, and this is with a system which still has had no formal proof methodology applied to the actual code of the software. They have been able to certify the design of the system,[39] which is a positive step toward a certifiable system, but the proof of the code is still at least 3 years away.[48]

The applications planned for the DOD KSOS appear to be in some respects incompletely developed. The Guard application, described previously, is a valid

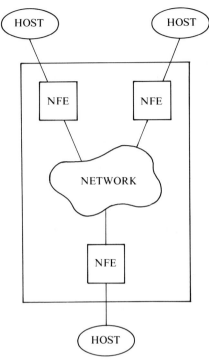

Fig. 9-9.   Security environment using network front ends only.   (From Hein.[23])

automated adaptation of an existing technique which will provide significant security improvements to links between two systems with differing security levels.
The network front-end concept, however, with its "set of cooperating secure network
front ends" [56] and claim of improvement to the "system-high" or benign environment appears to be incomplete.   The security environment established as shown
within the dotted line in Figure 9-9 implies the establishment of some network
operating system in which each network front end (NFE) is cognizant of the security
requirements of each of the hosts—a most complicated process in a network of any
size.

One alternative for reduction in the size of the workload required for the NFE
is the proposed network shown in Figure 9-10.   A security kernel would be added
to each host, and the workload required for each NFE in the network would be
shared with the security kernel.   If a Guard application were necessary for the host
to operate effectively in a multilevel security environment, it could be incorporated
into the host kernel, and the kernel would also enhance the network security by its
interface with the NFE's.   The NFE's could then provide network security functions while the host security kernel effectively screened the host environment from
the network.

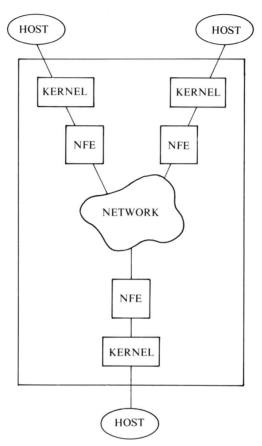

Fig. 9-10.   Security environment using security kernels and network front ends.

A second alternative presupposes the development of a data encryption algorithm which is certifiable by the DOD intelligence agencies.   None to date have certified any of the existing data encryption techniques as being secure and trusted enough to handle compartmented intelligence data.   FIPS Publication 46 states that the DES will be used by Federal departments and agencies when the data to be encrypted ". . . is not classified according to the National Security Act of 1947 . . . or the Atomic Energy Act of 1954 . . .".[19]   This effectively precludes the use of the DES in any DOD computer network where network computer security is badly needed at present.   This second alternative is described by Heinrich,[23] while Figure 9-11 illustrates the technique.   Heinrich's approach uses the NBS Data Encryption Standard (DES) for data encryption, but describes the network security center concept so that any certifiable data encryption standard could be used.

The basis for the concept is the authentication which is enforced by use of the data encryption algorithm.   The network security center as shown in Figure 9-10

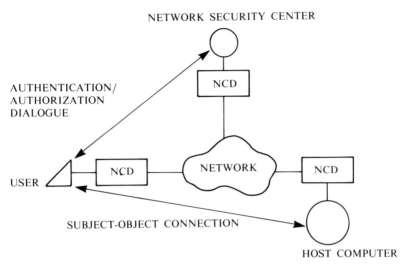

Fig. 9-11.   Network security center concept.   (From Hein.[23])

is the central repository for the keys to the data encryption system, and the NSC also provides network access control and collects audit trail data for the network security functions.   In the example given by Heinrich and illustrated in Figure 9-11, each user and host in the network is connected through a data encryption device called a network cryptographic device (NCD), which is remotely keyed from the NSC.   The NCD is initially keyed so that the user or host may communicate only with the NSC, which performs network authentication and authorization checking prior to allowing entry into the network.   After a user or host is checked, connection is established to the desired location or the requestor is informed that the connection cannot be made and the attempt is logged as a security incident by the NSC.

The subnetworks connected to each host are kept logically isolated, even though they share a common communications net, because the NSC allows communication only between NCD's which have been given access permission to other NCD's.   If additional security were required or if the subnetworks were very large, a concept similar to that shown in Figure 9-12 could be established, with each subnetwork having its own NSC and these NSC's providing any cooperation required for internetting between hosts.

Other Unresolved Security Issues

Several unresolved issues of computer network security were raised at the Second US Army Automation Security Workshop and these problems need research support for solution.   Dr. Willis Ware of the Rand Corporation, in his keynote address to the Workshop, stated that no comprehensive DOD plan is available to integrate the solutions being found to computer network security.   The DOD Se-

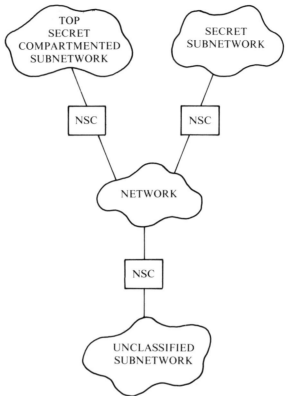

Fig. 9-12.   Compartmentation with network security centers (NSC).   (From Hein.[23])

curity Initiative is a step in the right direction, but Dr. Ware felt that more positive effort was needed in this area.   Dr. Ware also brought up the problem of hardware certification.   Once the program proving enigma is solved and the software does what it is supposed to do and nothing more, the hardware needs to be tested and certified for the same thing.   Presently, some hardware devices can be "spoofed" into performing actions that they are not supposed to perform, and this problem must be solved before a totally trusted system can be devised.

The evolution of trusted software and hardware will also place special restraints on operating procedures at computer installations.   Maintenance procedures will have to be certified or post-maintenance certification tests will have to be designed to re-verify the system, and installation of new hardware will have to be done from the perspective of integrating the hardware into the security design of the total system.

Conclusions

Because of the critical need for secure operating systems and the rapid and voluminous proliferation of computer systems and networks, the DOD began research into secure operating systems before most of the industry and before much of the academic community. The research programs in secure operating systems sponsored by the DOD are on the forefront of research in this field, and the DOD is making a concerted effort to get the computer manufacturing community much more heavily involved in computer security. This involvement effort is slowly paying off as more manufacturers initiate internal computer security development programs. Secure operating systems have not been successfully implemented to date, but they are slowly becoming a reality. The current trends in hardware improvements will help the effort as more and more software functions become implemented cost-effectively in hardware form. Application of secure operating systems will be limited at first until the systems are certified and accredited.

The "hand-waving" and rationalization that most vendors offer with respect to program proving cannot be allowed to continue. If software is ever to be able to be certified as secure, it must be mathematically provable. Efforts in this area should be emphasized and accelerated, the goal being the development of proof techniques which can be automated and which are inextricably combined with design techniques so that design and proof proceed simultaneously. If a proof does not check, the design must be further decomposed or altered until the proof does check. When Dr. Ware gave his keynote address to the Second US Army Automation Workshop, he also stated the difficulty of the software certification effort: "It isn't clear whether the country has the intellectual capital to do the job more than once." Since the DOD is presently driving the effort, the leader in the field by default may well be the DOD, with industry and other users adapting DOD secure operating system developments as needed.

REFERENCES

1. Abrams, M. D., et al.: Tutorial on Computer Integrity and Security. Long Beach, CA., IEEE Computer Society, 1977. This tutorial and the readings associated with it provide a practical background to the state of the art in computer security. Included is a section specifically addressing network security.
2. Anderson, J. P.: Planning Study, Computer Security Technology Planning Study, Vol. 1. US Air Force Electronic Systems Division, Report No. ESD-TR-73-51-1, October 1972. A study recommending research needed to provide secure ADP systems for command and control applications; basis for much of the secure O/S work.
3. Anderson, E. R.: Standards for Specification Languages. Paper presented at the Second US Army Automation Security Workshop, September 1979. This paper reviews a number of desirable specification language properties and proposes them as standards. It suggests that for implementation verification applications, a verifiable implementation language be extended to or designed with a matching specification language. It will be included in the proceedings of the Workshop.
4. Attanasio, C. R.: Operating System Architecture and Integrity. IBM Data Security Forum, September 1974. This paper outlines the strengths and weaknesses of the IBM OS/MVT and the VM/370 operating systems through a discussion of penetrations of these systems.

5. Beach, M. H.: Computer Security for ASSIST. Master's thesis, Ft. Leavenworth, Kansas, US Army Command and General Staff College, June 1977. A brief description of the Army Standard System for Intelligence Support Terminals (ASSIST) and the application of current computer security research to it.
6. Biba, K. J.: Integrity Considerations for Secure Computer Systems. Report by the Mitre Corp. for ESD, AFSC, Hanscom AFB, Ma., Report No. ESD-TR-76-372, April 1977. This report examines computer system integrity in light of current operating system mechanisms. It identifies sources and types of threats and examines several integrity policies.
7. Bushkin, A. A., and Schaen, S. I.: The Privacy Act of 1974: A Reference Manual for Compliance. Santa Monica, California, System Development Corporation, 1976. This publication provides a reference for implementation of the Privacy Act. It has guidelines for privacy implementation on computerized information systems, and it addresses the problems involved in accidental or intentional violation of the act.
8. Carlstedt, J., Bisbey, R., and Popek, G.: Pattern Directed Protection Evaluation. Information Sciences Institute, Univ. of Southern California, June 1975 (NTIS AD-A012 474). This paper develops patterns of error types in operating systems based on errors found in OS/360, GCOS, MULTICS, TENEX, and EXEC-8 operating systems.
9. Worldwide Military Command and Control System Intercomputer Network User Handbook, Vol. 1. The Pentagon, Washington, DC. Defense Communications Agency, CCTC (Code C400).
10. Comptroller General: Report to the Congress of the United States, Challenges of Protecting Personal Information in an Expanding Federal Computer Network Environment, April 1978.
11. Davis, R. C.: A Security Compliance Study of the Air Force Data Services Center MULTICS System. Report by the Mitre Corp. for ESD, Hanscom AFB, Massachusetts, AFSC, Report No. ESD-TR-76-165, Dec. 1976. This report by the MITRE Corporation supports claims that the MULTICS operating system at the US Air Force Data Services Center complies with the multi-level security requirements of DOD 5200.28-M.
12. Denning, D. E., and Denning, P. J.: Certification of Programs for Secure Information Flow, CACM *20*(7): 504, 1977. Presents a certification mechanism for verifying the secure flow of information through a program.
13. *DOD 5200.28-M EDP Security Manual,* published by Department of Defense, Jan. 1973.
14. Ekanadham, K., and Bernstein, A. J.: Conditional Capabilities. IEEE Transactions on Software Engineering *SE-5*(5): 458, 1979. This paper considers protection in capability-based operating systems and proposes the concept of a conditional capability, on which other security features can be built.
15. Feiertag, R. J., Levitt, K. N., and Robinson, L.: Proving Multilevel Security of a System Design. Proceedings of the Sixth ACM Symposium on Operating Systems Principles, November 1977. This paper presents a technique for accomplishing the security proof for the design of a multi-level security system. It does not approach the proof of the actual programs involved in implementing a secure system.
16. Federal Information Processing Standards Publication 31. Guidelines for Automatic Data Processing Physical Security and Risk Management, US Dept. of Commerce, NBS, June 1974.
17. Federal Information Processing Standards Publication 41. Computer Security Guidelines for Implementing the Privacy Act of 1974. US Dept. of Commerce, NBS, May 1975. Provides a set of guidelines for selecting safeguards for protecting personal information in automated information systems.
18. Federal Information Processing Standards Publication 39. Glossary for Computer Systems Security, US Dept. of Commerce, NBS, February 1976. Contains a vocab-

ulary of terms related to privacy and computer systems security derived from diverse sources and refined by FIPS Task Group 15 (Computer Systems Security).

19. Federal Information Processing Standards Publication 46. Data Encryption Standards, US Dept. of Commerce, NBS, January 1977. This publication provides a description of the data encryption standard which is to be used by almost all Federal departments and agencies.

20. Flato, L.: Navy Sinks 1108. Computer Decisions *8*(7): 35, 1976. This article provides a brief review of a US Navy penetration of the EXEC III operating system on the UNIVAC 1108 computer.

21. Gasser, M., Ames, S. R., and Chmura, L. J.: Test Procedures for MULTICS Security Enhancements. Report by the Mitre Corp. for ESD, Hanscom AFB, Massachusetts, AFSC, Dec. 1976. This report describes actual procedures used to test a US Air Force MULTICS system. The majority of the report is listings and actual test documentation.

22. Gold, B., et al.: VM370 Security Retrofit Program. Proceedings of ACM Conference, October 1977. This paper gives an overview of the Kernelized VM/370 project and discusses how the security flaws discovered in previous penetrations can be overcome.

23. Heinrich, F.: The Network Security Center: A System Level Approach to Computer Network Security. NBS Special Publication 500-21, Volume 2. Washington, DC, Dept. of Commerce, January 1978. This publication provides a tutorial on an approach for achieving computer network security using a data encryption methodology coupled with a network security center computer to manage all network security.

24. Hemphill, C. F., and Hemphill, J. M.: Security Procedures for Computer Systems. Homewood, Illinois, Dow Jones-Irwin, 1973. Security text for managers with no detailed knowledge of computer systems. Covers physical, organizational, and parts of ADP security, with security checklists in each area covered.

25. Hoffman, L. J.: Modern Methods for Computer Security and Privacy. Englewood Cliffs, New Jersey, Prentice-Hall Inc., 1977. This book is a text on computer security which provides up-to-date coverage of current security technology. The book presents its material in a technical manner and assumes a basic reader knowledge of computer hardware and software.

26. Hsiao, D. K., Kerr, D. S., and Madnick, S. E.: Computer Security. ACM Monograph Series, New York, San Francisco, and London, Academic Press, 1979. This book was subsidized by the Office of Naval Research and constitutes an up-to-date survey of research in computer security. It is not written at a high technical level, and it presents excellent annotated bibliographies at the end of each chapter.

27. Joint Chiefs of Staff Memorandum 593-71: Research, Development, Test and Evaluation Program in support of the Worldwide Military Command and Control System (U), September 7, 1971. This document states the objectives of the RDT&E program in support of WWMCCS ADP program and establishes the need for an intercomputer network.

28. Joint Chiefs of Staff Memorandum 286-75: Prototype WWMCCS Intercomputer Network Development Plan, July 7, 1975. This document provides a plan for the technical development of the intercomputer network and for its test and evaluation in a user environment.

29. Jones, A. K.: Protection Mechanisms and the Enforcement of Security Policies. Lecture Notes in Computer Science: Operating Systems, Berlin, Heidelberg, New York, Springer-Verlag, 1978, pp. 228–250. This set of notes discusses information control and access control policies and describes protection mechanisms used to provide security for them. It assumes a basic knowledge of computer operating systems.

30. Kampe, M., and Popek, G.: The UCLA Data Secure UNIX Operating System, UCLA, 1977.

31. Karger, P. A., and Schell, R. R.: MULTICS Security Evaluation: Vulnerability

Analysis. Report for ESD, Hanscom AFB, Massachusetts, AFSC, Jun. 1974. This report gives the results of penetrations of a US Air Force MULTICS system.
32. Kert, M.: Secure Communications Processor (SCOMP). Paper presented at the Second US Army Automation Security Workshop, September 1979. This presentation covered a brief history of the SCOMP project, described the SCOMP hardware, and summarized the status of the project development. It will be included in the proceedings of the workshop.
33. Lackey, R. D.: Penetration of Computer Systems—An Overview. The Honeywell Computer Journal 8(2): 81, 1974. This paper provides a taxonomy of penetration techniques and recommends measures that should be taken to secure computer systems.
34. Linde, R. R.: Operating Systems Penetration. AFIPS Conference Proceedings 44: 361, 1975. This paper explains the Flaw Hypothesis Methodology used in computer system penetrations and describes some basic vulnerabilities of operating systems. It includes some of the specific attack methods used on operating systems.
35. Linden, T. A.: Operating System Structures to Support Security and Reliable Software. NBS Technical Note 919, US Dept. of Commerce, National Bureau of Standards, August 1976. This survey describes capability-based addressing as used to implement secure software modules. It assumes a general knowledge of operating systems concepts on the part of the reader.
36. Martin, J.: Security, Accuracy, and Privacy in Computer Systems. Englewood Cliffs, New Jersey, Prentice-Hall, Inc., 1973. A good introduction to security subjects and an excellent reference for physical and organizational security. Some of the operating systems material is out of date, but the book contains extensive security checklists.
37. Mathieu, H. F.: The GYPSY Software Design and Verification System. Proceedings of the First US Army Automation Security Workshop, December 1978. This paper outlines the development of the GYPSY specification language and describes some of the features of the language.
38. McCauley, E. J.: KSOS Executive Summary. Proceedings of the First US Army Automation Security Workshop, December 1978. This paper provides a summary of the Progress in Phase I of the KSOS development by Ford Aerospace and its subcontractor SRI International and outlines the plans for Phase II work.
39. McCauley, E. J.: Status of the KSOS Effort. Paper presented at the Second US Army Automation Security Workshop, September 1979. This presentation covers the status to date of the Phase II (implementation) work on KSOS and presents efforts at program verification. It will be included in the proceedings of the Workshop.
40. Military Handbook (MILHDBK) 232: RED/BLACK Engineering—Installation Criteria. Washington, DC, Defense Communications Agency, July 1975. This Confidential document outlines the measures to be taken to prevent electrical crossover of classified information in communications facilities.
41. Neumann, P. G.: A Position Paper on Attaining Secure Systems: A Summary of A Methodology and its Supporting Tools. Proceedings of the First US Army Automation Security Workshop, December 1978. This paper provides a summary of HDM and describes its use in development of secure operating systems.
42. Neumann, P. G.: A Second Position Paper on the Attainment of Secure Systems: Recent Advances in the State of the Art. Paper presented at the Second US Army Automation Security Workshop, September 1979. This presentation outlines SRI's advances in automated development tools and proposed needs for further research into program verification techniques. It will be included in the proceedings of the Workshop.
43. Patrick, R. B. (Ed.): AFIPS System Review Manual on Security. Montvale, New Jersey, AFIPS Press, 1974. The results of a 2-year study, it consists of a set of guides in specific computer security areas (e.g., physical, administrative, and personnel) as

well as extensive, detailed checklists in each area. A definite aid to the manager or supervisor in establishing a security program.

44. Popek, G. J., and Kline, C. S.: Design Issues for Secure Computer Networks. Lecture Notes in Computer Science: Operating Systems, Berlin, Heidelberg, and New York, Springer-Verlag, 1978, pp. 517–546. This section of notes describes the design problems and alternatives available for secure networks, discusses network use with respect to data security, and provides a discussion of the use of encryption in a network. It assumes a basic knowledge of computer operating systems.

45. Public Law 93-579: The Privacy Act of 1974. 93rd Congress, S.3418, December 31, 1974. This is the actual text of the law as passed by the Congress.

46. Ritchie, D., and Thompson, K.: The UNIX Timesharing System. CACM, *17*(7): 365, 1974. This paper covers implementation of the UNIX file system and the user command interface with the system.

47. Robinson, L., and Levitt, K.: Proof Techniques for Heirarchically Structured Programs. CACM *20*(4): 271, 1977. This paper details a method for describing and structuring programs which simplifies program proving. Only manual proofs are outlined, but the methods used may be applied to automated proof techniques.

48. Robinson, L.: HDM—Command and Staff Overview. Technical Report by SRI International for Naval Ocean Systems Center, February 1978. This report provides a description of HDM suitable for managers or higher-level executives who are planning to use HDM for development projects.

49. Roubine, O., and Robinson, L.: The SPECIAL Reference Manual. SRI International, January 1977.

50. Rzepka, W. E.: Considerations in the Design of a Secure Data Base Management System. Report by the USAF Rome Air Development Center, Griffiss AFB, NY, Report No. RADC-TR-77-9, Mar. 1977. This report covers problems which arise in DBMS design and operation because of security requirements placed on the system.

51. Saltzer, J. H.: Protection and the Control of Information Sharing in MULTICS. CACM *17*(7): July, 1974. This paper covers the information transfer control mechanisms of MULTICS and discusses vulnerabilities in the MULTICS protection mechanisms.

52. Schroeder, M., Clark, D., and Saltzer, J.: The MULTICS Kernel Design. Proceedings of the Sixth ACM Symposium on Operating Systems Principles, November 1977. This paper summarizes the result of the MULTICS Kernel design project and reports on the conclusions drawn from the project. The project was terminated before formal specifications for a new security kernel could be finished.

53. Schwartz, M.: Computer Communication Network Design and Analysis. Englewood Cliffs, New Jersey, Prentice-Hall, Inc., 1977. This book is oriented primarily toward communications network design, but the author addresses computer networks. Written in technical terms, the book presupposes only a knowledge of basic probability theory on the part of the reader and provides explanations and examples for the concepts presented.

54. US Senate: Computer Security in Federal Programs. Report prepared by the Committee on Government Operations, Feb. 1977.

55. Short, G. E.: Outstanding Issues in Certification and Accreditation. Paper presented at the Second US Army Automation Security Workshop, September 1979. This presentation summarizes the unsolved issues facing the DOD and the computer community in general concerning the certification/accreditation of secure, trusted EDP systems. It will be included in the proceedings of the Workshop.

56. Walker, S. T.: The Advent of Secure Computer Operating Systems. Proceedings of the First US Army Automation Security Workshop, December 1978. This paper outlines the development of the DOD KSOS effort, and describes a technology transfer program to foster the development of trusted software by computer manufacturers.

57. Walker, S. T.: DOD Computer Security Initiative. Paper presented at the Second US Army Automation Security Workshop, September 1979. This presentation describes the Initiative, reviews its progress with emphasis on the involvement of computer manufacturers in the development of trusted software. It will be included in the proceedings of the Workshop.
58. Ware, W. H.: Keynote address to the Second US Army Automation Security Workshop, September 1979.
59. *WWMCCS ADP System Security Officer's (WASSO) Manual,* Joint Chiefs of Staff Secretary's Memorandum 635-77, 25 July 1977. This document is the security "bible" for the WWMCCS computer network. It provides extremely comprehensive coverage of security requirements, and has been the model for computer security implementation documents in many of the departments and agencies of the DOD.
60. Woodward, J., and Nibaldi, G.: A Kernel Based Secure UNIX Design. The MITRE Corporation, November 1977.
61. Worldwide Military Command and Control System (WWMCCS) Intercomputer Network (WIN) User's Guide. Defense Communications Agency Command Control Technical Center, Mar. 1977.
62. Worldwide Military Command and Control System (WWMCCS) Intercomputer Network (WIN) Programmer's Guide. Reston, Virginia, Defense Communications Agency Command Control Technical Center, July 1977.

Chapter 10

THE FEDERAL AVIATION ADMINISTRATION COMPUTER SECURITY PROGRAM

Lynn McNulty

Federal Aviation Administration, Washington, D.C.

The experiences of the Federal Aviation Administration (FAA) in developing and implementing a comprehensive computer security program provide insight into the problems that civil agencies of the Federal government have encountered in addressing the complex security issues resulting from the large-scale use of computers to perform essential administrative and operational functions. However, the FAA experience is also somewhat different from that of other civil agencies in that the FAA uses computers extensively to perform a unique function, the real-time control of aircraft. In this sense, the FAA computer security program indirectly contributes to the safety of the flying public.

Computer security has long been a topic of interest and activity for those Federal agencies involved in national security matters. Until recently this concern for computer security was not shared fully by the majority of Federal agencies and departments. This indifference came from many different sources, such as the pressure just to make systems perform the function for which they were developed. For the most part, the impetus for the civil agencies to address computer security has resulted from external rather than internal stimuli. The Congress has been particularly active in stimulating interest in the issue of computer security. Congressional pressure upon the Executive Branch to improve the level of security for Federal computer systems has been applied through public policy legislation, the appropriation process, and agency oversight responsibility.

In the legislative arena, the Privacy Act of 1974 stands as a significant landmark in the development of Federal agency computer security programs. This law requires that appropriate physical, technical, and administrative safeguards be implemented to protect the personal information contained within agency computer systems. It represents the first specific statutory requirement that obligates all Federal agencies to address the problem of providing security for their automated information systems. In the context of the appropriations process, the failure of Federal agencies to address the computer security issue adequately has also resulted in the denial of funds for major computer acquisitions. The FEDNET controversy

of 1973 was a significant milestone as Congressional opponents of this system acquisition focused upon the lack of safeguards as one reason why the proposals should
not be approved.   The security issue has also surfaced in large computer procurements requested by the Internal Revenue Service and several other agencies.   The
final area of Congressional involvement in Federal agency computer security
programs involves the oversight of the bureaucracy.   In exercising this function
Congress has been particularly effective in focusing attention on computer security
program deficiencies throughout the Executive Branch as well as in specific agencies
or departments.

In exercising the oversight responsibility, Congress has relied primarily, but not
exclusively, upon the General Accounting Office (GAO), which serves as the investigative arm of the Congress.   Beginning in 1973 GAO released a series of reports which cited major problems in the physical, managerial, and technical controls
used to protect Federal data processing installations and systems.   The deficiencies
cited in these reports included the incidence of computer crime in Federal programs,
the lack of adequate physical protection for data processing installations, and the
vulnerabilities of data communications links to interception.   Another example
of oversight activities in the computer security area occurred in 1977 when the
Senate Committee on Government Operations held a series of hearings on the status
of Federal computer security programs.   At these hearings the positive efforts of
the Defense and Intelligence communities were contrasted with the generally low
level of positive accomplishments by the civilian agencies to provide an adequate
level of security for their computer systems.

In response to these Congressional pressures to take positive action to improve
the level of computer security within the Federal Government, the Office of
Management and Budget (OMB) issued, on July 27, 1978, Transmittal Memorandum No. 1 (TM No. 1) to OMB Circular A-71.   Entitled "Security of Federal
Automated Information Systems," this directive established basic computer security
program requirements for all Federal agency administrative data processing operations.   The impact of this policy upon FAA will be discussed in a subsequent
section of this chapter.   However, at this point it is important to note that the OMB
directive was a supplement to a regulation that applies only to computers used to
perform administrative data processing operations.   Computer systems, such as
those used by the FAA for air traffic control purposes, are classified as "technical,
special-purpose" computers.   Consequently these systems technically fall outside
the scope of TM No. 1.   Most agencies, including FAA, have chosen to include
these technical special-purpose systems in the coverage of their computer security
programs implemented in response to TM No. 1.

Whereas the computer security program for many agencies dates from the issuance of TM No. 1, the inception of the FAA effort precedes the issuance of this
document by several years.   In mid-1973 the initial step to address the problem
of providing adequate protection for FAA computer installations was taken by Alan
Read, then Chief of the FAA Security Division.   By rewriting the Position Description to emphasize the computer security responsibility, Read correctly foresaw

the requirements for his Division to become involved in this new and complicated security program. Although it was envisioned that this would be part-time responsibility for the incumbent, the degree of effort which this program has absorbed has grown steadily in the succeeding years. At present two full-time security specialists are dedicated to data security activities. The volume of work is such that several others could also be gainfully employed in this program.

FAA COMPUTER SECURITY ENVIRONMENT

In order to appreciate the magnitude of FAA computer security requirements, it is necessary to have insight into the FAA computer environment. As previously mentioned, the FAA is somewhat unique among the civil agencies of the Federal government as it is a heavy user of computers for both administrative and operational purposes.

In the administrative computing section FAA has one principal data processing facility which supports national FAA requirements. Located at the Mike Monroney Aeronautical Center in Oklahoma City, the FAA uses two IBM 370-155s to process such applications as:

- FAA Personnel Management Information System
- National Aircraft Registration System
- FAA Uniform Payroll System
- National Airmen Registration System
- FAA National Supply System

These applications are all FAA-wide in scope and provide essential data processing services needed to support internal administrative and logical operations and FAA's regulatory mission. These computers also provide local data processing services for the Aeronautical Center.

Seven of the eleven FAA regions also have their own computer systems to support regional requirements. The EDP equipped regions also provide support to those regions which do not have their own data processing capabilities. Five of the regions are currently using Spectra 70/45 systems. The Alaskan and Pacific-Asia regions are using IBM 1401 systems. The Alaskan region 1401 is reported to be the only 1401 still being used in the State of Alaska. The agency has, for the past several years, attempted to replace these outdated systems with some sort of minicomputer network. However, given the complicated state of Federal computer procurements, this "no procurement" action has been initiated despite the need to modernize regional data processing equipment.

The use of computers to support air traffic control operations is widely varied and quite extensive. Computer systems are used to support both en route and terminal air traffic control operations. En route air traffic control is performed at 20 Air Route Traffic Control Centers (ARTCC) where hybrid IBM and Rathyeon computers are used to provide real-time displays needed by the controllers to maintain aircraft separation. At 65 of the largest airports in the country, smaller UNIVAC computers are used to control aircraft in the terminal area. Over a hundred other airports will be equipped with smaller versions of this terminal computer system. The National Aviation Facilities Experimentation Center at Atlantic City, New Jersey, plays an essential role in the automation of air traffic control operators. Using duplicate hardware configurations, master national programs are developed and tested for the terminal and en route systems.

FAA is somewhat unique among user organizations in that hardware maintenance for all air control computer systems is performed by FAA employees. Hardware maintenance procedures are taught at the Aeronautical Center where duplicate systems have been installed to provide realistic training. Air traffic controllers also receive computer-assisted instruction at a new Radar Training Facility that will go into operational use in 1980. This facility will use computer-generated displays to simulate various air traffic environments that en route and terminal controllers must be familiar with before completing their training. Finally air traffic control communications are processed by Phillips computers located at the National Communications Center in Kansas City.

Given the many diverse uses of computers within FAA, the challenge has been to develop a security program that is sufficiently flexible while at the same time being comprehensive. The security concerns for administrative computer systems differ significantly from those for air traffic control systems:

SECURITY PROGRAM INITIATION

Beginning in late 1973, the Office of Investigations and Security began to conduct formal and informal security evaluations of various FAA data processing installations. The purpose of these evaluations was to gain an understanding of the current security environment at these facilities, and to develop the information needed to plan for implementation of a comprehensive computer security program. The principal thrust of these inspections was to examine the physical and administrative security controls currently in place. The more technical aspects of the security problem were not addressed at this time. The results of these inspections disclosed several common security deficiencies that needed correction on an agency-wide basis. Of greater significance was the negative attitude displayed by most data processing and management personnel toward the subject of security. Citing the lack of any previous security problems, these individuals were not very enthusiastic about the need to increase the level of security at their facilities.

While it was not possible to visit all of the administrative data processing installations, it became evident during these initial surveys that the majority were being operated as "open shops." The following security problems were identified for the administrative systems:

- The data processing room was not made secure upon completion of daily operations.

- The computer room at one regional office was used as a shortcut to the employee parking area.
- Fire detection and suppression equipment were not available at regional data processing facilities.
- Little or no contingency planning existed.

The problems just cited do not reflect a deliberate pattern of neglect, but rather a failure on the part of management at all levels to appreciate the true organizational value of the data processing function. To this point there had been no major security problems or independent audit which focused upon the poor security environment. In the great majority of the facilities visited, data processing management took a fairly narrow view of their security responsibilities. Security also finished fairly low on the list of priorities when compared with the pressure to provide essential services. In addition, there appeared to be a universal lack of concern on the part of user organizations as to how their data were handled by the data processing organizations and what arrangements had been made to overcome the effects of a catastrophe.

The one bright spot in this preliminary analysis of FAA administrative computer facilities was the computer complex at the Aeronautical Center. The generally excellent conditions found there resulted primarily from the concern for security by appropriate management officials at the time that a new computer center was built. In 1972 the Aeronautical Center contracted with a security consulting firm to obtain their guidance as to what physical security measures should be incorporated into the new facility. One lesson that the Aeronautical Center group learned is the importance of making security a design criterion when the facility is undergoing initial construction. It was also readily apparent that security and operational efficiency were not mutually exclusive, for this installation was very efficient while maintaining an excellent security posture.

The early visits to the technical special-purpose computer installations also uncovered similar problems to the ones identified for the administrative data processing locations. However, the problem of controlling access to air traffic data processing facilities surfaced repeatedly. The Central Computer Complex at each of the 20 en route air traffic control centers was not controlled by any physical barriers or administrative restrictions. These conditions were also found in many of the major air traffic control towers equipped with the terminal computer system. In several instances the doors to the terminal computer area were found propped open, with no one in the room to monitor access to the operating hardware. The temporary interruption of air traffic computer operations can have significant air safety implications. The lack of fire protection for the air traffic computer rooms was also determined at this time. Fire extinguishers which had not been inspected for several years were found in more than one air traffic control computer installation.

The conclusion of this initial effort to review the security environment at FAA computer facilities produced several benefits. Of most importance was that security managers had a greatly improved understanding of the true nature and value of the security environment at most major FAA data processing installations. Again it is necessary to emphasize that this early review was an installation-oriented approach. Little time and effort was expended in determining what system type problems existed within these installations. The series of inspection reports that resulted from these evaluations also served an educational function in that data processing, user, and regional management were provided with reports that stressed the need to improve the level of security at computer installations within their sphere of responsibility. This series of inspections was also a learning process for those involved in developing a comprehensive automation security program within FAA.

SECURITY POLICY DEVELOPMENT

Work on translating the results of this initial evaluation program into an FAA-wide computer security policy directive was begun in October 1974. FAA is a highly decentralized organization with the Washington headquarters components being responsible for national policy development and program management. Since field elements are responsible for program implementation, the objective of this next phase was to publish a comprehensive security directive that would establish FAA-wide standards for EDP security. As this document would require the approval of the FAA Administrator, it was recognized that it would also be a budgetary document as other components would have to allocate future resources in order to comply with the standards established in this order. At the beginning of this effort a fundamental question concerned the approach that should be used in policy development. Recognizing the two distinct data processing communities within FAA, air traffic control and administrative, the question arose as to whether there should be one comprehensive directive or two, one for each community. Each alternative had certain advantages and disadvantages, but finally it was decided that the use of one agency-wide directive would be the best approach, particularly at the inception of the FAA computer security program.

The complexity of the computer security problem became apparent during the writing process of the first draft of this directive. Drawing upon experience gained from surveying most of the major types of FAA computer installations, corrective measures were written into the directive. What started as an attempt to address the physical security aspects of the problem, quickly widened as it became necessary to deal with such related issues as fire protection, administrative controls, password protection, and the other concerns inherent in assuring the security of such a diverse FAA data processing environment. For example, when this project was initiated, it was not intended to address the problem of fire protection. However, after reading the various fire codes and comparing these with the conditions observed at the installation level, it became evident that this area needed national standards. Interestingly, research conducted at this time disclosed that no single organizational element had the fire safety responsibility with respect to establishing standards for protecting physical assets. The primary thrust of the FAA safety program was compliance with the Occupational Health and Safety Act.

The first draft of this directive was sent to the field for review and comment by FAA region and center security elements in April of 1975. After comments were received from these components, a formal coordination version was transmitted to all FAA components by early summer. While the comments to this directive were largely positive, several non-concurrences came from major data processing organizations within FAA. The draft order did create enough interest and controversy that senior agency management became aware that some problems did exist with respect to the security of FAA data processing installations. Essentially the draft directive served as a catalyst for a broader examination of the entire issue. As a response to this interest, an ad hoc group was created. Its membership included representatives of the various offices and services having a direct interest in the computer security problem.

The study group conducted a comprehensive examination of the issues that had surfaced in the coordination of the initial version of the computer security directive. This involvement of a number of individuals from different organizations was highly beneficial for the long-term objectives of the security program, as the members gained increased appreciation about the requirements for an effective automation security program.

By June of 1975, a staff study report had been prepared and transmitted to the Associate Administrator for Administration, Mr. Gene Weithoner. This document concurred with the fundamental premise that had predicated the earlier efforts of the Office of Investigations and Security, namely that a problem did exist with respect to the protection of FAA computer assets. The study recommended that an FAA-wide corrective action program be undertaken. One important element of this staff study was the recommendation that a collective approach be taken to managing the agency computer security program. Under this concept not a single component would have overall responsibility for coordinating the entire program. Mr. Weithoner, expressing the opinion that he had enough of these type of organizational arrangements, which in his opinion led to collective irresponsibility, approved the basic findings of the staff study but designated the Office of Investigations and Security to function as the lead element within FAA for this program. Having obtained the approval of senior agency management for its responsibility for this program, the Office of Investigations and Security again turned its attention to producing an FAA-wide security directive. A final draft version of the ADP security directive was written and circulated for formal comment in June of 1976. This document contained major revisions to the responsibilities section. These changes resulted from a better understanding of organizational interests in this area which had been gained through the staff study process. The comments resulting from the interval staffing process were incorporated into the final version of the document, and the FAA EDP security directive was signed by the Acting Administrator in March of 1977. The approval of this policy order represented the first major milestone in the evolution of the FAA computer security program. With the approval of this policy document, future efforts would be directed at assuring compliance with the standards established in the order. The EDP security function would no longer be a part-time responsibility; it would require more and more resources to the point that resource needs would soon conflict with approved staffing levels.

ARTCC SECURITY IMPROVEMENT PROGRAM

Following the completion and approval of the security directive, the next major phase in the evolution of the FAA security program was a major effort to improve security at the 20 Air Route Traffic Control Centers (ARTCC). Given the limited resources available for the EDP security program, it was felt that efforts in this area would produce the most significant results. In addition, the publication of the directive provided a sufficient level of guidance that region and center security personnel could apply to the administrative data processing facilities located in their area of responsibility. In some instances, a significant security improvement could be achieved through the installation of good door locks.

In keeping with the basic purpose of the ARTCC security enhancement program, a fundamental re-examination was conducted of the security posture of these important facilities. The last thorough analysis of security requirements for these installations had taken place approximately 15 years earlier. However, the nature of these installations had changed in terms of both size and complexity during that period of time. Much of this change revolved around the introduction of computers as an integral part of the air traffic control process. The importance of the computers in these facilities had grown to the point where they had become absolutely essential to the safe and efficient movement of all commercial aviation. Yet the rooms which housed these critical systems were virtually open areas as no additional precautions had been taken on either a local or national level to provide an adequate physical security environment for the equipment being used in real time to control scores of aircraft. To illustrate the wide open nature of these facilities, it was found that at many ARTCCs the computer room was used as the shortcut to the employee parking lot. It was also recognized that, given the size and complexity of these installations, it would be an exercise in short-sighted futility just to focus upon the automation aspects of ARTCC security. Thus the decision was made to undertake a comprehensive re-examination of the entire ARTCC security program with major emphasis on improving the protection data processing assets.

The study was initiated in early 1977. From the beginning, what was desired was a significant improvement in the level of security at these facilities, in particular, in the computer areas. It was evident that when the automation wings were added to these ARTCC's in the early 1970s, no thought had been given to the question of how these areas should be protected from security-related events that might interfere with the vital services performed by these computers. The Central

Computer Complex is immediately adjacent to the control room floor, and the medical complex is also in the automation wing. It is the colocation of these two areas which produces the security problem that has not been corrected to date. The crux of the issue has been the requirement for air traffic controllers to have ready access to the Flight Surgeon's office. Thus the easy solution of securing the doors to the entire automation wing was not acceptable to the controllers as they would have to use an indirect route to reach the medical office. Management officials were not particularly anxious to incur labor problems by securing the previously wide open Central Computer Complex.

Falling back to the next alternative, the ARTCC Security Study, as finally written, called for erection of floor to ceiling partitions in the interior of the room. These partitions would form passageways, thus permitting unrestricted access to the medical offices but significantly reducing potential access to the computer equipment. The use of the proposed barrier system was further complicated by environmental considerations. As a result, the final recommendation included in the study document called for the use of an expanded or decorative metal partition in the computer room. While this solution is not fully satisfactory from a security standpoint, it represents the types of trade-offs that must be made during attempts to retrofit security into an existing facility. It is also indicative of the need to reconcile conflicting interests of various parties who have a legitimate concern in the operation of the facility.

This example has been chosen to illustrate one of the frustrations of the FAA computer security program. Although the formal study, which incorporated this recommendation for improving the level of protection of the Central Computer Complex, was sent to responsible management in July, 1978, no positive action has been taken to correct this significant vulnerability. In fact a budget request that would have implemented all of the ARTCC Security Staff Study recommendations did not survive the Fiscal Year 1980 budget process. This underscores the lack of perception on the part of management of the risks involved in the use of the computer. A typical reaction which illustrates this last point is the response, "We've never had anything like that happen here before." It is sad to have to acknowledge that nothing works wonders for a security program like a major catastrophe or compromise that could have been prevented if some degree of foresight had been exercised.

RISK ANALYSIS

In Federal Information Processing Standard 31, "Guidelines for Automatic Data Processing Physical Security and Risk Management," the concept of risk assessment was first advanced on a Federal government wide scale as a methodology to be used in making and justifying security resource allocation decisions. This return-of-investment approach had been developed in private industry to handle the complex resource problems that arise when the security requirements are addressed for sophisticated computer systems. In FAA this concept was not incorporated into the computer security program until several years after this methodology was introduced in the Federal sector—for several reasons. Given the lack of any external stimulus to adopt such an approach, the use of risk assessment techniques was not strongly pursued. It was felt that some of the security problems were so obvious that it was not necessary to use a time-consuming process to prove something that the staff already knew. Being human, they also preferred not to become involved with something with which they had no experience. However, in the summer of 1977, the draft version of TM No. 1 circulated among the various agencies and departments for comment. One requirement contained in this draft version called for the completion of a risk analysis at each data processing installation at least every 5 years or sooner, if certain conditions occurred. It was recognized that the continued avoidance of the risk assessment question would have to end.

Recognizing its deficiencies in this area, FAA entered into a contractual relationship with a computer security consulting firm, Computer Resource Controls, in late 1978. The president of this company, Peter Browne, was one of the leading authorities in the risk assessment approach to addressing computer security issues. The contract with Computer Resource Controls called for the company to perform a risk assessment feasibility study. The objective of this study was to have the consultants examine the FAA data processing environment and provide guidance as to how the Office of Investigations and Security, the FAA computer security program manager, could implement a comprehensive risk assessment strategy. It is also necessary to admit that the use of these consultants was perceived as having the secondary benefit of giving the computer security program some visibility within FAA in a manner that could not be accomplished through personnel resources. Within the Federal government, and perhaps other large organizations, the words of a consultant seem to have more impact than the same words coming from within the organization.

In the course of this study such diverse installations as the Leesburg, Virginia ARTCC, Chicago O'Hare Tower, Aeronautical Center and Kansas City Regional Office were visited by joint FAA-Computer Resource Control Teams. At each installation the management was given a briefing on what the risk assessment process involved. Following this introduction, the Computer Resource Control people attempted to identify the information sources that were available and would be needed if a risk assessment were to be conducted at this type of facility. The final report from Computer Resource Controls was submitted to FAA in May, 1978. It contained the conclusion that a risk assessment strategy was indeed feasible for both of the different types of computer communities within FAA. The report also contained suggested strategy for implementing such a comprehensive risk assessment program.

One of the significant milestones in the implementation of such a program was the development of an FAA risk assessment methodology. Given the wide functional and geographical diversity of FAA data processing facilities as well as the decentralized responsibility for conducting these security analyses, it was desirable to develop a common methodology that could be used throughout FAA, and it was hoped that this methodology would yield a standardized approach and consistent results. Again FAA turned to the consultant ranks for the development of this methodology. As it wanted to obtain the best available expertise in this field, the solicitation was issued as a competitive procurement. Interestingly, over 70 different companies wrote to the FAA contracting office to obtain copies of the Request for Proposals, but of this number only three submitted final proposals for evaluation. Of these, the bid submitted by Computer Resource Controls was judged by an evaluation panel to be the best. Serving as members of the evaluation panel were representatives of the Air Traffic Service and the Office of Management Systems as well as the Office of Investigations and Security. The contract was awarded to CRC in July of 1979. The initial draft of the methodology handbook was delivered in December, and it was immediately circulated within FAA for comment.

The contract also requires Computer Resource Controls to perform at least two methodology validation demonstrations. One will be conducted at the principal data processing facility at the Aeronautical Center, and the other will be of the Atlanta Air Route Traffic Control Center. These demonstrations will not only serve as a test of the methodology, but also provide case study material that can be used in training FAA personnel in the use of this methodology.

FAA is also examining another risk assessment technique developed by Robert Jacobson of International Security Technology Inc. of New York City. A significant advantage offered by this concept is the automation of the many calculations that are involved in performing a risk analysis. The Risk Analysis and Management Program (RAMP) developed by Mr. Jacobson allows the analyst to collect the necessary raw data and enter them into three automated data bases. The two primary RAMP programs, Damage and Delay, calculate the expected loss from physical damage and delayed processing using the data bases (threats, rooms, and applications). Our initial review of RAMP also indicated that it might serve a slightly different purpose as a security modeling tool. The system held the potential of allowing security planners to obtain cost/benefit information about various security measures implemented at a data processing facility.

To determine the utility of RAMP as a risk assessment and security modeling tool, FAA let a contract to Mr. Jacobson in May, 1979. Using the Chicago ARTCC as a test site, the FAA hoped to obtain additional exposure to a different approach to real assessment while obtaining data that would be useful in the project to enhance ARTCC security. One of the key elements of the RAMP process is the delay loss file. In the case of an ARTCC, the losses from a security event were difficult to determine, as the sole product of the facility is the safe, efficient movement of aircraft. During the study, information was obtained that showed the direct loss to FAA in the event of a catastrophic event at a center was approximately $40 million. However, the indirect losses to the air carriers and the flying public were potentially greater as there are potentially significant costs for delayed flights, extra fuel costs, and additional crew overtime. It is in this area that the real loss potential for an ARTCC appeared to exist. The figure calculated by Mr. Jacobson, using a modified version of RAMP, for indirect losses resulting from a 2-month outage of the Chicago ARTCC turned out to be $500 million. Using RAMP, the FAA obtained cost/benefit data on the installation of such security measures as a HALON fire suppression system in the Central Computer Complex, the use of an automated access control system for the entire ARTCC, and the erection of a barrier system in the Central Computer Complex. For each of these measures, RAMP quickly generated the data needed by the security analyst to identify those security alternatives that warranted further investigation.

The Chicago Center study demonstrated the feasibility of the RAMP methodology. It offers significant advantages in processing data generated in the risk assessment process. It also appears to be manpower efficient, as a single analyst can perform the initial information collection process and then involve those with specialized knowledge in the final refinement of these data. RAMP appears to be of particular value in conducting risk assessments of FAA air traffic computer installations.

THE IMPACT OF TRANSMITTAL MEMORANDUM NO. 1

As mentioned previously, the Office of Management and Budget issued a Federal government-wide computer security directive in July 1978. It required all Federal agencies and departments to initiate a security program that extended to all aspects of administrative data processing operations. Several of the component parts of TM No. 1 exceeded the standards that FAA had imposed upon itself in the Agency order issued in March, 1977. In some areas, full compliance will require significantly new investments of time and resources as well as substantial changes in attitudes and practices. The basic requirements of TM No. 1 are:

- Appoint a security officer for each data processing installation.
- Implement a comprehensive personnel security program for all data processing personnel, contractor employees and system users.
- Assure that appropriate security measures are incorporated into application software through a process that includes a security design review, a test of the security controls, and a certification as to the adequacy of these controls by a management official.
- Conduct periodic risk assessments of data processing installations.
- Assure that security requirements are included, when appropriate in all procurements for equipment, software and services.
- Perform periodic audits/evaluations of all applications used to process sensitive data.
- Assure that appropriate contingency plans are developed and tested for all ADP installations.

After the release of TM No. 1, the initial priority was to advise senior FAA management and those individuals engaged in data processing operations of the existence of this policy. Despite the fact that the OMB policy had been announced with some degree of public fanfare, FAA management was largely unaware of its existence. After a series of briefings on the requirements of TM No. 1 and the potential impact on FAA, management seemed skeptical that the goals of TM No. 1 could be achieved. Their attitude apparently resulted from several factors, including the lack of resources committed to the computer security program. The success of this particular program is dependent upon the existence of a sufficient number of motivated, knowledgeable people. Due to the existence of a hiring freeze for the FAA internal security program since April 1977, there presently exists a very limited ability to respond adequately to the challenge of TM No. 1. In addition, the Department of Transportation has shown a decided absence of guidance and leadership in the computer security area. Without some emphasis on this program from the Department, it was difficult for people located in a subcomponent to become overly interested in getting too far out in front of the Department of Transportation. Finally, within FAA there had been no major fraud or security-related outage that would produce enthusiasm for a new, more active computer security program.

Another problem that complicates the implementation of the OMB policy within FAA is the manner in which the directive was promulgated. It is obvious that the purpose underlying Transmittal Memorandum No. 1 was to improve the security of all Federal data processing activities, not just those involved in administrative data processing operations. However the basic OMB Circular, to which the computer security program was attached, applied only to administrative computers. Thus the FAA Air Traffic elements were able to respond to a request for comments on the OMB directive, by stating that it did not apply to the special-purpose computers used for and in support of air traffic control operations. While some of the software security provisions of TM No.1 clearly applied to such applications as payroll and inventory control, it is difficult to understand how or why a certain category system should be exempt from such fundamental security concerns as contingency planning and facility security controls. The Office of Investigations and Security did request that the Department of Transportation rule on this issue, and some time later a letter signed by a Deputy Assistant Secretary was sent to FAA expressing the position that such operational systems were in fact covered by TM No. 1. There has been no occasion to test the strength of this letter by having to cite it as the sole authority for some particular policy requirement with which the air traffic components disagreed.

The first significant impact of TM No. 1 was the issuance by the Office of Personnel Management (OPM) of personnel security standards for all Federal employees involved in the management, operation, and use of Federal data processing systems. Differing investigative standards were established based upon the sensitivity of the data processing, the degree of access, and the level of responsibility inherent in the position. To implement this policy an FAA-wide notice was issued in April 1979.   The controversy that quickly developed from this notice involved the type of positions that should be designated as being of sufficient sensitivity to warrant a background investigation of the selectee before the position can be filled. Another factor was the $900 cost of these investigations.   The FAA approach was to balance cost and operation inconvenience with the legitimate need to screen employees holding truly sensitive positions.   However, given the pervasive use of computers within FAA, the full implementation of this policy resulted in the designation of about a thousand individuals as requiring these intensive, and costly investigations.   The OPM guidelines on personnel security standards for contractor employees have just been issued.   The implementation of these guidelines holds the potential for being even more controversial than the earlier standards for Federal employees.

Transmittal Memorandum No. 1 also contains other provisions in the areas of contingency planning, risk assessment, audit/evaluation of operational systems, and inclusion of security in the procurement of software, equipment, and related EDP services.   Rather than handle these on an incremental basis, a comprehensive TM No. 1 implementation plan has been developed and coordinated throughout FAA.   In this manner it is possible to involve other organizational components that have responsibilities for achieving compliance with the OMB directive.   At this point in time it appears that FAA can achieve compliance with TM No. 1, although not within the immediate future.

The most difficult requirement to implement is the one dealing with the development of application software.   The OMB directive specifies a set of fairly rigid procedures to be followed from the time of the initial system design to the first operational use of the application.   It appears that compliance will be difficult for a variety of reasons; the principal one being that it will require a revolution in the attitude of FAA data processing personnel.   Heretofore, security has not been a priority concern in the development of applications software.   As a matter of fact it is safe to say that it probably has not even been considered in the overwhelming number of systems developed in FAA.

FAA has not taken any substantive steps to incorporate these software security standards into its spectrum of software development.   Rather the approach for the short term has been to select certain software development projects that definitely fall into the type of system covered by the OMB directive and use these as case studies for developing a compliance strategy.   The first project selected is the new national FAA Uniform Payroll System.   This application will soon become the single payroll system for all 58,000 FAA employees.   Approximately 2 billion dollars a year will be processed through this application.   Using the assistance of a highly qualified contractor, EDP Audit Controls of Oakland, California, FAA will conduct a comprehensive security analysis and design review of the system software.   At the conclusion of the study the contractor will provide FAA with an advisory opinion as to whether security certification of this system should be granted.   They will also thoroughly document the entire process so that FAA can use this study as a potential model for complying with the application software requirements of TM No. 1.

CONCLUSION

This chapter has provided an overview of the FAA computer security program. No claims are made that this is the best Federal agency computer security program; only that it is representative of the effort being made within the Federal government to meet the computer security problem. Given the limited FAA resources that have been dedicated to this effort, a significant amount of progress has been made in laying a firm foundation for assuring the integrity, reliability, and protection of all FAA computer systems. One factor which makes the FAA computer security program unique is that two distinct data processing communities exist within the agency. This factor complicates all aspects of the program, as it is necessary to be sensitive to these fundamental differences at all times. Recent events have demonstrated to management that security problems exist for each category of systems. The episode involving the Soviet aircraft near New York City illustrates that computer abuse is not confined to administrative systems.

Given the impetus provided by Transmittal Memorandum No. 1, it is hoped that the FAA computer security program will continue to improve in both qualitative and quantitative terms. The use of computers within FAA is just too widespread to accommodate these new requirements without some modest increases in staffing. To date the FAA computer security program has not been able to compete effectively with other staff and support programs for staffing. The program has matured to the point that a definite need exists to include a systems-oriented individual as part of the program team. Another factor which complicates the future of the FAA computer security effort is the result of a recent intra-agency reorganization. The Office of Investigators and Security has been abolished and its functions transferred to the Office of Civil Aviation Security. This Office has quite successfully managed the FAA anti-hijacking effort. It will be quite interesting to see what the relative priority of the computer security program will be after this reorganization is accomplished.